9/91

The Bug in the Martini Olive

The Bug in the Martini Olive

And Other True Cases from the Files
of Hal Lipset, Private Eye

PATRICIA HOLT

Little, Brown and Company
BOSTON   TORONTO   LONDON

First Edition

"I've Got a Gal in Kalamazoo" (Harry Warren, Mack Gordon), © 1942 WB Music Corp.
(renewed). All rights reserved. Used by permission.

Library of Congress Cataloging-in-Publication Data

Holt, Patricia, 1944–
    The bug in the martini olive : and other true cases from the files of Hal Lipset, private
eye / Patricia Holt. — 1st ed.
       p.   cm.
    ISBN 0-316-37161-0
    1. Lipset, Hal. 2. Private investigators — United States —
Biography. I. Title.
    HV8083.L56H65   1991
    363.'89'092 — dc20
    [B]   91-9014

BIO
LIPSET

10 9 8 7 6 5 4 3 2 1

MV NY

*Published simultaneously in Canada
by Little, Brown & Company (Canada) Limited*

PRINTED IN THE UNITED STATES OF AMERICA

BIO
LIPSET
            9/91

Contents

To the memories of

Evelyn Lipset
Jim and Edith MacInnis
Fritz Holt
Leah Holt

Acknowledgments

Near the end of my four-year stint as an agent at Lipset Service, Hal remarked half jokingly that I seemed to have the brains but not the stomach for general detective work. I had to agree. In fact, the truth of that statement made me all the more sensitive to the brilliant work of four very different yet equally effective detectives in Hal's office: Sandra Sutherland, a fearless investigator who told me how to cover the noise of opening a medicine chest by dropping my car keys on the bathroom counter; David Fechheimer, Hal's most creative detective, ever; Ralph Bertsche, the true genius behind Hal's electronic inventions; and Ellen Eagleson, intellectual-turned-operative.

These four shared many of their secrets for this book, as did Dorothy Jansizian, the true keeper of the keys at Lipset Service and a loving presence for everyone there. Thanks, too, to other investigators working with Hal in the mid-1970s, such as Jack Palladino, Sam Webster, Dash Butler, Ed Heller, Vance and Grayce Morris, John and Leslie Eppick. Members of the World Association of Detectives, in particular Zena Archer, David Almog, Dolf and Vera Schenkel, Vincent and Sylvia Carratu, Peter Heims, and Henry Bawa were more helpful than they knew.

Bill and Dorothy Raggio contributed much more to this book than the information about Bill's run-in with the vice king chronicled in Chapter 1. Sam and Sara Dash were both gracious and insightful in discussing the Teamsters case and early days of Watergate. Friends and colleagues of Hal's — Mel Belli, Bill and

Lynne Cahn, Phil Rosenthal, Bob Scherman, Carol Wetmore, David Pham, Kyle Rimdahl, and Carole Ritts — offered vital information at key moments. Dave and Rose Stadtner could not have been more generous with their friendship and help in the early days of this project.

Hal's younger son, Larry, was as much a friend in the early days of research as he was a subject, and the openness and continued support of Hal's older son, Louis, have contributed to the weave of case detail and family intimacy in these pages. Hal's sister, Roz, provided invaluable background and terrific blintzes during my visit to her home, and her daughter, Debbie, and nephew-in-law, Don, made one New York send-off very special for both Hal and myself. It was not easy for any member of this family to permit an outsider full use of the treasured diary of Hal's late wife, Lynn, but they opened old photo albums, letters, and journals to me as well.

Peter Handel provided brilliant assistance in condensing hundreds of pages of transcripts and case files into succinct description. Doris Ober, perhaps the most fastidious and compassionate manuscript consultant I know, was an invaluable guide. Special thanks to Alix Madrigal for her enthusiastic readings of the manuscript — and her impeccable taste — as well as to Bill Chleboun and Bob Thompson for their friendship and encouragement, and to Rosalie Wright, the *San Francisco Chronicle*'s Features and Sunday editor, who published my first article about Hal while still an editor at *New West* magazine in the late 1970s.

My father, George Holt, has seen the many incarnations of this book and supported each one with equal care. Thanks also to Chip Demarest and Giorgio Pizzato, to Cheri Bailly and Bob Jacobs, and to Marya Grambs and Jan Montgomery.

I don't think this book would have been completed were it not for the conscientious advice of literary agent Frederick Hill or the steadfast love and editing help of Terry Ryan. Thanks, too, to Pat Mulcahy and Christine Archibald at Little, Brown for their graciousness and professionalism in advising me on revisions and vision.

Finally, to Hal, an original thinker as well as the nation's first true detective, my deepest thanks.

The Bug in the
Martini Olive

True Detective

One needn't be a mystery buff or true-crime fan to be attracted to the world of the private detective. The classic image of a lone man facing adversity has universal appeal, especially if by his wits alone he succeeds in piecing together a complex and often dangerous puzzle of many twists and deceptions.

Best characterized by the "hard-boiled" detectives (Sam Spade, Philip Marlowe), this is also a man whose constant exposure to the sordid side of human nature has endowed him with a certain world-weary wisdom. Better than all of us, he understands how anyone, including himself, might easily fall prey to what his "betters" would call evil. A pragmatist, an original, and (in his way) a moralist, he is honorable yet deadly, stoic yet tenderhearted, objective yet involved.

But this is fiction, critics say, having nothing to do with the private investigator in real life. As mystery scholar Jacques Barzun writes, "Murder and detection in real life can give pleasure to very few. The one evokes anger and misery, the other boredom."

So it would seem: The real-life detective is too bogged down in paperwork and office procedures to play the romantic hero. If we were to follow him on an investigation, we would probably weary of the drudgery of it all — the constant checking and rechecking, the reports, phone calls, files, records, follow-ups, secondary interviews, and the like. It is only when such realities are "transmuted by literature," Barzun says, that they begin to "afford delight."

Such crosscurrents of fact and fiction — and the possibility that something of deeper significance was behind it all — started to occur to me when, like a literary sleuth for my own purposes, I began to investigate the world of Hal Lipset, a private detective whose forty-four-year career is something of a legend in his field. By the time I started working for him in the mid-1970s, Lipset had more than once been called by his private-eye colleagues America's "master detective," and looking through the files of some twenty thousand cases he kept stored in his basement, I began to see why.

The nature of these cases ran the gamut from simple surveillance, security, and process serving to matters of blackmail, embezzlement, kidnapping, and murder. He worked primarily for lawyers but often said he would take "any case that walks in the door." Although it appeared to his clients that he worked on one case at a time, in fact he supervised the work of four full-time agents on more than fifty cases at once, and most of these were concluded within a few days.

Lipset's most widely publicized defense cases included investigations for such clients as Angela Davis, Huey Newton, the San Quentin Six, the Soledad Brothers, Los Siete, Wendy Yoshimura, and Stephen Soliah. He was chief investigator for Sam Dash on the Senate Watergate Committee, undercover agent for a variety of federal, state, and local agencies, security adviser to such underground (at the time) political groups as the Black Panthers, the United Farm Workers, and the American Indian Movement, and "chief pooper snooper" for clients who received bomb threats and suspicious-looking packages at the front door — at least one of which turned out to be a gift box filled with dog feces.

Lipset has made much of his money as a professional "sweeper" of unwanted bugs and electronic surveillance devices in casinos, corporate boardrooms, and private homes, and he has also been hired as a "planter" of similar devices on the bodies of clients who are victims of blackmail and extortion. He was famous early on as the kind of investigator who could get you all the information you wanted on someone simply by investigating public records, and if you needed more, he had contacts in police departments, post offices, hospitals, banks, universities, city halls, and data processing centers who understood his needs and the services he rendered.

The agency he founded was soon known for its eclectic assortment of cases: It was Lipset Service whose undercover investigation of prison conditions in New York resulted in the indictment of twenty prison guards; Lipset Service that salvaged William Randolph Hearst's People-In-Need program during the Patty Hearst kidnapping by hiring former thieves and drug addicts at San Francisco's Delancey Street organization to deal with the vandals in their own way; and Lipset Service that first exposed the federal government's famous "alias program" by uncovering the true identity of an embarrassed Mafia stoolie–turned–government witness.

Historically, Lipset's career reflects a number of American milestones. In the mid-1940s, he commanded an army Criminal Investigation Division (CID) unit charged with solving crimes committed by American soldiers following the Battle of the Bulge and during the Rhineland and Central European campaigns in World War II. In the 1950s he handled defense investigations for several alleged Communists, including longshoreman and union organizer Harry Bridges. In the sixties he became known as "master tracker" of runaway teenagers in San Francisco, having convinced his contacts in the Haight-Ashbury district that he would never turn a runaway over to police or parents without the youth's consent.

In the 1970s Lipset emerged as one of the country's leading experts on electronic surveillance, having appeared as a witness before a Senate Judiciary Subcommittee hearing on eavesdropping in Washington, D.C. There he fooled everyone by bugging his own testimony with a transmitter hidden in front of the committee chairman. Some years later he was invited back to testify and again surprised everyone by taping his testimony with a transmitter hidden inside a fake martini olive, which in turn sat inside a martini glass from which Lipset pretended to sip his favorite gin.

This futuristic gadget (the toothpick was the antenna) so fired up the imagination of the national press that for weeks afterward Lipset was credited with ushering in a real-life James Bond era in which hidden bugs, wiretaps, and infinity transmitters threatened (or promised) to take over the world.

Lipset has been president of the World Association of Detectives, a director of the Suicide Prevention League, the only private eye ever appointed to the Penal Reform Committee of the San Francisco Bar Association, and the only nonlawyer on the board of directors of the College of Trial Advocacy of Hastings Law School. He acted as technical consultant for Francis Ford Coppola on the award-winning movie *The Conversation,* now teaches investigative procedures at the University of San Francisco Law School, and was described by Calvin Trillin of *The New Yorker* as being "widely credited with raising the standards of private investigation." His list of credits goes on and on.

Yet rummaging through the case files I discovered a flip side to Lipset's character that seemed bent not on "raising the standards" of his profession but on lowering them for his own profit. Case after case came out of the files showing Lipset to be the kind of investigator who had barged into cheap hotel rooms to photograph adulterous couples in bed; chased ambulances in search of prospective clients; kidnapped children in some of the most bitterly contested child-custody cases on record; withheld evidence from the police to protect a client; taken money from nuts and cranks who believed that Martians or the CIA were after them; bribed prison guards in foreign countries to return known drug dealers to the United States; and used hidden tape recorders and bugs to trap unsuspecting adversaries.

He was indicted twice, sued dozens of times, but convicted only once, on a misdemeanor, for conspiring to bug a hotel room in New York. Worst of all (some would say best of all), he has worked for a variety of religious, political, and "psycho-social" organizations, including some outright cults and their leaders: Jim Jones of the People's Temple, Charles Dederich of Synanon, Werner Erhard of est, the Hare Krishna Society, and the Reverend Moon's Unification Church.

The seeming mixture of sleaze and prestige in Lipset's career fascinates observers. While Hal fends off questions from the press that he thinks might make him look greedy or seedy, he has continued to take in the "wrong" kinds of cases without a hint of apology or defensiveness. In fiction, of course, there is precedent for detectives who disguise their intentions, as Dr. Watson or Archie Goodwin often point out in describing their bosses. But in a business such as Lipset Service, any notion that the head of the agency has some kind of heroic impulse or personal code of honor is the farthest thing from anyone's mind.

There were, however, his military records, much discussed but "up in the attic somewhere," he always said, and finally available to me only when I insisted they would surely be as valuable to my own "investigation" as his case files. A partition had to be broken to get into the space where they were stored, and once there, past decaying file folders and rotting rubber bands, I found them, stacks and stacks of filmy-thin carbon copies, written by or addressed to Lieutenant Harold K. Lipset.

Hal had saved every order, field report, procedure form, investigation record, witness interview, and court-martial testimony ever submitted to him by agents under him or officers above him during the war. Most of the papers described investigations of murder, sodomy, rape, arson, burglary, housebreaking, forgery, larceny, robbery, manslaughter, and "mayhem."

Even more fastidiously preserved were glossy black-and-white photographs of victims, most of them naked, most of them women. Expertly photographed in the crude laboratories of a moving army or the blood-spattered kitchens and bedrooms of victims' homes, the pictures revealed the exact nature of knife wounds, broken bones, dismembered limbs, caved-in skulls, swollen bruises, and gunshot wounds that could be traced up one side of their bodies and down the other like a child's connect-the-dots puzzle.

Even forty years after the fact, these garish photographs struck a nerve. It was as though the person who stored them had once cared deeply about these people, not as victims but as comrades in arms. Looking at them in that dim and dusty attic was like reading *True Detective* magazine without the exclamation points or little arrows pointing to this slashed neck or that missing foot. The message was: This is a crime against nature.

More intriguing was the structure of army CID reports. In almost every way — the formal language, the precise details, the case names and numbers — these documents had clearly been used as models for operatives' reports at Lipset Service for the succeeding forty years.

The attic tops off the four-story Victorian house that functions as Lipset's home and office in San Francisco's elite Pacific Heights neighborhood. For visitors it is an astonishing place, filled with elements that seem to pertain to detective work but are distant, somehow, from the mysterious goings-on of the people inside.

To some, even the simple act of climbing the front stairs and crossing into the formal entryway is like moving backward and forward in time. Foghorns groan from the bay below as the floating gray mist thickens. Inside, high ceilings, hardwood floors, intricate moldings, sliding doors, Persian rugs, and antique furniture reflect the world of Charles Dickens or Sherlock Holmes.

Yet equally visible are banks of sophisticated electronic and sound equipment that instantly evoke the futuristic spy world of James Bond. Desks and computers have been carefully positioned to blend with the elegance of the two front living rooms, and as a result the visitor at first glance finds little evidence that there is an office here, or that it is peopled by investigators, secretaries, bookkeepers, and typists.

Nevertheless, there in the midst of it all is Lipset himself, working on his files at an enormous antique desk in full view of everyone. From here he receives an endless stream of visitors ranging from lawyers to derelicts, cops to prostitutes, mayors to down-and-out stoolies. Watching this procession, the visitor may be reminded not of Sherlock Holmes or James Bond but of Dashiell Hammett's world of the Continental Op, where the Old Man himself still walks those mean streets.

Lipset rises to meet his visitor, file in hand, eyes obscured behind owlish glasses. One notices immediately a clump of bushy hair covering the back of his head, as if it had been mowed there from the top, and a slightly paunchy six-foot frame that still moves with athletic authority. He appears rather bland on first meeting, smiling kindly as if you have come to vote, but he listens carefully, taking notes in detail and asking questions as though you were the only client he ever had.

Clients are always surprised at Lipset's deep, gravelly voice with its coarse yet sophisticated Bogart sound, and there is a kind of battered look about his face that suggests he has been around the block enough times to know the score. (One magazine writer observed that Lipset's face looked so *used* he resembled the victim in one of his own personal injury cases.)

Yet his been-through-the-wringer face and roughshod manner of speech (he often talks in *dese* and *dose*, as in "dis must be da place") make it apparent to people who seek his help that for all his professionalism, this is somebody who is human, after all, and capable of human error. If he has looked at the world from the gutter up a few times, so much the better: It means that in his life he has seen it all, that nothing you can say will surprise or offend him, and that perhaps more than anyone else he can get you out of a jam.

The relief that hits prospective clients when they first realize this about Hal Lipset is overwhelming, as if a sudden reprieve or instant absolution has just been granted. Hal's late wife, Lynn, who was his partner, office manager, secretary, and bookkeeper for eighteen years, left a diary after her death in 1964 in which she draws an insightful analogy between detectives and psychiatrists.

> *Many times I would pick up the phone and find someone stammering and embarrassed and unable to actually come right out and say he needed a private detective. People are fearful of calling an investigator for the same reason they are fearful of calling a psychiatrist. It's not so much that they are mentally slipping but rather that they finally feel forced to admit failure.*
>
> *I'm sure some of them have lifted the receiver off the telephone a dozen times before having the nerve to dial the number. So I try to make them feel they are one of thousands who have felt the same way. There is always great comfort in knowing you are not alone, and by the time they come here and talk to someone who can help them* do *something about their problem, they walk out as if a ton of troubles has been lifted off their shoulders. It has, of course — they've left it sitting on Hal's desk.*

The idea of the detective as psychiatrist is nothing new in fiction or real life, but it pertains in a significant way to Lipset's reputation in his own community, where he is privately an admired citizen yet publicly one of its most controversial. Although thousands of people in San Francisco have received his help in confidential matters, perhaps because he refuses to fit a fictional mold or because he is outspoken on unpopular issues, Lipset sometimes appears to be full of contradictions.

He is, for example, highly protective of the confidential relationship he shares with his clients, yet he's constantly in the public limelight and delights in sharing his "secrets" with the press. Famous for his defense investigations in civil rights cases, he is vehemently in favor of what most people believe are invasions of those rights (bugs, wiretaps, hidden recorders).

While he is strongly supportive of the trial-by-jury system of American justice, Lipset often says he will "use any trick in the book to beat the system." An acknowledged master of his trade, he is disliked by many of his peers for his associations with political radicals and his many "embarrassing" cases in court. And as indicated by some twenty volumes of scrapbook clippings he keeps hidden in a closet, he is both incredibly vain and incredibly shy.

When asked why he is a private eye, Lipset says, "I'm only in it for the money," as if to bait his questioners into believing the worst about him — that like the stereotypical down-and-out detective he really is greedy, sleazy, and out to take you for all he can get — when it is obvious to people near him that what he craves most is acceptance and respect.

Nevertheless, it's true about his obsession with money. He has a lot of it and wants more. Reputed to have been worth millions when he reached sixty, Lipset is adamant about such seemingly unimportant details as the arrangement of bills in the reports his office mails out to clients.

"Look, you put the invoice on top of the report so it's the first thing the client sees when he opens the envelope," he instructs a new secretary. "Some people think you should bury the bill underneath because it's ungentlemanly to show it or something — and then they wonder why the guy 'mislaid' it after ninety days. Not us. We put the bill right on top so they get the hard part over with. Then they read the report and know we're worth it."

It's this kind of attitude that both separates and unites Lipset with his fictional counterparts. Money to Sam Spade or Philip Marlowe, for example, is one of the few constants in a world of no absolutes, where good and evil have merged in some tangled, vague way. Like them, Lipset has an old-fashioned idea that money in his business is symbolic of a trust or bond between detective and client. You need a lot of it to get him working on your side, but once that bond is made, Lipset, like a modern-day paladin, is your man.

Unlike many detectives in fiction, however, Lipset does not care if you are guilty or innocent, right or wrong. To him it would be inexcusable for a private investigator to intrude himself on a case as arbiter of human behavior. "Judgments belong in a court of law," he tells his agents over and over again. "Our job is to earn the fee."

The fee, though, has become Lipset's famous smoke screen. When asked by the press what sort of man would *do* this kind of work for a living — kidnap children, photograph couples in bed, chase ambulances — Hal throws the line out again and again: "The kind of man who wants to make a lot of money."

Some reporters take Hal's comments at face value, but generally, Lipset and the press have carried on a mutual love affair for over forty years. "All publicity is good publicity," he likes to say, and if you don't believe it, he'll recite the names and addresses of every new client who ever asked Lipset Service for help after reading newspaper accounts of Hal's latest indictment or arrest. Similarly, reporters love him because he's an authority on investigation who's notorious for adding color to otherwise mundane interviews.

One television reporter — thinking his approach was original — suited up in a trench coat and had himself filmed slouching into Lipset's office with cigarette dangling and lips twitching as though he were Humphrey Bogart.

Sitting down to grill Lipset like a tough-guy detective, the reporter was startled to find that Hal, tipped off to the ruse, had run a routine background check on him a few days before the taping and had uncovered "just a few facts": the reporter's date and place of birth, family background, names and dates of schools and colleges, childhood sweethearts, sports interests, two ex-wives, employment history, military records, property owned and sold, lawsuits and other court actions, medical history, political affiliations, sexual interests, books read, movies seen, recent telephone conversations, arrest records, and parking-ticket history. Some of it apparently proved embarrassing to the reporter, who interrupted Lipset to ask, "How on earth did you find all this out?"

"Public records, mostly, a few contacts here and there, and then there was this," Lipset replied, pulling a large paper bag out from under his desk and spilling its contents onto the floor so the camera could zoom in closer. What appeared on screen was a random assortment of old beer cans, newspapers, cigarette butts, eggshells, coffee grounds, wadded-up papers, empty packages, used napkins, and pencil shavings. "Recognize this?" Lipset asked blandly.

"My garbage?" the reporter asked incredulously. "You went through my garbage?"

"Sometimes it's helpful," said Lipset, his hand puttering around in the mess. "Now here are some papers that might be of interest — telephone bills, old letters, notes to your lawyer about a certain misunderstanding. . . ."

But reporters are not quite so charmed when they question Lipset about the ethics and morality of his daily work. Then the romance disappears. As he has often said privately to his agents, "In this business, you're either a hero or a bum," meaning that to the press as well as to the client, the detective is a success if he solves the case and a failure if he doesn't.

The comment also quite accurately describes the image of the private eye in fiction, where he is almost always seen as a hero, as opposed to the stigma of the private eye in real life, where he is almost always stereotyped as a probably crooked, certainly corruptible bum who has failed at everything else — otherwise, why would he be in the business of making money off other people's pain?

Lipset stands apart from these stereotypes yet is trapped by them as well: On the one hand, his office and professionalism indicate to clients that here at last is one private eye who is not going to take the money and run. On the other hand, his controversial cases and checkered past suggest that maybe he is as tainted as private eyes in real life are supposed to be — otherwise, how did he make all that money?

If critics believe that private detectives in fiction have little connection to private detectives in real life, a look at Hal Lipset's career may shed new light on comparisons that Jacques Barzun and others find so odious. As we will see in subsequent chapters, Lipset's operating methods — his Jigsaw Puzzle theory, his Detective as Salesman approach, his principle of the Complicated Lie, his American Flag speech, his notion of the Detective as Manager, and his theory of the Lying Client — are all concepts that could have come directly from mystery fiction. The only difference is, Hal made them up in real life.

In fact only two things separate the true detective from his fictional counterparts. In Hal's case, it's hatred of guns and devotion to family. Philip Marlowe or Mike Hammer might sneer at him for that, but had they been caught in a hotel room with a voluptuous witness who, peeling off her clothes, threatens to cry rape, it's a safe bet they would have been relieved to have Lynn walk in with her tape recorder running and offer sweetly, "May I help you undress, dearie?" (see Chapter 2). Certainly Nick Charles would have spotted the plucky humor and innate courage of Lynn Lipset from afar and fallen just as hard as Hal did in 1942.

What is perhaps most surprising is the ordinariness of Hal and Lynn's attempt to find the American Dream — the kids, the house, their own business, two cars in the garage, and security for their old age. Their story, so typical of millions of households starting anew after World War II, parallels that sense of rebuilding America that inspired such disparate writers as Ross Macdonald and Rex Stout.

It's not just that aspects of their life seem to resemble aspects of mystery fiction, it's rather that they always quite unself-consciously represented something larger than themselves or their agency. If you asked Hal today what that larger thing was, he would answer, "Money, what else?" But to many of his investigators the real answer is free will, a concept that happens to be the foundation of all detective novels.

These simultaneous notions of fact and fiction, when applied like a grid to Lipset's many cases, begin to elicit truths about human nature and society that neither mystery nor true crime reveal alone. Finding that grid and interpreting it is the investigation you are now invited to join as Lynn and Hal stumble into the electronic age in Part I of our story, "The Art of Listening In."

PART I

THE ART OF
LISTENING IN

Chapter 1

The Electronic Witness

"Bugs?" He shook his head. "Not often. Cameras with telescopic lenses are better. Catch the claimants walking around on their paralyzed legs."

— Dick Francis, *Blood Sport*

San Francisco private eye Hal Lipset takes a seat at the bar of a financial-district restaurant with Dorothy Jansizian, his bookkeeper of nearly twenty years. Two cash registers are set up at the back of the U-shaped bar, each with its cash drawer slightly open.

It's a few minutes past five o'clock on a Friday night, and executives, stockbrokers, lawyers, and clerical workers are pouring into the place for their ritual end-of-the-week relief. The bartenders leave the cash drawers open so they can make change more quickly when the crowd gets four-deep around the bar.

Hal and Dorothy have arrived a few minutes early to position themselves at the curve of the U. As they talk, Dorothy glances to the side of Hal at one cash register, and he looks past her at another. Hal hasn't done a "bar check," as it is called, in many years, but his agent is stuck in a freeway jam in San Jose and two others are on surveillance in Marin County. Downtown on a case anyway, Hal takes the chance of being identified by people who might have seen his picture on TV or in the newspapers. As long as he and Dorothy keep their heads low, seeming to discuss some crucial bit of office gossip, nobody will see him.

Dorothy doesn't often do bar checks, either. Her work keeps her in the basement office most of the day, near Hal's giant walk-in safe and the banks of files holding nearly all Lipset Service's cases from 1947 to the present. Although she works at her desk most of the time, Jansizian has a kind of omniscience about the rhythm and flow of the cases under way at Lipset Service. She knows who's on the telephone when the secretary picks up the receiver and which clients are arriving upstairs before anyone opens the front door — this last because she sees their feet going up the front steps from the basement window.

But doing a bar check is kind of fun. You can have a drink, straighten out some matters with a co-worker (going alone is too suspicious), keep your eye on the cash, and get paid for your time all at once. By now, waiters and customers alike are shouting their orders to the bartenders behind the U-shaped bar. Piles of money have accumulated on the ledges above the cash drawers. It is from these piles that the bartenders make their change.

Hal and Dorothy are looking past each other to see if the bartenders ring up a sale every time they put more cash on the pile, or if some of the bills are finding their way into a separate stack to the side or underneath the register. Dragging on her cigarette, Dorothy makes a knowing wheeze. "This guy's incredible," she tells Hal. "He'll skim off a hundred bucks tonight at least." Jansizian is terrific at bar checks no matter how tricky they get. A professional bartender is like a sleight-of-hand artist — he can remove any number of bills off the pile every night, but if he sees anyone looking, he'll shuffle the stolen cash back in.

Hal's bartender keeps stacking and fingering the pile each time he comes back to the register — a good sign he's palming some of it. "Not exactly a class act going on up there," he mutters to Dorothy. In a way, he feels sorry for his client, the owner of the bar, whom he's known for several years. If the client hired these two amateurs knowing that she had a problem with bartenders ripping her off, she's only going to repeat the error next time. Tomorrow Hal will talk to her about hiring somebody else to do the hiring.

Meanwhile, keeping their heads low, Hal and Dorothy have begun to discuss a story in the morning newspapers about police officers who placed an open wallet hanging conspicuously out of the pocket of an undercover cop pretending to have passed out on the sidewalk. The idea was to capture the "criminally minded" in the act of stealing the wallet, but the reality, critics were saying, was that cops were committing an illegal act of their own called *entrapment* — seducing otherwise innocent people into committing crime.

"That was not a smart move on the part of the cops," Dorothy suggests. "But it occurs to me, sitting here: Wouldn't it be the same thing, if we hired these two bartenders to work at a party at your house so we could watch them skimming off the cash?"

"I don't think so," says Hal. "I think that would be a very old-fashioned but still legal procedure we used to call 'roping.' " He signals the bartender for another round, leans closer to Dorothy, and begins, as he often does in these wait-and-see situations, a story about the early days at Lipset Service.

> Lynn and I had barely been making ends meet when we got this big case — well, it was a big case at the time, because we got to charge our full fee of $2.50 an hour. We had gone through most of our savings from the war and Louis [their first son] was on the way, so we wanted to do a good job.
>
> An insurance company had a client, a real estate salesman, who claimed he had a permanent back injury. The company's doctors said the salesman was probably lying, but they couldn't prove it.
>
> We were hired to take movies of the salesman whenever he did anything strenuous, like shovel dirt or climb a ladder, that would show him up as a phony. We used the best machine money could rent (there was no credit to buy anything then) — a large, heavy movie camera with a built-in motor that made choking sounds as loud as an air compressor.
>
> I set up the surveillance and began watching the real estate salesman wherever he went. I filmed him never picking up a shovel, never going up a ladder, never so much as taking the garbage out. All this time, the clock was ticking away, and the insurance company was getting antsy.
>
> In those days, private investigators had a worse rap than they do now — they were seen as disreputable types who

couldn't hack it as cops and thought nothing of charging clients a lot of money without doing any work. Lynn and I were determined to change that image by showing the insurance company how reliable and efficient we were.

To save time, we decided to help matters along a bit. Lynn called the salesman and said she had some property she wanted to sell in a desolate spot in the San Carlos Hills. Since it was difficult to find, she offered to pick him up in her car and drive him up there to take a look at it. He agreed.

The next day, as Lynn drove up the windy dirt road to the property, I was hiding in some weeds about a hundred feet away from the spot where I knew she would park the car. The movie camera was camouflaged in the weeds on its tripod, ready to go.

We had the whole thing timed to twenty minutes: Lynn led the salesman up the hill for a tour of the property that took ten minutes. I left my hiding place and let the air out of one of her tires, which took another five minutes. Lynn returned five minutes later with the salesman and was about to get into the car when — oh-oh — he stopped her and pointed to the flat tire.

Lynn could change a tire faster than a team of gas-station attendants, but she feigned helplessness well. He took off his coat and asked her to open the trunk so he could change the tire himself. This was perfect. Not a word was mentioned about a bad back. Just as he bent down to pull the spare out of the trunk, I turned on the movie camera.

That nearly ruined everything. Through the lens I saw him stop, look around curiously, and, I thought, glare straight at me. Lynn touched his shoulder and pointed to her watch, trying to get him back to the tire business. I started to sweat. We had tried to absorb the noise from the motor with cotton webbing, but it seemed the choking sounds were floating across the field right at them.

Lynn talked louder and louder until the guy started changing the tire faster and faster, probably thinking he had a nut on his hands. We got clear shots of him bend-ing, lifting, cranking, hurrying. The insurance company showed the film to the IAC (Industrial Accident Commission) and easily won its case. Later I asked Lynn how she had explained the noise, and she said, "Oh, I told him it was a rare highland cricket."

Dorothy bursts out laughing. Stories about Lynn Fast, the Mennonite from a Minnesota farm who became the wartime lover of Hal Lipset, a Jew from urban New Jersey, and married him twice at war's end (once as a Jew, once as a Mennonite) continue to float around Lipset Service like pleasant ghosts. Although her tragic death in 1964 devastated the family and stunned the detective community throughout the world — Hal and Lynn are still remembered for single-handedly raising the standards of detective work in the postwar era — her original style and no-nonsense ways left a legacy of compassion and humor that are fondly recalled even today.

Thanks largely to the diary Lynn kept faithfully during her eighteen years of marriage as agent, office manager, wife, mother, and sharpshooter extraordinaire at Lipset Service, Dorothy and a few of Hal's long-standing operatives have gotten a glimpse of what it was like to start out in the detective business over four decades ago with no money, contacts, credit, reputation, or business experience — much like the Sam Spades, Philip Marlowes, and Horatio Algers of previous eras.

Since the Lipsets opened their agency at a key moment in history — the end of World War II and the beginning of the electronic age — their experience and vision paralleled an important coming-of-age period in America. Lynn's diary reveals the immediacy of that era as she describes another milestone that occurred early in the history of Lipset Service:

> *Insurance companies were the best bet for a newly licensed detective since they were always looking for cheap labor, and a new investigator could not afford to put much value on his services. After all, our fee of $2.50 per hour included use of our own automobile about town and office supplies at home. We were lucky to own a small tract house in south San Francisco, which we bought on the GI Bill, but mortgage payments of $57.50 per month were draining us.*
>
> *Hal made the rounds of lawyers' offices to get what he*

called "real work," but often he came home so discouraged I know it took great effort to open the front door. Then one day he walked into the office of Hallinan, MacInnis and Zamloch, a prominent law firm in San Francisco. It was five P.M. At that moment Archer Zamloch was wondering how to preserve the testimony of several witnesses in a criminal case.

Zamloch asked Hal if he was trained to use a recording machine. Hal replied he most certainly was. Archer told Hal to be ready to record three witnesses in three hours. Hal paled and tore out of the office, looked in the telephone directory for a store that handled this kind of equipment, and fifteen minutes later laid his eyes on a recorder for the first time in his life.

Lynn's diary account becomes a bit sketchy at this point, but Hal's recollection of his "day of desperation" has the clarity of a good detective remembering both context and detail of a recent case.

Hal: The store's name, F. A. Thomas, sounded professional to me and was nearest to Zamloch's office — that's really the reason I went in there. The salesclerk brought out what he said was the state-of-the-art machine, a Pierce wire recorder, followed by a fifteen-minute lesson on how to use it. With the last of our cash, I bought the recorder and returned to the law firm, where the secretary showed me right in to Zamloch's office. I placed the microphone in plain sight on his ink blotter, though partially concealed by books and papers, then ran a wire down the leg of his desk, under the carpet, and out the window and fire escape to an upstairs office he had given me to work in. Upstairs I set up the recording equipment, tested it, made sure it worked, and went home to have some dinner.

The plan was that Zamloch would interview the witnesses while I sat upstairs monitoring the equipment so that nothing could go wrong. In those days, the wire used in Pierce recorders was so thin and threadlike that it would snap in the middle and knot up all over the place. You'd open the lid and a tangled mass would pop out. The clerk at F. A. Thomas showed me how to feed the wire by hand in case it crinkled up or tore.

I was back by seven P.M., when Archer walked in and announced that his wife had tickets for the symphony so he wasn't going to make the interview tonight and wanted me to do it. "Certainly," I said, although I didn't know the case and couldn't figure why he was so blasé about missing this crucial part. Archer briefed me for half an hour and left.

When the witnesses arrived at eight, I sat them down, excused myself, ran upstairs, and turned on the recording equipment. Then I ran downstairs, walked in with a professional air, and started the interview. When it was over I thanked them all, leisurely ushered them out the door, ran upstairs, and turned the equipment off. I opened the lid of the Pierce and — *sproing!* — it was like a wig bouncing out of there.

Lynn: *Hal was crestfallen when he arrived home that night with this box of black spaghetti. We decided to try unknotting and splicing the wire into a single strand. It took hours, but with the help of tweezers and a magnifying glass, we finally had one long thread winding all over the living room. We rethreaded the spools and hoped for the best. By today's standards, the conversation was nearly unintelligible, but by playing it over and over again, we got enough words transcribed in readable format to satisfy the client.*

Archer was so impressed with Hal's ingenuity that the Hallinan office became our first big account. With this, a health and accident insurance company for which Hal checked out claims, and a life insurance company for which he investigated applicants' backgrounds, we were launched.

Hal: The reason Archer wanted to duck out of the interview was that lawyers were beginning to realize how compromised they'd appear if they interviewed witnesses before meeting them in court. The opposition could say these witnesses had been coached if a lawyer had seen them too many times. I felt this was an ideal entry for us: A good detective could take care of that part of the strategy and do the legwork that paralegals do today. But at the time, to find witnesses and interview them right there in the field — even take statements and brief them on court procedures — all that would be a huge departure from the kind of work private detectives had done before the war.

But if private eyes were considered "disreputable types" before then, Lynn and Hal had nearly double-crossed their own good intentions in the earlier case, when they filmed the real estate salesman changing the flat tire. The very shortcut they had used to prove Lipset Service so reliable and efficient was exactly the kind of quasi-unethical approach that had tainted the image of private eyes for decades.

Hal: The practice we used with the real estate salesman was called "roping," and it was fairly common in investigations of insurance fraud. Essentially, by letting the air out of Lynn's tire, we "roped" the insurance agent into performing the kind of strenuous work that he had concealed from public view during the course of daily life.

Lynn: *I felt badly about roping at first because it meant we were out to trick people, and this was hardly an honorable thing to do. Then I realized that these subjects were trying to trick their insurance companies, and I enjoyed the thought of having outwitted them.*

Hal: Eventually, the practice of roping was considered questionable because the subject was placed in a situation not of his own making, and juries don't look too kindly on that sort of thing. But there's a fine line of distinction. If it takes a manufactured job to get someone to do something he's capable of doing, what's the harm? It's faster than conducting a long, tedious surveillance, and the outcome is the same.

Finding that "fine line of distinction" between legal, ethical, and practical procedures became more important in detective work than the actual investigations, the Lipsets found. Some shortcuts were seen as models of efficiency, some as examples of corrupt thinking. The conscientious private eye was considered both businesslike and sleazy. And a common practice such as roping soon became confused with entrapment.

> *Hal:* Roping is still thought to be a kind of progenitor of entrapment, but here again is that fine line. With entrapment you lure people into doing something illegal they wouldn't ordinarily do. With roping we helped the person do something he could do and wanted to do but wouldn't do in front of the company he was defrauding.

There was also the question of the privacy of insurance claimants. They might have been guilty of attempted fraud, but weren't they still protected by the law?

> *Hal:* Roping had elements of invasion of privacy but was never considered a true violation. If you trespassed on people's property to photograph them, that would be illegal. But if you stayed across the street and caught them on film doing pirouettes when they told the insurance company they couldn't walk, that was OK. I think what happened to roping was that insurance investigators got carried away with increasingly elaborate ploys that got them into trouble.
>
> One insurance company employed an investigator who talked a woman named Jane, also claiming a bad back, into going water-skiing so he could arrange to have another boat with a photographer go by and take pictures of her on skis. It turned out that he had the wrong person — her sister was the claimant. Nevertheless, Jane went skiing, fell and injured herself, and put in a claim with the same company. The ensuing investigation revealed that the insurance company's own investigator had in effect caused the accident by roping the wrong person. This became a big case and cost the insurance company a lot of money.

No wonder it was difficult for a private investigator like Hal Lipset to get lawyers to take him seriously. The image of the stumblebum antihero from pulp novels of the thirties had merged in public consciousness with unorthodox-to-unethical investigation methods in the forties to make the idea of hiring a private eye to do legal work for lawyers a ridiculous notion. Until Hal proved he could handle witnesses and secretly record a conversation at Archer Zamloch's office, few private eyes had ever been allowed inside a law firm, let alone given employment. Even if a lawyer did hire one, what kind of credibility could the *private* detective sustain when he took the witness stand?

> *Hal:* Private investigators were seen as easy pickings by opposing counsel in those days. In court, you'd be accused by the other side as being a "hired gun," meaning that because you were paid, you might destroy or change evidence to suit your client's case. I could claim until I was blue in the face that I would never lie to protect a client — that I was there to investigate only the facts for my client — but I wouldn't have any proof.
>
> So when recorders came along, Lynn and I thought well, here was incontrovertible proof that what we said and heard in the field was true. It was like hiring a witness for every investigation, every interview we conducted, only the witness wasn't human — it was electronic and so, we felt, more reliable.

Ironically, the very means Lipset used to upgrade his business would be the basis of later accusations that he himself was sleazy and unprofessional. What he saw as a protection of civil rights would be considered by his critics a violation of the Fourth Amendment's right to privacy. At the beginning, however, his belief that recorders could be a tool for the respectable investigator made life on the witness stand much easier.

> Lynn and I proved the point when we got a case for an attorney representing a Mr. Chekhov, a former polio victim who had a pronounced stutter and a wooden leg that caused him to walk unsteadily. Mr. Chekhov was driving his car late one night when he got into an accident with an elderly woman named Mrs. Varig. She wasn't injured, but her car had to be towed, and she was angry. She told

the police that Mr. Chekhov was a drunk driver. He was arrested that night and called his attorney the next morning.

I went out that same day and interviewed Mrs. Varig. I
wore an early prototype of a miniature recorder in a holster
under my suit and rang her doorbell, told her I was working for the defense, and said that Mr. Chekhov insisted he
hadn't been drinking at the time of the accident.

I said I wanted to interview her and find out why she
thought Mr. Chekhov was drunk. She said, "Oh yes, he
was definitely drunk." I asked her how she had known
that. She said, "He walked very unsteadily, and he slurred
his words when he talked." Then I asked her the key question: "Did you get close enough to smell alcohol on his
breath?" Mrs. Varig said, "Oh, no, it was after midnight
on a dark street, and I didn't want to get too close to him."
I thanked her and left.

When the case came to trial several months later, Mrs.
Varig decided she had developed a back injury from the
accident and had brought a case against Mr. Chekhov's
insurance company for compensation. When the district
attorney asked how she knew Mr. Chekhov was drunk, she
said, "Well, he walked unsteadily, slurred his words, and
reeked of alcohol." The D.A. said, "You mean you could
smell alcohol on his breath?" "Yes," she said, "that's exactly what I mean."

Next the defendant, our Mr. Chekhov, took the stand.
He said he was not drunk the night of the accident. He
pulled up his pants leg to show his wooden leg, and said,
"This is the reason I have an unsteady gait." He stammered when he spoke and said his polio had left him with
a speech impediment he was still trying to overcome. The
jury, of course, was able to see and hear all of this.

Then I was put on the stand for the defense. I testified
that Mrs. Varig told me she hadn't smelled alcohol on Mr.
Chekhov's breath because she had never gotten that close
to him. I described her statement about the lateness of the
evening and her fears about the dark street, and I even
sneaked in my opinion that she seemed to have made up

her mind that Mr. Chekhov was drunk when he hit her car. No question about whether I had recorded the interview came up during direct examination by our client's attorney.

On cross-examination, the prosecutor got very sarcastic. He wanted to know if I was alone in Mrs. Varig's house during the interview. I said I was. Did I have any witnesses to this alleged conversation? I said no. Had I looked in Mrs. Varig's kitchen or any other rooms to see if maybe someone else was in her house? No, I hadn't. So there was no one else who might be called upon now to back up my story? No.

He kept at it for some time, trying to get at my credibility as a defense witness. Wasn't I being paid by Mr. Chekhov's attorney? Wouldn't it serve my interests to have Mr. Chekhov go free instead of to jail? All of my answers were basically the same: "It is my job as an investigator to go out and get the facts. If Mrs. Varig told me that she smelled alcohol on his breath, I would say so."

The prosecutor was ready to dismiss me when the arresting officer, who was seated beside him, whispered in his ear. The D.A. then asked, "Did you in any way preserve this conversation on some kind of electronic device?" I said, "Yes, I made a recording of the interview, and counsel at the defense table has it. We can play it for the jurors if you'd like. Then they will hear whether or not Mrs. Varig told me she smelled alcohol on Mr. Chekhov's breath."

The D.A. refused to play the recording because he knew I wasn't lying. The only reason he brought it up was in the hope that I had *not* recorded it. Then he could have inferred that I had the capability to record it but, not getting what my client wanted, had destroyed the tape. Mr. Chekhov was acquitted.

The important distinction here is that the value of a recorded conversation in court is to prove the truth or falsity of what a witness said, not the truth or falsity of what happened. I don't know if Mr. Chekhov had been drinking that night or not. I do know the credibility of Mrs. Varig was diminished the moment the existence of the recording was known.

"The truth is not the same as facts," Lipset often tells his agents. "The truth is a relative thing that a court is supposed to determine. Our job is to get verifiable facts." But the question is often posed: If you want to be so aboveboard about taping conversations, why hide the recorder? Why not put the machine on the table and say, here: I'm going to turn this on to make sure I understand you perfectly so that I can represent the truth of what you say in a court of law. The reason, says Lipset, is simple: "People who lie would refuse to talk to an investigator like me if I said I was tape-recording the interview. A recording does nothing more than establish what was said; it doesn't alter the facts of the case. That's why you keep the recorder concealed."

Perhaps the best and most enduring use of Hal's "electronic witness" occurred in a ground-breaking case that freed a lone district attorney from the trap set for him by a local vice king.

The case was eventually to receive national attention because of Hal's unprecedented use of recording equipment, but San Franciscans heard about it first from the headline of the evening *News Call-Bulletin:* RENO D.A. ACCUSED OF S.F. GIRL "KIDNAP."

Anyone who's watched private detectives in the movies or on TV will find this case familiar — the maligned, heroic district attorney, the mysterious client, the undercover private eye, the expertly placed "bugs," the crime boss out for blood. The fact that it all happened in real life — and that it would be rewritten in more lurid prose in *True Detective* magazines later on — makes the case both a myth and a mirror of the good detective in action.

> *Hal:* The city of Reno was not very large in 1960, and at that time, small-town district attorneys were allowed to have a private practice on the side. One afternoon just after five, a young woman named Julia walked into the office of Reno D.A. Bill Raggio looking visibly upset.
>
> She told Raggio that her husband, a sailor with the navy who served on the USS *Enterprise* in San Francisco, had been cheating on her with a woman named Beverly Larsen, who had been seen with him at the Peek-A-Bye Motel, and

that even after they moved to Yuba City, California, and she went to work at Mom's Diner, and his ship moved to Oakland, he still cheated on her, and she couldn't take it any longer, especially after they had gone to Bernard Hays, a Reno marriage counselor, and she had sought help from Leland Fitzgibbon, the minister at the Little Prairie Church, while her husband got drunk on Cuba Libras at the Ship2Shore Bar, and so on.

It was quite a litany of details, and the gist of it was that Julia wanted a divorce and was asking Raggio to be her attorney. He took extensive notes throughout all this and agreed to take the case. Then, quite unexpectedly, she stood up and asked him out for a drink. He declined.

The next day Julia called to say she had more information and wanted to know if he'd take her up on that drink. He agreed, made sure a friend would act as a kind of male escort, and drove to the Riverside Hotel cocktail lounge to meet with Julia, who turned "pouty and seductive," according to Bill, when she saw the friend. Even when Bill escorted Julia to her room, the friend didn't leave. A few days later, just about the time Bill had started the paperwork on her divorce, Julia disappeared.

Raggio had smelled a rat, and now he was worried. He was currently involved in an increasingly violent battle with the local vice king — let's call him Frank — who ran the houses of prostitution that in Nevada operate legally by county option. Only a few days before, Raggio's office had initiated a series of busts in which Frank was arrested for vagrancy and thrown into jail twice.

The rumor going around town was that Frank had switched the tables — he was telling people he had evidence that Raggio was corrupt and unfit to serve as Reno's D.A. Now the target of some kind of conspiracy, Raggio searched around to see where he was vulnerable. The only suspicious thing that had happened to him recently was Julia's visit and disappearance. If Frank was cooking something up, Raggio thought, Julia, who might be one of his prostitutes, could also be a part of his plot.

Raggio called me into the case because he was afraid to assign his own detectives to investigate the problem. Frank's connections had spread inside the Reno Police Department before. My advice was that Raggio should have a face-to-face meeting with Frank, which I would secretly record, so we could find out just what Frank had in mind. In a way, it was very much like roping: Somewhere in Frank's desire to ruin Raggio, he was aching to tell Bill off. We were going to give him an opportunity to do just that, and maybe use some of it to convict Frank of blackmail in court.

Raggio called Frank's lawyer, who agreed to set up a meeting between Frank and Bill. It was very stupid of Frank to agree to this meeting, but he was such an arrogant SOB, Raggio said, that he relished the thought of taking Bill on in private. The meeting was to take place at the lawyer's office late at night. I toured the building looking for empty offices and Raggio got a court order allowing me to trespass legally in the attorney's office.

I called my engineer in San Francisco, Ralph Bertsche, who flew up to Reno with the recording equipment. I found an empty office near the one where the meeting would take place, and a few hours before the meeting, Ralph and I, dressed as janitors, let ourselves into the building and set up our headquarters in the unused office space. We found the back stairs in the dark, picked the attorney's lock, and let ourselves into his office. Ralph planted a microphone in an air conditioner we knew wouldn't be turned on and, just to be sure, another in a law book on the wall. This way we would have two simultaneous recordings made.

Ralph and I then returned to the empty office where we draped the windows with heavy cloth and sat down with miniature flashlights to listen to the conversation and make sure both recorders were picking it up well. We heard Raggio and Frank arrive, search each other for microphones, and begin talking. As I had coached him, Raggio started asking questions that were designed to elicit incriminating statements from Frank.

True to form, Frank said that Julia was "a friend" of his, was now pregnant, and about to sue Raggio in a paternity case that was going to hit the newspapers from Reno to San Francisco. However, if Raggio quit harassing Frank and his friends and withdrew the vagrancy charges against Frank in particular, maybe he, Frank, could convince Julia not to sue.

That was it, I thought — the threat of blackmail we were waiting for. I waited for Raggio to make some conciliatory remarks that would close the conversation when Frank raised a legal point that infuriated Raggio, who said that Frank didn't know what he was talking about. Frank started screaming at Raggio and started pulling law books off the shelf, looking for verification. Ralph and I looked at each other in a sweat as we heard him getting closer and closer to the book with the mike hidden in it. I could swear I felt his hand around my ears as he pulled "our" volume out, but Raggio, who didn't know where the mikes were hidden, happened to accuse Frank of something else, and the book was shoved back in in the nick of time.

The wire recording was clear as a bell, but it wasn't enough. We could play it to the grand jury and get Frank indicted, but Bill's career as D.A. was in jeopardy. The word had gone out by Frank and his goons that Raggio had fooled around with a client, gotten her pregnant, and abandoned her. Sending Frank up the river would not fix that. We had to find Julia to prove Raggio had done nothing wrong.

All we had were Raggio's notes on the lengthy story Julia had told him at their original meeting. Bill doubted everything she said, but I was operating under a long-held theory of the Complicated Lie: When anybody tells a lengthy and detailed untruth, there are always going to be elements of truth in it. Julia made up the lie to drag out the meeting and confuse Raggio with her barrage of details, but she had to start from somewhere.

From the USS *Enterprise* to the Ship2Shore bar, from a stakeout of Frank's hideaway apartment in San Francisco to interviews with a number of sailors, one of whom led me to Julia's parents, we slowly sorted out the lies from the facts. The trail ended when Julia's mother called me a few months later from San Diego to say that Julia had just telephoned her from a phone booth in the Haight-Ashbury section of San Francisco. She had convinced the girl to wait at the phone booth until she heard from me. I raced over there, found the daughter, and got her into my car. She told me that she was afraid of Frank and his gang.

I took Julia to an employee's house rather than my own home because I figured that Frank knew my name and might come looking for her. That night she told me she had been conned into the whole mess by her older sister, who was Frank's girlfriend at the time. The plan was for Julia to go to Raggio's office and give him the divorce story, then try to get him in a compromising position so Frank's men could photograph them. She was very young and very sorry, and she said she would testify on Raggio's behalf in court.

That's when the "kidnap" headlines hit. Her sister had the audacity — prompted by Frank, of course — to hire a lawyer and file suit against Raggio and me, accusing us of kidnapping Julia. We denied this but did admit to reporters that we knew where she was staying.

What changed the tone of this case from tacky sexual scandal to a serious legal action against attempted blackmail were the recordings we made of Frank and Bill the night they met in the attorney's office. Ralph and I were able to equip the entire jury with headphones so they could listen in on that conversation and pick up every nuance of threat and extortion in Frank's voice. This was such a new procedure in court at the time that it made as many headlines as the alleged "kidnap." Frank was easily convicted of conspiracy and ended up in the penitentiary.

In a sense, a mythology about the case had already begun. Raggio's encounter with Julia was just lurid enough — and Hal's use of bugs and headphones just high-tech enough — that the case was given full-page pictures and an evocative text in *Inside Detective, Startling Detective,* and other true-crime magazines.

Here, next to pictures of a Riverside Hotel room, its bedsheets unaccountably mussed, we meet "handsome" and "courteous" Bill Raggio, whose sterling reputation remains untarnished when Julia, within minutes of their first meeting, "allowed her skirt to hike itself up her leg so that an ample amount of silk stocking, a gracefully curved knee and part of a well-proportioned thigh were revealed.

" 'Now, how can I help you?' Raggio asked.

"The beautiful young woman leaned forward so that her white leather coat parted. A black sweater clung like adhesive tape to her voluptuous bust. Her lips parted and she purred. . . ."

It was the purpose of true-crime magazines to sell their readers on the idea that real life via a police blotter was as interesting (and dirty) as any sex scene you could find in fiction. But there always had to be a moral. Raggio, who stood for good, untempted by evil, might yet have been slain if it hadn't been for Lipset, a kind of Sancho Panza of the eavesdropping trade, so that Judeo-Christian values could be aroused and sustained along with other, more primal instincts.

The legitimate press disguised its own bent for scandal with seeming journalistic objectivity, but photos of pouty Julia in tight-fitting sweaters and pictures of a woman standing in the closet of the Riverside Hotel carried the same prurient invitation. Throughout all the coverage, Lipset's recording equipment — those buxom earphones, those tumescent mikes — had a seductive authority of its own. What a thrill it was for jurors to find their own earphones awaiting them as they returned to the jury box, or for reporters to feel Hal slip the heavy leather headsets over their ears while instructing them in the careful turning of dials ("a little to the left . . .").

The Raggio trial convinced Hal and Lynn that they had found a way to upgrade their profession through emerging technology. From then on, they embraced the idea of electronic surveillance as a terrific tool for business. That great foresight was to prove both a curse and a blessing.

Chapter 2

"May I Help You Undress, Dearie?"

"Do you know what you sound like?" said Mrs. Oliver. "A computer. You know. You're programming yourself. That's what they call it, isn't it? I mean you're feeding all these things into yourself all day and then you're going to see what comes out."

"It is certainly an idea you have there," said Poirot, with some interest. "Yes, yes, I play the part of the computer. One feeds in the information —"

"And supposing you come up with all the wrong answers?" said Mrs. Oliver.

"That would be impossible," said Hercule Poirot. "Computers do not do that sort of thing."
— Agatha Christie, *Hallowe'en Party*

Hercule Poirot takes his morning stroll in the garden of an English country home, pondering a recent murder. Passing a rosebush, he comes upon the sound of whispered voices. An exclamation point appears over his head: What luck, he thinks. Whoever is whispering may be exchanging information on the current case.

Without questioning his right to do so, Poirot edges nearer to the rosebush that separates him from the people talking and positions his ear as close to the thorns as safety and hiding permit. The very best pieces of the jigsaw puzzle, he thinks with delicious anticipation, are secrets about to be imparted.

Throughout detective literature, the art of listening in has been given as much prominence as the art of deduction. Hidden information is often the last piece in the jigsaw puzzle, and the detective — literature's agent of good — entertains few compunctions about invading anyone's privacy in his quest to terminate evil. For him, listening in is the equivalent of spying through a keyhole. It offers a chance to uncover hidden information without anyone guessing what information *he* is hiding.

Poirot understands that if he leans too far into the rosebush, he may startle the speakers, causing them to stop the conversation and cover up whatever secrets they think he might have heard. This fact — that the detective's very presence may cause people to cover up, to lie — doesn't bother the likes of Hercule Poirot. After all, every case begins as a lie, and lies are the fiction of everyday life. To get to the truth, he must often lie himself.

That's why listening in has such a timeless presence: It doesn't matter if the detective's ear is aided by electronics or stuck naked against a rosebush wall. If he seeks to be invisible so that people will exchange secrets in what they think is the privacy of their own conversation, he becomes more powerful, and they more vulnerable, in his effort to solve the crime.

Does it matter to Poirot that listening in during a conversation like this is illegal — an invasion of the privacy of the people talking on the other side?

Poirot knows this, but he doesn't care: In mysteries, pretending invisibility is a time-honored tradition of getting at the truth. Radio character Lamont Cranston exploited this method for years as "The Shadow," that "mysterious presence [who] invoked mechanical aid to place himself where he could hear without being seen," as Maxwell Grant's book *Kings of Crime* explains. Because of his ability to listen in on evil in the making, "The Shadow, more than any other person, was equipped to battle crime."

In real life, governments attempt to give law enforcement — society's agent for good — the edge on this "mechanical aid" (electronic surveillance) to monitor criminals in its unending battle against evil. As Yale law professor Charles A. Reich said about federal use of wiretapping, "The argument is always made that what Government does is for the public good. Yet this can justify anything

Government does. It is the very argument that is used in totalitarian countries to justify practically any kind of invasion of personal liberty."

Congress appeared to both agree and disagree with that line of thought in passing the Federal Communications Act in 1934, which made it legal for the police and FBI to intercept information electronically — but illegal to divulge that information in a court of law. The theory was that eavesdropping could be used by the forces of good to combat crime but not to jeopardize civil rights along the way. In reality, however, such empire-builders as J. Edgar Hoover, who consolidated the FBI in the 1930s to overtake the Treasury Department, which he considered inept, ended up secretly wiretapping political activists, criminal figures, and personal enemies at will.

To Hoover and his successors, any threat to national security — bootleggers and bank robbers in the thirties, spies and aliens in the forties, Communists "under every bush" in the fifties, the antiwar movement and civil rights riots of the sixties, radical feminist and gay dissenters of the seventies, Central American refugees and radical environmentalists of the eighties, and environmental protesters of the nineties — justified increased wiretapping by government agencies for the good of the country.

Federal law today — originated by the Omnibus Crime Control and Safe Streets Act of 1968 — defines the phenomenon of listening in under two categories:

No-party consent. Eavesdropping on a conversation in which *no one* has given consent is considered an invasion of privacy. This means an outside party cannot secretly record the voices of two or more people who are having a conversation except in extreme instances, such as mobsters talking about selling drugs or conducting a prison break, and only then by law enforcement operating under court order.

One-party consent. Eavesdropping on a conversation in which *one or more persons* have given consent is considered legal by federal law and in many states. The thinking here is that you have a right to record what you say, and what is said to you, in your own conversation.

Thus law-enforcement informers or undercover operators wearing "wires" (recorders or radio transmitters) to tape conversations with mobsters do not need a court order and are acting legally because they have given consent to record their own conversation. While J. Edgar Hoover's many buggings — the ones without court approval — of Martin Luther King's telephone conversations were illegal, had King taped his own conversations, even without the consent of the people with whom he was speaking, his recordings would have been legal under federal law. Further, had Hoover called up King and taped their conversation, that would have been legal.

The distinction between no-party and one-party consent recordings is worth exploring because few people in the private sector have been credited with as much daring — or heaped with as much abuse — in the area of listening in as Hal Lipset. In fact it was exactly in this tangled thicket of definitions that Hal and Lynn built their reputations as the Paul and Paula Drake of San Francisco. To be regarded as professionals whose word could be trusted, they had to change the status quo:

> *Hal:* Insurance companies stopped using Lipset Service after we started working for independent law firms — apparently the word was out that I had jumped to the "other side" because I sometimes conducted investigations for lawyers representing people who sued insurance companies.
>
> The idea that we were choosing "sides" was ridiculous, Lynn and I thought. The point we were trying to get across about our agency was that a good investigator gets *all* the facts so the client can determine the potential of his case in court. These are facts that will be challenged by the other side and tested by the court, so they better be right, and we better not fool around with them or try to falsify them in any way. This was why we could work for one attorney one day and find ourselves working on a different case against him the next. Our job, clearly, was to find out the facts, no matter what "side" we worked for.

It did not matter to Hal and Lynn that the cases they investigated for lawyers sometimes got as seedy and as distasteful as any taken on by Spade or Marlowe. To them, raising the standards of their profession meant using the best tools they could find on whatever cases they took — and in their efforts to operate a general detective agency, they prided themselves on taking every case that walked in the door. This included "wiring" clients in cases of scandal such as adultery and paternity, where lying had been elevated to a high art.

Hal: In the days before no-fault divorce, evidence of adultery was one of the few grounds that were admissible in court. Before the era of recordings, investigators had a tough time establishing the facts of a case.

A classic example was the man who admitted to his wife that he was having an affair but said he'd deny it in court and make her look like a fool or a slut if she tried to get a divorce. She felt she had no alternative than to hire us to follow him.

Every night we watched him leave home to go to a woman's house across town where he would spend two or three hours. He would knock on the front door and go in; the lights would go out; two hours later he would come out and go home.

His wife did sue for divorce, but when the case came to court, the man got on the witness stand and swore that he was building a ship model in the basement of the house as a Christmas gift for his son. That's why the lights were out — he and this woman were downstairs working painstakingly on this ship. The judge didn't believe him. I didn't believe him. But it didn't make any difference. The court ruled that there was no factual reason to believe adultery had been committed. So we lost the case.

Paternity cases were also unwinnable because if the woman was our client, the man she said had impregnated her might blithely announce they had never slept together, and she couldn't prove they had. Or he might threaten to have his buddies tell the judge they all slept with her.

I wanted to switch the tables. "Let's make a recording," I said. "Let's get his admission down on tape. He can deny it until he's blue in the face, but the court will know he's lying." It still wasn't easy hiding recorders in those days, so we began experimenting with our own designs, making body holsters out of elastic rib support belts. I coached our clients about steering conversations to get people to admit things. Then we were in business.

Former Mennonite Lynn somehow saw past the sordid details of paternity cases to develop a matter-of-fact sensibility very much like Hal's: "An investigator must know how to get information from people," she wrote in her diary. "This is an art often underestimated."

Lynn: *If the woman is our client in a paternity case and the culprit denies being the father, we install recording equipment in the woman's home and have her call the man to come over and discuss what she's going to do while we record the conversation. If he is difficult and denies having had intercourse with her — which is rare when the conversation is between the two involved persons — we tell her to have intercourse with him right then and there. Tell him, "Just one more time since I probably won't see you again, and I'm pregnant anyway, so no further harm can be done." A man who's guilty won't turn down this invitation.*

If the man is our client, occasionally we have been able to get him off the hook by interviewing all the fellows that the two had seen when they were dating. More frequently than you would realize, one of his buddies also dated the girl and slept with her.

Some people, she writes, were in it for the scam.

One lady-about-town named Suzie made it a point to date married men. She managed to get into a circle of affluent executives, including many from out of town. She slept with as many as possible and would send a letter to each man at his home. The letter invariably arrived after the man had gone to work, so his wife would be sure to see the envelope and question him about it when he arrived home.

At least two men we know of paid her some money, but not enough to work a financial hardship or cause them to see a lawyer. She was very clever. She pretended she did not want any money, but after some conversation she would just happen to remember that she had to fly to Mex-

ico City or New York the next week, and it would be nice not to have to purchase her own ticket. She would go so far as to pick up the phone and call the airline in his presence and book her flight. Then she would accept the plane fare and never bother the man again.

Suzie got tired of operating on this scale and went after a man named Bob, who fell for her almost immediately. A month later she told him she was pregnant. As time went by, Bob suggested she talk to his lawyer. This she did, looking about four months along.

We were assigned to observe her. We followed her going out to shop, having her hair done, having lunch with friends. Her size increased as expected, but we never saw her visit a doctor. One day as we were watching both the front and rear of her home, we got what we'd hoped for. She stepped out on her back porch wearing size-six slacks and a tucked-in shirt and was photographed by one of our agents. An hour later she left via the front door, again looking very pregnant.

We installed recording equipment in Bob's lawyer's office and called Suzie in for a discussion about financial arrangements. Shown the photograph, she admitted her scam but tried to shrug it off, thinking maybe she'd still get some cash. When Bob's lawyer told her a hidden recorder had just taped her admission and could be used as grounds for a blackmail charge, she left town and was never seen again.

The more they worked with recorders, the more powerful the Lipsets became. As the Reno brothel owner Frank (see Chapter 1) had discovered, recorders were like guns. When you were "armed" with a recorder, you carried it under your jacket in the same way detectives holstered a gun. Recorders weren't as violent as guns, but they were just as powerful, as Lynn's story about one mob-supported witness makes clear.

Lynn: *A man was accused by a woman of making her pregnant, and she asked him for a large sum of money. The woman, whose name was Helen, had quite a colorful* background, and our job was to document it. One lead took Hal to Las Vegas, where she allegedly had connections with the underworld.

Hal went there and soon realized that interviewing one particular man, Mr. X, was going to be a bit difficult. He had driven out to Mr. X's home, which was in the country, only to find that the ranch was enclosed with a high electric fence and a guard on duty at the front gate with a pack of dogs to aid him. Hal did not speak with the guard at all and returned to town.

He spent several hours nosing around Las Vegas and returned to his hotel room about one in the morning. As he pushed the door open, he smelled heavy cigar smoke. When he turned on the light, three men were in his room. They were big, tough, surly characters who suggested that for his own good, Hal get out of town and stay away from Mr. X. Hal left that morning.

The next lead took Hal to Los Angeles to talk to a woman who was believed to be a former friend of the accuser. He telephoned her on his arrival, and she readily agreed to come to his hotel room and talk — too readily. Hal called me, and I flew down with recording equipment to check into the room he had rented next door. We set up our gear, with the microphone in his room, the wire running under the connecting door, and the recorder in my room where I could monitor the conversation.

The woman arrived at the appointed time, and Hal started to ask questions about Helen. She answered a few, but when the questions became more pointed, she suddenly stood up and started to undress.

I heard Hal say, "Hey, what are you doing?" The woman replied, "You think you're going to make Helen out to be a bum so she will lose her paternity suit against Sam? Well, I'll fix you. I'm going to accuse you of raping me." I opened the connecting door, quietly walked into the room and said, "May I help you undress, dearie?" She was a bit aghast but then looked past me at the recorder in the adjoining room. That terrified her. She started screaming

and crying. Hal told her to get dressed and get out or he
would call the hotel detectives.

That was the end of that witness. With her tape, we
developed evidence that Helen was trying to blackmail
Sam and was not pregnant, nor had she been pregnant.
The case never went to trial.

Developing the power to record a scene or conversation for
legal purposes soon became the Lipsets' stock-in-trade. They were
resourceful and dedicated — and sometimes too ingenious. Early
one morning, Hal was arrested on a New York grand jury indictment of twenty-eight suspects in a four-state "sweep" of alleged
wiretappers initiated by the New York district attorney. "I think it's
pretty chicken," he joked to the press on the way to jail, "to be
rousted out of bed at six in the morning."

It was also pretty serious. One of Hal's codefendants had been
arrested on similar charges before and sentenced to two to four years
in prison. Hal himself was charged with eavesdropping, conspiracy,
and possession of eavesdropping equipment — charges that could
put him away for half a decade.

Hal: In those days the distinction between no-party and
one-party consent was still pretty fuzzy. In some courts, it
was thought that an investigator could take the place of
his clients by acting on their behalf as a witness to private
conversations. The reasoning stemmed from a legendary
story about Mrs. Warren G. Harding, who at one time paid
Secret Service agents to hide behind the drapes in the Oval
Room to listen in on the President's phone calls to his mistress. She felt there was no other way to get the information she needed to sue him for divorce, so she believed she
was justified in her action by giving the Secret Service
agents a kind of unofficial power of attorney.

The idea of placing a microphone *for* a person rather
than placing a microphone *on* the person was a familiar
one to me almost from the beginning of our involvement
in recording conversations. On many occasions, I had
brought tapes into court that revealed admissions by errant
spouses or blackmailers and was not asked how I acquired
them. The attorney for our client would say, "Now, Mr.

So-and-so, is that your voice?," and the witness would stammer, "Yes, that's me," and try to explain what he had said on tape. The opposing attorney would never rise and object to the admissibility of the tape because everyone was in a state of shock that the actual voice had been preserved for the court. That's how new it was then.

The only question of legality that occasionally came up was whether I was guilty of breaking and entering to place the mike on private premises. "No, sir," I would say to the judge. "I used a fishing pole from the window of the room above to fly-cast the mike down and attach it to the drapes that were accessible through the open window of the subject's apartment." To me, this was the same as hiding behind the drapes of the Oval Office for Mrs. Warren G. Harding. On the occasions where I had paid a maid to let me in, I would say that I had found the door unlocked, which was technically true, because I didn't want to get the maid in trouble. I would explain that I had walked in, calling out my name to see if anyone was home. This often got a laugh from the jury.

This was the legally cloudy atmosphere that surrounded the issue of tape-recorded conversations when a woman named Mrs. Hillerton came in to talk about getting a divorce. Her husband, she said, would not give her a divorce and would not discuss in front of her the fact that he had been having an extramarital affair. It would do no good to engage him in conversation while wearing a tape recorder, because no admissions would be made. "Why not photograph him with his mistress?" I asked. "Because the affair is over," she said. "Oh, he'll go on to somebody else eventually, but who knows when that will be? Our marriage ended long ago. I have to get on with my own life."

The next weekend, she said, Mr. Hillerton was going to New York on business, in part to see an old friend with whom Mrs. Hillerton was sure he would discuss his most intimate secrets. If I could record their conversation from the next room, she was certain I would get the evidence she needed to begin divorce proceedings.

Today I would tell her we couldn't do it. This would

constitute a clear violation of the no-party consent laws, and we both could be thrown in jail for it. At the time, however, before the 1968 law had passed, it seemed routine. I called an associate in New York City who hired a technician to set up his own equipment in the room adjacent to Mr. Hillerton's at the Plaza Hotel. The husband's "friend" turned out to be a woman with whom he had a sexual episode while the recorder was running. I flew to New York to see what had been recorded and found the tape almost indecipherable. "If I had known you were using such lousy equipment," I said, "I would have brought my own." Little did I know the technician himself was wired and was now recording my voice. I flew back with the tapes, having no idea that the technician was a convicted eavesdropper who had been granted immunity when he turned informant. Almost a year later, the police made their arrest.

I felt that I could convince a jury I was acting in my client's best interests. Whose rights were at stake, I would have argued — a woman who couldn't get a divorce any other way or a man who had lied his head off about extramarital affairs but swore he'd never give her a divorce?

My attorney thought we could win such a case because I hadn't bugged the room myself. I had made a statement that he would argue was too vague to be termed "tacit agreement," which was needed for a conviction of conspiracy. Still, he said, he had to agree with the attorneys for the other twenty-seven suspects that the D.A. had his eye on the mayor's seat and was pinning his chances on the headlines this "sweep" would generate. Apparently, my case was one of the lesser ones — the D.A. was not interested in sending me to jail, but he did want a conviction, however minor, and he was going to get it. I ended up pleading guilty to a misdemeanor.

Ironically, instead of returning home with a blot on my record, I found the phone ringing off the hook with new clients. Lynn said people who heard about the indictment had decided we must be right at the cutting edge of our profession, which was true — in fact, at that point it was painfully true.

The Lipsets were soon regarded as experts on all phases of electronically recorded evidence — legal or otherwise — and as a result, lawyers in San Francisco began turning to them for advice and direction on the presentation of taped materials in court. In postwar San Francisco, still a wide-open port, some of Hal's assignments took on the comic qualities of a French farce.

San Francisco had a number of burlesque houses, not what you'd call strip joints, but shows where the women would take off most of their clothes and dance around on stage. Every so often, the police would go through these places and make arrests. Marvin Lewis, a lawyer I did a lot of work for in those times, represented the dancers in court.

It happened at the time of these raids that there was a play in town called *Remains to Be Seen.* This was a legitimate stage show at a grand old theater called the Alcazar. I had seen the play, and I said to Marvin at the time, "Gee, Sally Forrest, who is an MGM starlet under contract, takes off more clothes in *Remains to Be Seen* than your dancers do in their entire burlesque routines. She got all the way down to her underwear, then she slipped on a very sheer nightgown, then she took off her panties and bra under the nightgown and got into a bed onstage."

Marvin's eyes widened, and he said, "Do you think we can prove it?"

"Why not? We'll buy some tickets, put some people in the audience as witnesses and have the proof," I replied. That wasn't enough for Marvin. He wanted something more dramatic.

"Let's get movies," he said. "Let's get pictures of just that part of the play."

Taking movies inside a theater had never been done before, but with all that light on stage it didn't seem impossible. I wasn't sure what the Alcazar's management would think, though, so I bought box seats — the whole box, so I'd be alone. I took a cameraman with me, and when Sally Forrest started taking off her clothes, he started filming. We had tried to insulate the sides of the machine with cotton, but we hadn't had the time to devise some kind of box to cover up the motor, so you could hear this loud whirring noise all over the theater. People below us made angry shushing sounds, and in a very few seconds, somebody from the theater came over and whispered in a loud voice, "What's going on?"

The cameraman kept filming while I got up and whispered to the guy, "It's OK, we're just taking movies." He left, but pretty soon another guy came through the curtain and said, "What's going on?" I got him out of the box to distract him.

"It's OK — I already told the other guy we're just taking movies." He wasn't budging.

"Who gave you permission?" he asked.

"Randy Hale," I said. Lynn had called earlier to find out the name of the theater manager.

"No, he didn't," the man said.

"Of course he did. If you doubt it, why don't you go ask him?" Another second and Sally Forrest would be down to her skivvies.

"Because I'm Randy Hale, you jerk."

I could see there was no more stalling. "OK, do you want us to leave?" I asked — by now we'd gotten the part we needed.

"Yes, I want you to leave now or I'll call the police," he said, "and I want the film. This is a private theater. You can't just walk in here and take film of this play."

"Well, I think you're wrong," I said, "but I don't want to make any trouble. Give him the film," I told the cameraman, who had replaced the Sally Forrest reel with a blank one. "If you're going to make such a fuss about it, we'll leave right now." I wanted to get out before the audience recognized us as the troublemakers in the box. They would have stoned us, they were so mad.

After Marvin got the processed film, he made a statement to the press that in a legitimate play here in town, MGM starlet Sally Forrest revealed more of her body than did any of his burlesque clients, and he wanted to go on record to say the arrest of these dancers was an improper use of police power and an offense to human decency.

By the time we got to court and subpoenaed Sally Forrest, MGM's lawyer, a legendary San Francisco attorney named Jake Ehrlich, was so happy about all the free publicity that he milked the court proceedings for even more headlines. Jake hollered at Marvin; Marvin hollered at Jake. After seeing the film and hearing testimony from the arresting officers, the judge threw the whole thing out and dismissed charges against all the burlesque dancers. Everyone was happy — Sally loved it, Marvin loved it, Jake loved it, the San Francisco newspapers got their fill, and I got more business — except the theater manager, who posted a big sign in the lobby prohibiting the taking of pictures or tape recordings while the play was in progress.

Other theaters around the country heard about the Sally Forrest case and put up signs of their own, and that's why you'll still see a sign similar to that original warning that the taking of photographs or recording of voices is illegal whenever you go to a stage or movie theater. Even tickets have that warning on them. I guess you could call this a landmark case in that respect.

Such high jinks seem harmless now, but at the time they contributed to a vague uneasiness among Americans about electronic eavesdropping. In a country where pulp novels and true-crime magazines offered the few glimpses of sex America allowed itself in the conservative fifties, newspaper stories about secret microphones recording illicit affairs and peeled underwear had more than a sensational appeal — they offered lurid thrills unknown even in the pulps.

At the same time, there was something dirty and gutter-ridden about the kind of technology (and the detectives who used it) that snooped into people's private lives with hidden mikes and lenses. Dime novels portrayed private eyes in earphones as seduced and fallen men who, like drug addicts and sex fiends, needed to be saved — but first, the authors would say, let's listen in on the wild sex scene that's coming over their headgear from the nymphomaniac stewardesses' apartment above. . . .

Such an act was called voyeurism, not a new word in the American lexicon but newly applied in the press and in fiction when it went beyond peeking to listening in. The idea of being as close to a subject as you could stay distant from it heightened the thrill of violating people's privacy, especially when hidden tapes were used by the media in what one newspaper called a new "pornography of the earwaves."

Listening in offered an intoxicating power that made voyeurs of everyone — readers and participants alike — except those who made a living at it. For professional private eyes such as Lipset and his engineer, Ralph Bertsche, pioneering advances in the science and the commerce of hidden recorders made every impossible assignment a billable challenge. Thus the quality of the recording — more than the meaning of the conversation — soon became the central focus of electronic surveillance.

Francis Ford Coppola considered the implications of the professional eavesdropper a dozen years later when he made *The Conversation*, a motion picture in which private investigator/recording expert Harry Caul says to his technician, "I don't care what they're talking about. All I want is a nice, fat recording." It should come as no surprise that Hal Lipset was hired as technical consultant for the picture.

Coppola makes voyeurs of us all when he opens the film on San Francisco's Union Square, where three "units" of Caul's eavesdroppers, including a futuristic parabolic mike the size of a small satellite dish, monitor the conversation of a pair of lovers who are dodging the woman's husband and his detectives. Unlike his assistant, Stan, who takes pictures of women who unknowingly apply lipstick in front of the two-way mirrors of Caul's disguised Pioneer Glass van ("Show me some tongue!" Stan says, snapping away), Caul has no curiosity about the meaning or importance of the conversations he records. "Listen," he tells Stan, "if there's one surefire rule that I have learned in this business, it's that I don't know anything about human nature. I don't know anything about curiosity. I don't — that's not part of what I do. What I — this is my *business*."

Inarticulate and reclusive, Caul feels the world turning on him when his girlfriend and his assistant leave him and the competition moves in. His guilt emerges over an earlier, hideous triple murder for which he believes his recordings were responsible, and his rather primitive Catholicism — that need to confess secrets to a Poirot-like presence — overwhelms him with panic. "You're not supposed to feel anything about it," says a call girl who physically pulls him away from his agonizing obsession over the Union Square tapes. "You're just supposed to do it." Coppola makes it clear that she could be describing her own job as much as his; the detective as prostitute is a recurring theme throughout film *noir* and a nagging accusation in the mind of the real-life private eye.

The movie is one big jigsaw puzzle on the invasion of privacy, yet it is really about the voyeur-turned-paranoid in all of us. Caul represents that part of human nature that wants to live as a recluse inside society. His sophisticated locks, hidden microphones, and high-tech devices — all created and used in real life by Lipset and Bertsche — signify the child inside cringing against moral choice in a repressive society. Like Lipset, Caul masters and advances the technology of electronic eavesdropping as a way of taking control over his universe. But by cutting out all emotion, Caul, unlike Lipset, becomes a kind of closet fascist.

Hal's job as technical adviser began when Coppola dropped by unannounced one evening and said, "You Lipset? Somebody told me you should read this," and handed Hal a large brown envelope.

> I stayed up all night with that script. It was astonishing — here this kid out of UCLA film school had perfectly captured the kind of built-in paranoia that detectives wrestle with every day. We all feel it; you can't listen in on people's lives to the extent we do and not get the feeling people are listening in on you. Voyeurs in this business never make it — they're not interested in billable hours — but paranoia? That's something that creeps in like the fog.

Taken on one level as a conventional mystery, *The Conversation* could be a portrait of the real-life private eye. It shows the investigator trying to find the truth by working outside a system he hates. It shows both the promise and reality of high-tech surveillance hardware, its everyday penetration of privacy. More to Coppola's point, it suggests that Americans have jeopardized their own principles through their bedazzlement of gadgetry, capitalism, and big business.

On a more symbolic level, it is a fiction within a fiction, a waking nightmare, possibly acted out entirely in Caul's imagination as he plays his saxophone alone while the apartment around him — his moral environment, his privacy, his fate, his chance for autonomy — gradually falls into chaos. The question is, does he trash it of his own volition, or do "they" convince him to do it?

> I told Francis I'd oversee the technical aspects as long as we used state-of-the-art equipment — no James Bond stuff — and tried to show how a real surveillance might work. What you see in that movie is the best of the field at the time with only one fib — the pocket tape recorder does not have a playback function — and one exaggeration: the parabolic mike is too large to use secretly. I tried it once, looked through a telephoto lens, and saw my subject thumbing his nose at me.

Perhaps most important, *The Conversation* is one grand, timeless metaphor of the act of conversation and the impulse to listen in, with or without "mechanical aids." As Hal has put it, you can elect never to enter into a conversation and so never have to bear the responsibility for what you say or hear. But once you hear something, even if you're an eavesdropper like Caul, you've heard it. You know it. Now what are you going to do with it?

> What impressed me about the script was that Caul is both a detective and a kind of Everyman. He wants to deny that he heard something in the conversation that could lead his client to murder. He denies to his priest that he is responsible at the moment he realizes how responsible he is. He's like the witness who tells the private investigator she saw one thing and the court she saw another. A hidden recorder helps the court determine credibility. For me it's kind of an enforcer. It backs me up when I ask people to tell the truth. You can't just say, "I don't want to get involved." The universe got you involved.

Typically, Caul's epiphany does not come in an executive boardroom in confrontation with his client but under a hotel sink where a flushing toilet covers the noise of his drill as he inserts a listening device into the adjoining wall. The toilet — an apt Coppola image — provides the kind of plumbing connection between hotel rooms that investigators such as Hal Lipset use all the time, just as he did many years before in a case that bears a striking (though happily nonviolent) resemblance to events in *The Conversation*. This may be called "The Case of the Kinky Husband."

In my early days as an investigator I got a phone call from a man named Sam who wanted me to record a conversation he was going to have with his wife, Nancy. They had a troubled marriage, he said, and Nancy had recently admitted that during one separation, she had had an affair with an old high school boyfriend. Since he was still considering divorce, he wanted to get this admission on tape in case he needed it in court.

At the time, this was a very commonplace thing to do, and I agreed to set up the equipment to record the conversation. Sam had arranged for them to have dinner at a restaurant up in Santa Rosa and to spend the night in a motel room. He said they would check in early, so he asked me if I would rent two adjoining rooms for him beforehand, get the microphone in place in their room, and leave the key for him at the desk. He would try to get the conversation over with before dinner so I could retrieve my equipment and leave after they went out.

They checked in as planned. I had stationed myself in the bathroom where I began the recording as soon as they began talking. Sam started off by saying to his wife, "Honey, tell me again what happened when you and I were separated. You went home to your parents' house, right? And from there you went to a dance where you met your old boyfriend, and then you went out to the car and had sex with him in the backseat?"

Nancy told him the story and made all the proper admissions, but then Sam started asking her questions in more detail. I was much younger at the time — not that experienced in psychological matters — but I had a funny feeling that things weren't proceeding as they should. Sam kept asking for specifics. He said to her, "Now when he took your panties off, did he take your right leg out first or your left? When you were sitting in the car, did you raise up yourself to help him? Did he pull them off slowly, or did you do it for him?"

He kept asking her these sorts of questions, one after another. Then he stopped, suddenly, and to my complete astonishment, they began to make love. I didn't know what to do. The recorder kept running, although now I figured it was useless until they finished and left the room to have dinner.

While they were gone, Sam called me as we had planned and asked if I got a good recording (I was still using wire). This was even more astonishing. I told him what I thought was obvious; since he had sex with Nancy, it was going to sound on the tape as though he was condoning her past behavior. "You made love to her as though you forgave her," I said. "That's not what this tape's for — the tape is supposed to show that she caused you grave mental cruelty when she committed adultery."

Well, he was surprised to hear this but said he now understood how these things worked. He asked me to stay until they came back from the restaurant so he could start the conversation again. This time, once it was recorded, I could turn off the recorder and leave, and whatever happened between them after that would be his own business. So I put another spool of wire on the recorder and waited for them to come back.

They walked in chatting and again he got her talking about what happened when they were separated. By now it was obvious to me that this was maybe the twentieth or thirtieth time he'd had her repeat it. Nancy dutifully began to tell him again, almost word for word as he asked her the same questions over and over again, when all of a sudden, she broke down and started to cry. This stopped Sam cold.

"Nancy," he said, genuinely concerned. "What is it? What's wrong?"

"Oh Sam," she said. "All of this is a lie. I never had an affair with my old boyfriend. I just needed to get away for a few weeks and think things over." Then the really shocking part came out. She said to Sam, "I love you, honey, but you're ill. That psychiatrist you're seeing — I called him to ask his advice about your impotence. He said the only way for us to have a regular sex life was for me to pretend I had an affair with somebody else! I didn't want to, Sam, I didn't! So I left for a few weeks to think it over, and I realized I would have to make up the whole story. Now you keep asking for more details and I keep having to make them up — oh, I can't stand it, Sam, I love you too much to lie like this!" She burst into tears again.

At this point Sam became so upset I thought I was going to record the first murder in process; he was yelling and carrying on like a crazy man. I was too inexperienced to know what he was really angry about. Was it me, because the tape would not now give him the upper hand in the divorce case, or his doctor, who violated his confidence, or his wife, who hadn't really had the affair? The way he was shouting, it was everyone. It was the world. Clearly he forgot he had hired me to record his words for his own protection.

Eventually things quieted down, and they went to sleep. Per our agreement, I packed up my recording equipment and went home. I had never met this man in person. Everything had been handled by phone — he sent me a money order, and I didn't know his true name. I never allowed myself to get in this position again. I insist on meeting all clients, knowing their true identity, and getting a full picture of the case before I agree to take it.

A few days later, Sam phoned me and wanted the wires. Usually, when I make a recording, the tape or wire belongs to the person who hired me. But in this case, I didn't know what might happen — he was too volatile. I explained that we never let tapes out of our possession in instances like these — not that we had ever had an instance like this, but I did make it a policy to protect what lawyers call the "chain of evidence," which means you sign the object over to an attorney, he signs it over to the D.A., he signs it over to the court, and so forth so that no one can tamper with it in between.

I told Sam that the tapes might be important to him

down the road, and that while they were his property, we had them safely under lock and key in a fireproof, earthquake-proof, waterproof vault, and they'd always be there if he needed them. I wasn't about to send them to him, period. But I would hand them to him personally if he were willing to come over and identify himself and sign a receipt for them. He never did.

Could it be that precedent-setting techniques in electronic technology took place at the base of a toilet both in real life and in the movies? Absolutely: The reason Hal's office would leap ahead of government research in the field was that Hal was applying Ralph Bertsche's experiments to the needs of real cases in the private sector every day. And the reason Lipset Service would succeed was that unlike Lamont Cranston ("The Shadow"), the detective decided to step out of the shadows as his own lobbyist. How the public and the government became enchanted with a little gimmick called the "bug in the martini olive" is the subject of our next chapter.

Chapter 3

The Bug in the Martini Olive

Bugs . . . She had thought of the decade that the country had just sleepwalked through. Electronic surveillance wasn't exactly without precedent. As a matter of fact one could say that it had become an American tradition.
— Karl Alexander, *A Private Investigation*

Secrets became marketable commodities when hard-boiled detectives realized they were in the business not of solving crimes but of selling information. As technology in the fifties and sixties caught up with increasing needs for commercial data, a new industry developed in which investigators such as Hal Lipset discovered the Rosetta stone of the electronic age: the Japanese transistor.

The transistor, as Hal would explain it to a Senate subcommittee on eavesdropping, "allows the investigator freedom from wires and connections so that a microphone placed in a hotel room can pick up voices and transmit them by radio band to a recording device several blocks away. It also allows for miniaturization, making bugging devices so small they can be hidden almost anywhere without being detected."

By 1964, *Time* magazine estimated that the transistor had "virtually transformed . . . scientific snooping" and estimated that the federal government was spending about $20 million on "bugging gear a year." Even more was spent "by the bug-infested CIA, which likes to shop through dummy agencies." Nevertheless, the more significant progress in research and development was taking place in the private sector.

"To advance the art," *Time* wrote, "Hal Lipset, a seasoned San Francisco private eye, maintains a laboratory behind a false warehouse front where his eavesdropping 'genius,' Ralph Bertsche, works out new gimmicks such as a high-powered bug that fits into a pack of filter-tip cigarettes. It is padded to feel soft and shows the ends of real cigarettes to reassure a suspicious businessman or divorce-prone spouse. . . ."

These were heady years at Lipset Service. Bertsche could hide his transmitters in anything — hatbands, ballpoint pens, briefcases, tie clasps, wristwatches, the snap clasps of purses — and just about anywhere: in telephones, dashboards, air ducts, floral arrangements, kitchen sinks, electrical outlets.

Spike mikes, sugar-lump transmitters, floating rooms, miniature spy cameras, and infinity transmitters were all part of the exotica Bertsche fiddled with in his "laboratory," which in fact was a storefront on Bush Street he had made into a shop. Talk about fiction in the making: The words "genius" and "laboratory" in the *Time* article made Bertsche sound like a mad scientist plotting maniacally to destroy the world with miniature recorders. Hal loved the idea and the image.

In one case of long-running theft in a wholesale liquor firm, Hal's undercover agent clasped a bar of soap in the men's room each time he struck up a conversation at the sink with the gang's suspected ringleader. The bar was a tiny transmitting device made of plastic and coated with soap. When the ringleader asked the agent to join the racket, Hal and Ralph, sitting in a disguised van outside, recorded the conversation on a reel-to-reel tape recorder. Transcripts from the bar of soap, along with falsified delivery invoices, were introduced as evidence in the trial that convicted over a dozen thieves.

When a building contractor realized that his company was being repeatedly underbid by a suspicious few dollars on every new project, Lipset began monitoring company phones with hidden bugs and caught an engineer making the tip-offs to the company's competitors. At the time, the company was considered the consenting party because it owned the phones and allowed the hired help to speak on its behalf. A decade later, however, two Oakland, California, private investigators would be convicted of invasion of privacy in a parallel case. Such is the shaky legal firmament upon which the private eye trods at any given time.

At a trucking firm, an undercover agent offered his boss one of the two real Marlboro cigarettes that could be placed in Bertsche's ingenious transmitter/cigarette pack, and as the two shared a smoke, the boss offered to split "hidden income" from "extracurricular deliveries" shared by a ring of warehouse thieves.

At the home of a woman whose neighbor had approached her about buying stolen radios "hot off the waterfront," a lovely vase of roses was equipped with bugs that picked up a conversation in which she, carefully coached by Hal, prompted the neighbor to provide the names of accomplices and buyers.

If caught installing these devices, Lipset's agents had their stories.

> *Hal:* Ralph was installing recording equipment in the house of a woman who wanted to have a conversation with her husband to get him to admit that he had been having an affair. The husband came home early and found Ralph down in the basement with a flashlight running wires. He said to Ralph, "Who are you?"
>
> "I'm a termite inspector," Ralph answered.
>
> "Have you found any bugs?" the man asked.
>
> Ralph was kind of stunned at this. "Well, when you get our report," he said, "you'll know all about the bugs."

As cases of business theft and industrial espionage increased, Hal, with his flair for PR, seemingly made public all that was hidden. Every photographer, every TV cameraman, every investigative journalist who wanted to know just what was going on behind that secret "laboratory" was invited in with great ceremony to view and record the latest progress in listening in.

Bertsche himself shunned publicity — another quality Hal appreciated — so it was Hal who was photographed sliding on his back under a dashboard to plant a transmitter, holding up the pack of wired Marlboros, setting up headgear for jurors to hear recordings, examining telephoto lenses, opening the cabinet doors to his "electronic arsenal" as though inviting guests to view the Torah — and looking throughout like the respectable businessman he believed himself to be.

Hal tried to take advantage of the publicity because he felt it would attract more clients to Lipset Service, regardless of the morality of the times. "Bad publicity is good publicity," he liked to say, reminding his operatives that even in the worst of cases — when he was arrested, jailed, even convicted — his picture in the paper always drew more business. In one *Business Week* article about the latest bugs used in industrial espionage, Hal was, typically, the only private eye to quote the going rates (not his) of these illegal devices — "the cost for a telephone tap runs from $75 to $250 a unit, and room microphones from $150 to $350. . . ."

More important, Lipset knew that the proliferation of bugs and recorders in the fifties and sixties was making Americans nervous. If they didn't think immediately of voyeurism, reference to electronic eavesdropping in the press reminded people of George Orwell's prediction that government would one day become an oppressive Big Brother, not only watching your every move but listening in to your every conversation and thought.

Hal insisted he worried about Big Brother as well, with one crucial difference: Miniature recorders were on their way to the marketplace, not by the dozens but by the thousands. They would soon be affordable and easy to use, so Americans shouldn't stick their heads in the sand. Why wait for Big Brother to take them over when you, as a consumer, as a citizen, have a right to control the electronic age as well?

Hal believed citizens should require police to wear recorders so that whatever a cop said about an arrest on police reports or in court would be backed up on tape. (Now that they wear radios on their uniform, it would be simple to keep the mike on whenever they approach a vehicle or suspect.) He even suggested that people buy their own miniature recorders and hide them on their person to keep agents of Big Brother under control. If you had a tape machine handy, Hal said, every conversation, every telephone sales order, every run-in with the police, every threat, every declaration of divorce could be confirmed electronically.

"The basic issue," he told interviewers, "is not whether some private eye is going to invade your privacy by bugging your home, but how well you can *protect* your rights against the invasion of privacy by Big Brother. . . . If you get in trouble with the law, the prosecution has the investigative power of the police, the FBI, the Treasury Department, and private records to put you in prison. Your defense attorney has me. A recording of your voice or of someone making accusations could free you."

Look at Watts, he said: We'll never know what really triggered the riot and conflagration that followed the exchange between a police officer and a black citizen. A recording would tell us unequivocally how that riot started.

"Take the assassination of John F. Kennedy," he told a reporter. "Would you believe there was no recording made when the Dallas police were interviewing Lee Harvey Oswald? The police said they couldn't afford it, but the FBI was there. The public is entitled to hear the man's responses even if they were only denials. I see this as another dreadful example of ineptitude."

Hidden recordings were either taken too fearfully or too lightly at the time. Local columnist Herb Caen thought it funny to confuse the issue when he wrote, "Pvt. Eye Hal Lipset flies to N'York this wkend to tape a David Susskind 'Open End.' . . . There's hardly a privacy around town that Lipset hasn't invaded at least once. . . ."

Perhaps as a result of so much publicity, clients arrived at Lipset Service asking Hal to do the reverse of what was making him locally famous — to remove the bugs other investigators had planted in businesses, homes, and political meetings. Hal immediately dubbed this kind of work "industrial counterespionage," because the term sounded so professional, although the press would soon say that San Francisco's "super snooper" had now become a "super sweeper."

Sweeping was simply a way of placing a thirty-to-a-thousand-megacycle, very narrow-band, quality radio receiver in the suspect room, then sweeping the band carefully while causing a tone to be emitted in the room that we could pick up when a hidden transmitter was detected. In other words, the same receiver that you use to listen to a bug is what you use to check it out. Some people think you walk around with a little frequency meter in your hand that's going to beep loudly like a Geiger counter when you pass by a bug. In these situations, that's no good — you're just picking up something on the radio waves that already exists, and there's so much out there that it's impossible to know what you've got.

The more sophisticated the operation, the more sophisticated the sweep equipment — Bertsche could bring in everything from metal detectors to fault locators, X-ray devices, wire identification seekers, and tracers to trigger whatever remote controls might exist.

A union under investigation by the government was planning a big meeting of its hierarchy and needed a room secured at the Fairmont Hotel in San Francisco. In our sweep we came across a hidden camera that was to be operated by remote control from a room two floors below the meeting room.

Casinos in Las Vegas and Reno were some of the earliest clients looking for reliable "sweepers."

We worked successfully for one casino operation until the owners decided that if Lipset Service was hired to find out if other investigators could get at them, they should hire other investigators to check on us. One night we got a call from the security manager who said that newly hired "experts" had removed twenty-seven telephone taps we had obviously missed from executive offices and pit telephones. It turned out these "experts" mistakenly removed all the intercom buzzers in the phones.

Another time Ralph and I were sweeping a casino when we were told the owners had spent $35,000 to build a room within a room, impenetrable from electronic surveillance, where they had been meeting to discuss matters of the utmost secrecy. They were very proud of it —"You don't have to worry about bug-proofing *this* one," they said. We went exploring and found the job well done except that the contractor, who was not an investigator, had failed to secure the air-conditioning ducts.

Ralph climbed up in a crawl space and lowered a little radio transmitter down a piece of wire to the bottom of the duct, where a vent had been placed in the ceiling of the room-within-a-room. I called in the vice president and asked him how exactly they had made the room secure — if this was the place where they decided how much money they would steal, and a few other things for humor. After we left, Ralph met us and played the conversation between the vice president and myself in the room-within-a-room. The vice president was very surprised.

Hal made his views clear to the scholarly legal community by contributing an article, "The Wiretapping-Eavesdropping Problem," to the *Minnesota Law Review* in 1960. But his first chance to go public on the national scene occurred the previous year when he was invited to testify before the Senate Constitutional Rights Subcommittee, chaired by Missouri Democrat Thomas C. Hennings. "I had what I thought was a great idea," he remembers. "First I thought I'd dazzle them with an array of miniature devices they had never seen before; then I would surprise them by playing back my own testimony from a recorder I had hidden before the hearing."

The great idea worked too well. Lipset's appearance was seen as a clever but ominous sign of electronic snooping running amok. SECRET MIKES IRK SENATORS ran the understated headline of an Associated Press story, which stated that after viewing Lipset's demonstration, the senators were aghast at the "rampant" use of eavesdropping gadgetry and ordered an immediate investigation of "how many pocket-sized recorders Government agencies have bought and what use is being made of them."

Look, Lipset said, federal law had already made wiretapping without anybody's consent an illegal act, so it didn't matter how rampant the gadgetry was. What mattered was a proper understanding of one-party consent. Using a secret recorder was not an invasion of privacy, Hal insisted; it was a *protection* of privacy.

The committee was not impressed. Irked at having their questions taped without their knowledge, the senators were made to feel like fools in front of reporters and decided Lipset was exploiting the hearings for his own profit. So did the press, apparently, as a *St. Louis Post-Dispatch* editorial indicated a few days later: "Mr. Lipset . . . should know that eavesdropping is a furtive, dirty business against which honorable men instinctively revolt. No doubt there is money in stealing other people's secrets — and listening to perhaps thousands of personal conversations to do so — but it is not nice money, nor is it legal money."

There it was, the stigma of the private eye, whose lack of principles and lust for dirty money (two attributes Lipset has not-so-jokingly used to describe himself), contributed to that other stigma about the hidden recorder — a symbol of voyeurism and an insult to "honorable men." Nothing could be more un-American.

And yet "stealing other people's secrets" was a time-honored institution in American history, Hal believed. If you were going to write an editorial against it, you had to be against all of it.

> Here's a case in point: What would be the difference if I took your photograph with a hidden camera or taped your voice with a hidden recorder? There's no difference: The camera is hidden; the recorder is hidden. The photograph is made without your consent; so is the tape. Yet paparazzi make a million dollars hiding in the bushes to photograph Jackie Onassis; insurance investigators prove their case by secretly filming fraudulent claimants; but reporters and private investigators hiding a tape recorder go to jail.

If that's true, why are the laws different for hidden cameras than for hidden tape recorders?

> The reason — beyond the fact that insurance companies have a more powerful lobby than private investigators — is that to the public mind, photographs are safe, recordings are dangerous. A photograph, people think, can't be faked. An expert can always tell. But a recording is inexplicable. People are afraid of it, afraid that what they say in a moment of anger may be the painful truth; afraid their words may be misconstrued, or worse, may be altered by someone else.

So early on politicians say to me, through the legislature, that I'm developing a new investigative technique, the first new technique to come along since photographs — and I'm not working for an approved institution like an insurance company, mind you; I'm a private eye who snoops for money — and because this new technique may be misused, we'll make it illegal. That's why you can use a hidden camera today, but you can't use a hidden recorder in the same situation in many states.

But can't a tape be altered? Aren't there ways to change a person's meaning by changing the words recorded?

The technology is too sophisticated for that — any alteration would be instantly detected. If you don't believe me, ask Richard Nixon. Don't you think if it were technically possible to alter the White House tapes during Watergate he would have had them fixed? No, with the millions of dollars and state-of-the-art expertise he had at his disposal, the best he could do was to have Rosemary Woods "mistakenly" erase eighteen and a half minutes. It was impossible then to falsify a tape, and it's impossible now. It's our fear of falsification that's the real issue, not the reality.

To prove his point, Hal needed a big, headline-making case that would show the world just how valuable hidden recorders could be in protecting average people from law-enforcement oppression. The Raggio case had been splashy enough, but Raggio's role in law enforcement overshadowed the importance of one-party consent.

Then, as so often happened in the very worst (or best) pulp mysteries that preceded him, fate was to lend a hand with its own deus ex machina, Philadelphia attorney Sam Dash.

Dash: I was defending Local 107 of the Philadelphia Teamsters against investigations by the Senate Rackets Committee, the IRS, and the local district attorney's office when John J., a dissident inside the union, called me one day to set up a meeting. He said he had information that would help the union's case, but I felt it was just as likely he had turned government informer and was out to lay a trap. I called Hal, who strapped on a recorder-in-a-holster and went out to talk to John. J. It was the first time I had seen a tape recorder used this way.

Hal: The subject was mowing his lawn when I got there. He seemed friendly enough, but just after I identified myself, he excused himself and walked into his house. A moment later a police car rolled into the driveway. Out came John J., screaming that I had violated his rights and interfered with due process. "What can I do, John?" the cop yelled. John pointed to me and said, "Lock him up — I'll press charges." I looked at the cop and said, "On what charge?" The cop laughed and said, "Never mind. We'll think of something later."

These two were so obviously in cahoots and I had so easily caught them at their game that I was afraid they might pat me down, looking for a recorder. But the idea of preserving conversations was too new. They took no precautions.

Dash: Hal called me from the police station, and our conversation went something like this:

Hal: "I'm under arrest and at the station here."

Sam: "Have they . . ." (Meaning, have they searched you?)

H: "No, they haven't yet."

S: "Did they . . ." (Did they find the recorder?)

H: "No, they didn't."

S: "You can prove . . ." (You're sure the recorder was working?)

H: "As far as I know, yes."

S: "Great." (Gee, you pulled it off.)

Dash: The police charged Hal with offering a bribe, and the newspapers carried the headline, "Dash's Investigator Threatens Federal Witness." That kind of charge, that's prison stuff. It's very serious. We were cleared, but only because Hal made a transcript of his recording, which I made available to the FBI and the newspapers. It was a precedent-setting case.

Hal: Because of it, a lot of former skeptics turned believers in the value of recording conversations. Instead of being afraid of Big Brother, they saw that a recording could be used for a private citizen's protection. Without it, I certainly would have gone to jail from John J.'s testimony alone.

Zsa Zsa Gabor could certainly have used a recorder, Hal would point out many years later, during her infamous encounter with the Southern California cop who charged her with slapping him. Had both Gabor and the cop carried working recorders, they would have been more polite to begin with.

More important, consider the Los Angeles police officers who were secretly videotaped while mercilessly clubbing a motorist after a high-speed chase in 1991. Public outcry over routine police brutality would never have happened if the nation hadn't seen for itself, through the unquestioned veracity of a videotape, police officers nearly kill a civilian when they thought no one was looking.

Again and again, Lipset warned: These bugs are coming. Use them for your own protection, or the government will use them for you — and against you.

It all seemed so clear to Hal that the next time he was invited to Washington to speak before a Senate subcommittee — this one in 1965 to hear testimony specifically on eavesdropping — he renewed his efforts to convince the world of the value of hidden tape recorders.

The way these hearings worked, at least at that time, was that the chief counsel for the committee chairman — in this case, Bud Fensterwald — did a lot of preliminary work with witnesses because he was the one who opened the hearings and asked the first questions. Then he brought the senators in to do the probing, because it was their show and not his. He was like the producer of the show. It was all worked out beforehand so there wouldn't be any surprises and they'd know just how much advantage they could take of the press.

Fensterwald came out to San Francisco and told us that while the press always dropped in at these hearings, unless ours was exciting enough and caught their fancy, they might hear only the first ten or fifteen minutes and then drift off to other hearings. People in Washington were always worried about which hearing would get more coverage because, of course, every senator wanted as much coverage as possible.

So Fensterwald wanted to know what kind of clever ideas we were going to come up with to make the conference exciting. We got out the pack of cigarettes and the bugged lighter and the recorder in the book, which he thought were cute and nice but not quite eye-catching enough. He left us to come up with something better, and we sat around drinking coffee, whiskey, and lemonade for three days inventing new schemes.

One was to plant a bug on the chairman, Senator Edward Long of Missouri, but I thought we might get in trouble. Another was to put a bug inside some doggy-turds that we'd get from my dog, Lady, and take to Washington. No one would think of examining dog excrement for transmitters, but when it came to explaining to the committee what this dog shit was doing on the exhibit table, we were stumped. Somebody thought that maybe one of us could appear to be blind and we'd bring in this big seeing-eye dog . . . but that was getting too elaborate.

When we came up with the "bug in the martini olive" idea, it didn't seem all that unusual. We used a large bulletin board with all sorts of gadgets stapled or drawn or pasted onto it, and the martini glass was simply another example of how ingenious these devices could be. The glass held a facsimile of an olive, which could hold a tiny transmitter, the pimento inside the olive, in which we could embed the microphone, and a toothpick, which could house a copper wire as an antenna. No gin was used — that could cause a short.

Our point was that a host could wander through his own party, having drunk his own martini, and pick up the conversations that were directed at him, or leave his glass near a conversation he could then monitor in secret. We wanted to show the vast proliferation of this equipment, and the bug in the martini olive was one very feasible example of many.

When we got to Washington I told the security people that Ralph and I had to see the room in which this hearing would take place because we were having "acoustical problems," which meant Ralph had to get in there to plant the mikes. He did that relatively quickly and we got to bed relatively early — one A.M. Washington time — when Fensterwald called to say the room had been changed.

"We're going to the main caucus room instead — there's going to be more press than we thought, so we have to accommodate the TV and radio crews," he said.

"The main caucus room? What's that?" I asked.

"Well, it's larger than the one you saw."

I said that would be no problem if we could get in an hour earlier to fix our "acoustical problems" again. Fensterwald said he'd make the arrangements.

The hearings were scheduled to start at ten A.M. When we walked in at nine, I went into shock. The main caucus room was palatial by most standards, easily as big as a football field, with batteries of microphones down where I'd be speaking, and an armory of microphones up where the senators would sit. Ralph had to restructure his eavesdropping equipment, and I was just putting the roses back in place when everybody came streaming into the room to begin the hearing at precisely ten A.M.

"Nothing was sacred in the Senate Caucus room yesterday," wrote the *Washington Post*. "Even Long's opening statement was bugged . . . [by] a tiny microphone concealed under a rose petal. . . . Long, an obliging straight man . . ."

Hal: Long was terrific. He had been briefed beforehand about my testimony and was happy to feign surprise at some of our tricks. When Ralph walked out in the corridor and had a conversation with a capitol policeman, I played it on a loudspeaker so the senators could hear it. "You can imagine what would happen if I wanted to monitor a conversation you are having in your office," I explained. "I could be sitting in my car outside the building picking it up in this way."

Hal's testimony made it clear that he was on the side of the Constitution, the Founding Fathers, a man and his castle, and the right of every American to personal privacy — including the use of hidden recorders to protect that right. Once a conversation occurs, he said, people have their memories as witnesses — and they may, if they want to protect themselves, have a little backup in any of the dozens of devices pinned to a bulletin board to which Lipset directed the senators' attention with his handy wooden pointer. At one point, Senator Long leaned over and picked up the vase of roses that had been sitting in front of the dais all morning.

"Why, Mr. Lipset," he exclaimed, "did someone send me flowers?"

"That they did, Mr. Chairman," Lipset responded. "If you lift the large petal on the upper right, you'll see how I came by this recording." At that, Ralph began playing back Long's opening statement, while senators, reporters, cameramen, and photographers crowded around to peer at and photograph the hidden microphone.

But it was the bug in the martini olive that made Lipset "the real star of the day," as UPI reported. Hardly an ominous indication of private snoopers taking over the world, this little olive with its toothpick antenna became a "playful" and charming toy through which Lipset finally convinced his listeners that electronic eavesdropping in the private sector was both charming and patriotic.

> The senators kept asking about the martini glass. I had the pointer on it, then I'd move it away, and a question from yet another senator would bring me back. This was an actual martini glass? they would ask. Oh, yes, with an olive as a microphone and the toothpick as the antenna, I would answer. And would it work with gin actually in the glass, they'd ask, or with an onion, say, in a Gibson martini, or a lemon peel. . . .
>
> They were so entranced with the idea that I couldn't help romanticize it a little. A Gibson, a lemon peel, sure; gin would not work but maybe vodka . . . things got very congenial all at once, and then when the reporters and

photographers rushed up to get a photo, we were all laughing at how funny it was. I felt I had introduced a new toy, like a play-chew for a dog. They couldn't stop gnawing at it.

Nor, for months afterward, could the media. Headline stories about "The Tattler Martini" and "The *Pry* Martini" dominated newspapers around the country. One cartoon depicted two executives staring in horror at the martinis set before them in a men's club ("Before we talk," one says to the other, "check for antennas"). Another showed a senator on his hands and knees, looking up at a dozen microphones taped to the underside of a conference table while another senator overhead asks, "Perhaps you could tell this committee how widespread is the practice of 'bugging' in this country. . . ."

"To think that the martini, to which harried man turns for solace and comfort, should now turn on *him*," wrote Art Hoppe of the *San Francisco Chronicle* in mock horror. "A splendid development," wrote Russell Baker of the *New York Times*. "With his olive, an agent can pick up disloyal sentiments during the cocktail hour. . . ."

Fortified by Senate and public acclaim, Lipset continued his campaign to educate the world about one-party consent. When the Federal Communications Commission tried to pass a regulation banning electronic eavesdropping by private citizens, Hal called it "a very dangerous ruling" and charged the FCC with "making it safer for the bad guy but not for the good guy.

"If a policeman met you on the street and tried to extort you in violation of your rights, you would be violating the FCC ruling if you attempted to protect yourself by recording the conversation." Elected president of the Professional Investigators Association of California, Lipset mobilized his colleagues to call a press conference about the FCC ruling even as they were photographed holding up their own snoopers' gadgetry.

Reporters by this time didn't need much help understanding the issues: "Attempts by the federal government to protect you against the invasion of privacy could help land you in jail, a private investigator from San Francisco said. . . ."

If the cops can use it, we should be able to use it, Hal kept repeating. "One of the fundamental legal principles upon which our nation was founded is the idea that a suspect is innocent until proven guilty. So how can we allow certain tools to help the prosecution and then deny them to the defense?" Soon the FCC ruling disappeared in bureaucratic red tape.

But another one — far more damaging to Lipset — was to remain. A few years after the Raggio case, legislators in the state of California tried to pass a law making it illegal for private citizens to record a conversation without the consent of all parties involved. This meant elimination of one-party consent recordings in California and would have rendered all of the recordings described in this chapter inadmissible in state court.

That bill did not pass — thanks in large part to testimony and lobbying carried on by Lipset himself — but a similar one in 1967 (Section 630 of the California Penal Code) did pass and still stands as one of the most restrictive laws on listening in in the nation. When the bill became law, Lipset promptly called California "a police state" and told reporters, "Our right to record conversations in all civil cases has been completely taken away. That's the end of personal protection in this state." One small loophole still exists.

> There is an exception in Section 633.5 of the 1967 California law that says one-party consent recordings are allowed in criminal cases involving bribery, kidnapping extortion, blackmail, or a crime of violence against the person. There is also one last line that says nothing in this law shall preclude law enforcement from doing whatever it deems necessary in the course of its duty. That means the police can use hidden microphones whenever they want; we can't.

Pennsylvania has passed similarly restrictive legislation, as have increasing numbers of states.

> We now have a situation in which I can make a tape in Arizona, where it's legal, but not in California, where it isn't. I can play a tape in federal court but not in state court in California. I can play it in a criminal case but not in a civil case.

I can record a suspected blackmailer in California because of Section 633.5, but if he's acquitted in court, I can be charged with invasion of privacy. I can't record a police officer who walks in my front door because I would be breaking the law. But he can record me and any conversation I have with other people without getting anybody's consent but his own. He could even record himself asking me for money to see if I'd offer him a bribe. If I did, I'd be breaking the law; if I didn't, I'd have no proof of entrapment or extortion, except on the tape he's hiding, and he won't give it to me.

Hal's feverish defense of hidden recorders was to continue for the next decades, yet the question remained: Why would a private investigator who had done so much for the invention and proliferation of electronic eavesdropping devices be so concerned about police misuse of those devices? It didn't seem right. Reporters who did a little digging found out that Lipset had started out as a kind of cop for the U.S. Army during World War II — a decorated cop, even. He had been trained by the legendary FBI agent who captured John Dillinger and had been awarded the Bronze Star for criminal investigations following the Battle of the Bulge and during the Rhineland and Central European campaigns. That would seem to make him a proponent, not an enemy, of law enforcement. So what was his problem?

PART II

LEARNING THE ROPES

Chapter 4

The Broker

> *". . . the draftees weren't all choirboys, so there was a certain amount of pilferage. And there were wheeler-dealers who would've sold the bullets out of their buddies' guns for a buck. We caught the ones we could, but you don't have a lot of time playing policeman when you're fighting a war."*
> — Linda Grant, *Blind Trust*

Most of the hard-boiled detectives in fiction are former cops who quit the force in disgust because they believed the system was corrupt. Some are loners who never fit; some were fired for alcoholism or emotional instability. All look back with some astonishment that they ever willingly became a cog in the law-enforcement machine. Outsiders but not outlaws (yet), they stand for independent choice in a society that depends on institutionalization and conformity for its own stability.

Hal follows in this tradition, yet he considers his early experience as a military law-enforcement officer in World War II as perhaps the most valuable training of his career.

> I was a CID (Criminal Investigation Department) detective assigned to investigate crimes committed by American soldiers against civilians or against each other. When the Allies moved into Belgium and Germany, my unit moved almost directly behind them, setting up a kind of tempo-

rary detective headquarters every place American troops landed.

Say a company got involved in a firefight in a town where American soldiers had to go from house to house, pushing the Germans back. While most soldiers did what they were trained to do, there was always some kind of bad apple who would leave his buddies and find an important-looking German, someone who seemed to know something about the town.

He'd grab the man, put a knife to his throat, and say, "Who's the biggest stamp collector in town?" If the man knew, the soldier would get the stamp collector's address, go to his house, kill him if necessary, and steal the stamp collection. All he had to do was tear out the valuable stamps and mail them home to his family or himself in a V-mail letter. When he got home after the war, he'd have hundreds of thousands of dollars worth of stamps.

There were soldiers who knew about rare coins who would do the same thing to the local coin collector; GIs knowledgeable about art who would find a museum, cut valuable canvases out of the frames, roll them up in a cardboard tube, and mail them home. There were officers who packaged and posted the parts of a jeep, one by one, so that when they got home, all they had to do was assemble it, and they'd have a whole four-wheel-drive car. Nobody checked the mails at that time. It was a war zone. Everybody was moving, fighting, stopping, moving again.

A lot of gambling went on, which wasn't terribly illegal, but you'd get some soldiers who would owe money to a buddy, wait for a firefight, and kill the guy rather than pay him back.

Rape was very common. Some GIs felt any woman they saw was there to have sex with, regardless of consent or age. We learned right away that rape was a power thing. It was more about humiliation and control than sex, and that made it easier to find the men who engaged in it. They would brag to their buddies, and the word would get out.

The army, I learned, is just a mirror of the population

back home. You get a whole range of men. There were people who barely spoke English, or couldn't read, or always got in trouble. During one training period we had to put a guard in the latrine because we had men from rural areas who had never seen a chain toilet flush. The guard was there to explain how to use the toilet whenever someone came in.

Lipset's official title was First Lieutenant and he was leader of a ten-man CID unit attached to the 506th Military Police Battalion assigned to the Twenty-second Corps, which moved into the European theater during the Battle of the Bulge, and later to the Fifteenth Army during the Rhineland campaign. He was twenty-five years old.

I would go into a town, requisition any usable place I could find to set up our office and any private home large enough to billet the men. One German woman got very nervous when I walked into her home looking for five bedrooms. Without being asked, she said that I should look across the street where some Nazis lived — they had bedrooms enough for anybody.

Her home was empty, and she didn't like the idea of housing an Allied unit there. I explained we would bring our own equipment and wouldn't harm her furniture, which was sparse and meticulously cared for, but there was something about Americans, or maybe me in particular, that bugged her. She didn't like it when I inquired about several locked rooms — hell, what did I know she had in them?— so I made her open them and kept going from room to room until we got to the end of the third-floor hallway.

By this time I assumed the source of the problem was her hatred for Jews, especially American Jews, especially this American Jew who was ordering her to open the last of the closets. Finally she unlocked the door, and as it swung open I saw several sets of uniforms with swastikas sewn on the arms, all hung up neatly along the sides. The woman stammered something about the arm bands being necessary for the local cycling club. I didn't know whether to laugh or cry. We had no information about death camps at the time, but it didn't take much to sense the level of hatred in that closet. "The war is over," I said through my interpreter. "And this has got to go with it." I ordered everything in the closet removed. I did billet the men in her house, but the memory of that shrine is still chilling to me.

We always brought in our own typewriters, files, and office supplies, and we hooked up our phones to army power lines the signal corps rigged up outside. We had to scrounge for crime labs, polygraph experts, forensic doctors. We had the power of arrest, interrogation, detainment, and the taking of signed statements from witnesses, suspects, and victims. We wore no stripes or insignias and could pull rank on any officer in the course of an investigation, but of course that was rarely done if you wanted cooperation in the military.

Once we got an office operation under way, we'd let townspeople and military personnel know we were there to hear any charges of criminal activity that might involve American soldiers. There would be so many incoming cases that we'd have to conduct a kind of triage process. Petty theft, gambling debts, fraternization, absences without leave, drunkenness, and what civilian courts called misdemeanor cases we left to the M.P.s — they were like our local police. Larceny, assault, poisoning, rape, and murder were ours.

A typical crime might occur after the Allies took over a German town and established curfew. This was hard to enforce because the Germans weren't afraid of American soldiers. They might go inside when M.P.s drove around on patrol, but they'd come back out as soon as the streets were cleared. M.P.s were frustrated because they couldn't convince civilians that curfew was for their own good, since there was a remote chance that snipers could still be holed up and use the cover of a crowd to take a shot or two. So everybody was pretty edgy.

In one town, our first assignment was to investigate the

death of a German girl who had been shot through the eye while leaning out the window of a third-story apartment building. M.P.s who had been patrolling the streets had heard the shot. So had witnesses who then saw a German woman run into the street, waving a white handkerchief. The nearest M.P., Corporal Lundquist, had followed the woman to her third-floor apartment, where he found the twelve-year-old girl lying dead on the floor next to an open window.

Lundquist said he assumed a sniper had aimed at him or had fired off a wild bullet and somehow killed the girl. But a field autopsy showed a surprisingly upward wound to the brain — the bullet entering the victim's eye in a nearly vertical direction and exiting through the top of her head. This meant she was either looking up at the sky when the bullet entered from, say, an apartment across the street (there weren't any), or she had leaned out the window just as a bullet hit her from the street below.

It didn't make sense to me that the killer, if he was a sniper, had deliberately fired up toward her apartment rather than down toward M.P. Lundquist. "Everyone heard the shot," I said to him, "but no one saw the killer? Does that make sense to you?" He knew what I was getting at.

Lundquist blurted, "I got so sick of yelling at these — these faceless people who wouldn't move, wouldn't *do* anything. We had to keep to schedule, but they kept coming back outside. So I thought, well, I'll scare them, that's all, I'll fire my pistol in the air, and — and I did, and that hurried them up, but then this woman was running toward me with her handkerchief. I knew I shot the girl as soon as I saw her, but I never meant to. . . ."

My job was to write a report on each alleged crime and recommend whether the person be released or brought to trial via field court-martial. In Lundquist's case I recommended that he be charged but that no punishment occur, except perhaps to remove him from patrol and take away his stripes. Clearly this was a tragic and stupid accident; it was not a premeditated murder.

In another case — a brutal attempted rape and murder, where a twenty-year-old woman tried to escape from two soldiers by jumping out a second-floor window and was shot and killed by them where she fell — the investigation was surprisingly easy. We had very clear photographs of the exit and entry wounds, ballistic tests on the bullets, verified statements by witnesses, testimony that discredited the suspects, fingerprints at the scene. I recommended both a full court-martial and first-degree-murder trial.

Another time a Belgian couple was found leaning against each other in a sitting position on their bed, with a trail of bullets from an automatic rifle moving up the right arm of the woman, through her shoulder and neck area, into her husband's shoulder and neck area and down his left arm. They had been killed in this manner by a GI looking for jewels. He had mistaken them for the jewelers who lived next door. He thought they were lying when he killed them and took some of the woman's heirloom jewelry, which we later found sewn into the lining of his backpack.

Decades later a rumor would circulate among private detectives in San Francisco that the great Hal Lipset had gone into semiretirement by acting as "little more than a broker" of agents who reported to him from the field, while he, comfortable and declining in his later years, never stepped away from his desk.

What they did not know was that Lipset had started out as a broker in the war, orchestrating the movements of his CID agents on forty to fifty cases at a time. He kept the progress of reports, interviews, requisitions, orders, statements of testimony, and requests for recommendation clicking off in his head while he moved agents from one case to the next, from trial to trial, town to town.

> I reported directly to the commanding general. When I had a case I thought should go to trial, he would appoint a special investigating officer who would examine my reports with an eye to irregularities or errors in procedure, and concur or disagree with my recommendations. Sometimes he'd talk the case over with me, but my men knew how to conduct a proper investigation and present a case for the prosecution, and there was rarely a question about how

our evidence was gathered or how arrests were made. Most of the time there would be no trial — usually the defendant just pleaded guilty.

If the case did come to trial, the commanding general would appoint a court-martial board of five to seven judges, as well as a prosecutor and a defense counselor. A military court is really one of the fairest of all legal systems when it works properly because it incorporates at least three checks and balances. We were the first; the reviewing authority (the special investigator) was the second; the actual trial with opposing officers was the third.

During the trial, it was clear to everybody that the prosecution and defense could not be intimidated to bring in the kind of results the commanding officer wanted. Even a sentence by the court-martial board could be appealed to the secretary of defense, and this did happen. So there were several stages of recourse available to any man before he actually went to serve his time.

Due process was part of a system that we as Americans were supposed to feel proud of. In the same way, as a conquering army, we were trained not to behave like the barbarians many Europeans had been used to. We weren't supposed to rape and pillage; it was against our laws to loot and steal, and if anyone did, my office was the place townspeople could complain to. We were there to make a proper investigation.

At the same time, there was always a lot of talk about the effect of war on otherwise good men. Looting has been the prerogative of invading armies since wars began, but since Americans were forbidden to do it, the men grumbled about the difference between "souvenirs" and stolen items. You couldn't blame them: An enlisted man might grab a German Luger off a dead soldier and take it home (if nobody caught him), but a high-ranking officer might confiscate an entire room of furniture or crystal for himself and call it standard requisition.

This sort of thing led to territorial wrangles between CID and CIC (Counterintelligence Corps), especially during the

Battle of the Bulge. In one very large château in Belgium that had been turned into a headquarters for the commander, I was called to the general's office along with the head of the CIC. It seemed the castle's magnificent silver service, which the general had commandeered for his own use, had been stolen, and he wanted to know who would take responsibility for investigating the theft. Would it be me, since there were American enlisted men preparing the food and acting for the general on his behalf, or the CIC officer, since there were German civilians employed in the general's headquarters as well?

I said I thought it was better for the CIC to handle it, and the other guy said it was better for the CID to handle it. Obviously, neither one of us wanted the job, because we knew if we didn't get the silverware back, the general would be furious. Then suddenly everyone had to move on, and the general forgot about it. I think today some former GI is serving his family with that silver service. It would have made a hell of a souvenir.

Legal distinctions and matters of rank diminished the farther we got into Germany. The more Americans saw of other Allied armies, the better and more patriotic they felt about ours. At one spot near Düsseldorf, where American, British, and French armies came together, you could see the differences clearly. The U.S. Army made a point of bringing everything on its back; the army took care of its soldiers in every complete way. We took nothing from the land on which we were moving; everything came from home.

The British pretty well supplied their troops, but in Germany they did requisition food. The men were very strictly rationed and had to turn to civilians for basic staples. The French, who had been occupied by the Germans, came empty-handed. If the man had sheets, he got them from German civilians. If he had a blanket, he got it from a German. If they ate, the Germans fed them. They came with nothing except the clothes on their backs and their rifles.

But the closer to the end we got, the more that question cropped up about what war does to men. Did it make killers out of ordinary law-abiding civilians? What was the difference between sanctioned killing in the heat of combat and murder of civilians off the field of battle? For many of the men, the whole thing came to a head with what was later known as the Briggs Case.

Private Gerald Briggs and some buddies took the German weapons they had "liberated" off dead soldiers and used them to barter several gallons of cheap cherry brandy from another unit. Most of the men had gotten drunk and passed out, but Briggs allegedly staggered down the road, laughing drunkenly and asking other American soldiers, "Is it OK to shoot at civilians in a combat zone?"

Witnesses later testified they thought he was kidding. Some of the men did see him prop himself up on a fence and aim his carbine at a farmer working in an adjoining field. Before they could stop him, Briggs had shot and killed the man.

To my mind, this was an open-and-shut case of first-degree murder, but to many of the men in the company who had fought alongside Briggs and said he could be trusted under fire, it was a "bad accident," a result of what war does to otherwise normal men. I recommended full charges be brought against him. Thousands of other Americans were keeping their heads about who you could kill and who you couldn't in and out of combat. I didn't see why Briggs should be treated differently when he knew it *wasn't* "OK" to shoot a civilian in a combat zone.

To my own CID agents I made the point that you had to take the law-enforcement position. As investigators, we weren't scavengers who had to come in after an occupation and clean up the mess our men created; we were detectives bringing crimes to justice in the wake of the havoc created by conquering troops. The difference in approach was important: Seeing ourselves as part of a legal system we respected meant that we were never alone out there making things up as we went along. The disciplines, rules, procedures, and methods of investigation I had been taught in the States, I now taught my men in the field, and I emphasized the same premise: When there is chaos, the law gives you order. In the chaos of wartime, stick to procedure. You may think a man like Briggs is a comrade in arms in combat, but if he commits criminal deeds, he's a menace to society. That's the law-enforcement position.

Lipset trained his CID agents with a stripped-down version of an eight-week crash course in procedures of detection conducted by the FBI for military investigators in 1942. This course, itself a condensed version of the FBI's own six-month training program for new investigators, was a brainchild of the legendary FBI agent, Melvin Purvis.

Purvis had made headlines some years before by capturing John Dillinger, a famous criminal of the thirties. The rumor was that J. Edgar Hoover, piqued at all the publicity Purvis was getting, decided to get Purvis away from the press and farm him out to the military. But Purvis, piqued that Hoover was piqued, was determined to get himself back on the map by putting together the most rigorous investigators' course he could model after the FBI's program.

The school was one of two lucky things that happened to me during the war. I had just gotten out of O.C.S. (Officer Candidate School) and made second lieutenant in the M.P.s on Governor's Island in New York. An investigator's slot opened about the time Purvis's school started, and my commanding officer put me in.

Purvis, it turned out, was a stickler for by-the-book detail. Like the other recruits, I was sure going in that the instructors were going to teach us the basics — how to preserve and search a crime scene, interview witnesses, keep records, make arrests, write reports, and prepare cases for prosecution — which they did. What we didn't expect were daily drills on a vast array of specialized technical information — such things as the use of ethyl alcohol when testing for blood, or the effect of hydrochloride and oxalic acid on "questioned documents," or the identification of various criminal M.O.s (methods of operation) you'd rarely find in a combat zone, for example, the exact way a safecracker might use a "drag job" applying pressure to a lock or hire a "peter man" as a nitroglycerine expert.

We learned some things cold: determining symptoms of poisoning by arsenic, prussic acid, strychnine; identifying fingerprints — the radial loop, the ulnar pocket loop, the whorl, tented or arch type — and how to lift "latents" with paraffin or, as a last resort, cellophane tape. We had to know how to test for gunpowder burns, how glass fractures when a bullet hits it, how to mold a plaster cast on everything from a tire print to a battered face. We learned to use and dismantle explosives, to identify hairs and suspected fibers with and without microscopes, to conduct ballistic tests, initiate police raids, use a blackjack, frisk a witness, search a suspect.

We'd spend the morning in classes and go "window-shopping" with a partner, where one man would stare at a store window for thirty seconds and then be tested by his buddy on the exact number, identification, and location of the items in the window. We'd learn the theory of surveillance techniques, like the classic ABC (leapfrogging) or convoy (bracketing) methods, and go out to practice it in the field. We would look at faces and describe them "according to the book"— always "according to the book": Was the nose of the *snub, horizontal, Roman, concave, convex,* or *hook* variety, and what was the width across the nostrils? Were the lips *receding* or *prominent?* Were the earlobes *long, gulfed, descending,* or *medium?* What was the degree of baldness, if any, and was it *frontal* or *occipital?*

Some of the instruction was amusing. When removing a square of dirt that had blood on it from a field, our instructors told us, "be sure there are no worms or insects" in the dirt, as if that would never occur to us. They gravely announced that the Japanese government was responsible for 90 percent of illegal narcotics sales in the U.S. "Reason for

Jap interest in narcotics: 1. Source of revenue. 2. To en-
slave conquered countries. 3. To corrupt Western nations."

FBI agents today would smile at the state-of-the-art
technology at the time — of course there were no tape recorders, calculators, computers, electronic microscopes, or
digital equipment in those days — but even if Purvis could
have used modern methods then, his approach would have
been the same. The idea behind the school was to show us
the wealth of resources that ordinarily would be at our
disposal within the law-enforcement machine, and then to
say, you may not be able to use any of it. In a war zone,
chaos reigns. Follow procedure whenever you can and substitute your own intelligence for the missing parts. Stay
objective. Emotions may betray you, so "do everything by
the book."

We felt like a specialized but not an elite corps of investigators. We were supposed to have a certain humility
about our place in the hierarchy and pride in being a part
of the huge law-enforcement machine. Crime in any society was too extensive and various for any individual to take
on the burden of acting alone. Instead, if we all acted in
concert, many crimes — never all of them, of course —
would be solved and brought to justice because the system,
for all its imperfections, worked.

The instructors emphasized that a clear distinction existed between those who committed crimes and those who
didn't. People like Corporal Lundquist may make a bad
mistake once in a while, but the hardened criminals who
spend their lives hurting and stealing from others are
"criminally minded" before they ever step into a war. That
was the message. No law-enforcement agent ever believed
that war made criminals out of otherwise normal men. We
thought, in fact, it was the other way around: Criminals
used war as a cover for their bad acts. That was the principle Purvis stood for. He taught us that people who en-
forced the law were like scientists proving that same
principle over and over.

That was all fine in theory. But when we got into the

war, it was immediately clear that politics would often get in the way of legal procedure. The general's stolen silver service, for example: What was I doing wasting time on something the general had stolen in the first place? Playing politics is what I was doing. As much as the system tried to get favoritism and personality out of "doing it by the book," people did pull strings to get what they wanted, and sometimes, for the sake of the system as a whole, you just had to step aside and let a case you had worked very hard on go down the drain. That I understood.

What I didn't understand was how the system and all its principles could be thrown aside because somebody with connections decided it didn't suit his plans to keep a case open. We'd be in the middle of an investigation, and — *poof!* — the suspect would disappear, no explanation, because he had a powerful "friend" somewhere up the line. It wasn't just a matter of pulling rank or misuse of power, it was a belligerence that made the hard work and belief in "doing it by the book" so much naïveté.

The prime example for me occurred near the end of the war when we got an assignment to investigate a brutal rape and subsequent murder of an eighty-one-year-old German woman. The autopsy showed evidence of massive damage from sexual assault by at least three men, death by multiple knife wounds, most of them in the stomach, chest, and neck area, and assorted burns to the skin on the victim's arms and legs from lighted cigarettes.

The assault had taken place in front of the woman's retarded fourteen-year-old grandchild, whose statement, however thorough and unshakable to us, could not, we knew, stand up against an aggressive defense in court. An extensive search of the crime scene turned up our only other hope, an American helmet liner that seemed to have been discarded during the melee.

It was standard military issue, made out of glass fiber and resembling the kind of liner that fits into a batting helmet that professional baseball players use. This liner had a faint but detectable serial number, which we traced to a GI who insisted the liner was no longer his — he had lost it in a crap game to a paratrooper who had said that his head was a quarter inch smaller than the helmet liner *he* had been issued.

We got the names of other soldiers at the crap game and found a witness who had seen the paratrooper on the train with a special section of the 101st Airborne Division, which at the time had gone deeper into Germany to make a final jump in the Berchtesgaden area, where Hitler's mountain retreat was located. The witness, who had been transferred back to the infirmary near our headquarters for treatment of shrapnel wounds, said he had seen the paratrooper, Gene Albert, throw the knife off the train.

"Oh, it was the knife he used to kill that old lady, all right," he said. "Or at least that's what Gene kept saying. He had the idea you could trace it to the body or something, so he threw it into the bushes while the train roared past. I don't know where it is. I don't know how you'd find it. That train must have covered a hundred miles straight up the mountain that day."

"Who else was there?" I asked him. "Were you the only one who saw the knife?"

"Oh, no, his whole crew was there — his 'Commando Charlies,' he calls them. They're like a squad within a squad; they do whatever he says. I guess he told them to rape that old lady, because they sure were proud of themselves for it."

"How come they let you in on it?" I asked.

"Well, they didn't. The medic had put me in the back of the car where he could drain my leg and keep it elevated. I was on a cot behind this partition when I heard them come through — nobody else was in there. They were so plastered they didn't even take a look around. I could make out Albert and his 'chief buddy,' as he calls him, Jiggs Carter, and one of the others — Howie James. Howie, I heard, has been transferred back."

James, I discovered, had already been charged with another rape and was awaiting trial in a different division. I got in a jeep and drove the thirty miles to interview him in the other camp. He was so mad at Albert and the "Commando Charlies" for not backing up his false alibi about the new rape that he decided to tell me everything about the last rape. What was the difference between one or two rapes, he figured.

Everything James told me about the rape was consistent with what my investigators had found, and with two positive IDs I felt I now had a case. I took a military plane up to the 101st's launching zone in the mountains near Berchtesgaden.The day before they were set to make the drop, I found the commanding general and read him the charges against Albert and Carter. He laughed out loud.

"I don't know what you think we're up against here, Lipset," he said, "but I need every proven paratrooper I can get, and Carter and Albert are two of the best. This is Hitler territory; some crack German troops are still up here defending it to the death, and they know these mountains like the back of their swastikas."

"Well, general, these men raped, maimed and killed an eighty-one-year-old —"

"German woman. Nazi woman. Kraut woman. So what do you care? You want a big conviction to chalk up on your record, right? Well, go play detective with somebody else. These are my men. When they risk their lives for me, I'm not going to turn them over to some candy-ass detective like you."

"Then don't turn them over to me," I said, standing up. "As you appear not to know, I have the prerogative of preferring charges over your objections. This is what I am doing. My men have arrested Albert and Carter and are escorting them back to our base today." I left without saluting the son of a bitch.

That was bullshit about losing two of his "best" men: The army had already decided that people charged with major crimes had to be brought to justice and could not under any circumstances continue to fight, regardless of how major the battle. For one thing, they couldn't be

trusted; for another, that was the law. That's all there was
to it, and he knew it. Nevertheless, I got my men and the
suspects out of there as fast as army transport could carry
us.

We returned to our base and were awaiting trial for
Albert and Carter when V-E Day occurred and new orders
came in transferring us to Japan, where we were supposed
to link up with American occupying units, just as we had
in Belgium and Germany. I couldn't let this happen without seeing the Carter-Albert case to its conclusion. The
next day I flew to Paris and explained to the commanding
officers of the European theater under Eisenhower that my
men and I had to attend the Carter-Albert trial as witnesses, or there would be no case for the prosecution. They
hemmed and hawed and said there was nothing they could
do. "War's over, lieutenant," they kept saying. "Go do
your duty where you're still needed."

So we got shipped out. I was shaking my head about it
when word came while we were en route that Japan had
surrendered. A lot of cheering erupted on the ship, but by
this time I was like a cop who couldn't let go. Carter and
Albert were out there cheering somewhere, too. One day
they'd go home and rape or kill somebody else. Then
they'd go out and cheer again.

We were given ten days off when we reached New York,
so I checked in at the Commodore Hotel on Forty-second
Street, sort of an officers' playground at the time, to cheer
up. There I ran into a lawyer from the 101st Airborne
Division, and out of curiosity, I asked him about the case.
He had a good laugh.

"Well, look, the case wasn't mine," he said, "so everything I say is on the Q.T., right?"

"Sure," I said.

"OK. After you left, the general roared around about
protecting his men and never letting them come to trial.
We all heard him. He said if you took his key paratroopers,
and Carter and Albert were among the most vicious on his
team, he would turn the tables. Through some pretty fancy

string pulling, he was responsible for the next CID trans-
fer."

"What?" I said. "That's impossible. No one person has
that much power."

"Want to bet?" said the lawyer, still grinning. "Wait —
it gets better. The day after you left, a court-martial hearing was called in the Carter-Albert case, and when the
convening officer found no witnesses, he dismissed the
charges against both of them."

I was dumbfounded.

"Come on, Lipset — you gotta admit, it's funny. The
Old Man doesn't like you pushing him around, so he ships
you off to Japan and gets his men acquitted of murder."

"Very funny," I said, walking away from him. "It'll be
a riot when Carter and Albert meet their next eighty-one-
year-old lady."

"Hey, lighten up, soldier," he called after me. "Haven't
you heard? The war's over."

"Yeah? Which one?"

Two things about that case kept coming back to me as
the years passed. First, in a wave of postwar sentiment that
hit the States as American soldiers came home, clemency
boards started popping up in the War Department to help
"our boys" wipe the slate clean. Suddenly you'd see a
headline reading, "Army Trims Sentences of 20,000
Yanks," most of them "soldiers convicted of serious offenses, mostly in wartime."

Thinking of Carter and Albert, I started clipping these
stories out of the paper because I knew what the result
would be, and sure enough, in less than a year, the headlines started announcing things like "U.S. Murder Rate Is
Up Over 1945."

Was there a direct, causal connection between clemency
on "serious offenses" and a rise in murder? I would say
yes, absolutely. These men were criminals when they went
to war, they were criminals during the war, and because
nobody wanted to face the fact that Americans could be
guilty of personal atrocities in the "good" war, they were
allowed to be criminals after the war.

In the fifties and the sixties and the seventies, when Americans were shocked at the atrocities committed by our troops in Korea and Vietnam, I found myself shrugging. Maybe if the public had known about the one-on-one crimes Americans had committed during World War II, no one would have been surprised at the wholesale slaughters that occurred in places like My Lai.

Granted, these were very different wars, probably illegal wars, certainly insane wars. But that fundamental debate about whether Lieutenant Calley was a hero or a butcher never got beyond what to me was a pretty primitive question we had all discussed in World War II — does war make criminals out of otherwise normal men? A better question would be: Did Calley obey the law? If not, and we let him go, why have laws in the first place?

Second, it kept occurring to me over the years that law enforcement is not comfortable with agents who act or think independently. Although my outrage over the Carter-Albert case was a direct result of what I had been taught at Purvis's FBI school, I wasn't supposed to question how these cases turned out. I was supposed to go back to my caseload and continue plodding through the facts and gathering evidence like a good investigator who had learned his lesson about knowing my place. Well, I had learned a lesson, all right.

Awarded the Bronze Star for "exceptionally meritorious conduct in the performance of outstanding service against the enemy during the period of February 15, 1945, to May 8, 1945," Lipset later applied for employment as an agent with the FBI but was rejected in the first interview for being "immature," as the recruiting agent put it. By this time, however, Lipset had figured out that he had been twice blessed during the war — not only by the lucky chance of falling into the slot that led him to Purvis's school, but also for the incredible good fortune of meeting a young Mennonite off the farm from Minnesota named Evelyn Fast.

Chapter 5

A Real Pipperoo

Oh what a gal,
A real pipperoo
I'm going to Michigan
To see the sweetest gal
In Kalamazoo
— Mack Gordon and Harry Warren,
"I've Got a Gal in Kalamazoo"

To understand the phenomenon of the American private eye and the rise of detective work as a profession, it's important to examine the background of two who led the way. The drive that compelled the Lipsets to create a model detective agency had its roots in American traditions evolving from immigrants, capitalism, individualism, and, in a very emotional sense, the sounds of Glenn Miller.

Hal and Lynn met in December of 1942 across a room crowded with khaki and olive-green uniforms, a band playing "Kalamazoo," and Christmas decorations disguising an atmosphere of war and uncertainty.

Lynn: *I lived in a rented room above the library in Libertyville, a suburb of Chicago, but I belonged to a bridge club near the Loop. One Sunday a Mrs. Larsen called from the nearby officer's club with an S.O.S. There were many young officers but few girls. I was having a run of good hands and wanted to continue playing, but the others out-voted me.*

Hal: I had arrived in Chicago on a ten-day pass while Colonel Purvis moved the FBI school from Georgia to Fort Custer, near Kalamazoo, Michigan. Staying at the Knickerbocker Hotel, a buddy and I had seen a notice announcing a dance for officers, and decided to go.

Lynn: Dancing had been considered a sin in my family, so of course I hadn't learned how and felt that at my age, twenty-one, it was too late to learn. I had a very active social life, though, and had taught myself to be good at bridge (card playing was another sin left at home). However, a year after Pearl Harbor, when the military called, you went, and we did.

Hal: Everybody played Glenn Miller in those days, so no matter where you were, the sound of those moody saxophones made you feel at home. My pal and I were kidding around when I spotted this young woman sitting along the side, laughing with one of her friends. Sometimes you'd see an icy brittleness at these dances because the girls felt it was their duty to entertain boys in uniform. But this woman with the laugh — I looked at her and thought, well, here is no phony. She had the friendliest smile I had ever seen.

Lynn: A tall, slender, blond second lieutenant strode across the floor and asked me to dance. He was a most confident and cocky young man, impressed with that fresh gold bar on his shoulder. I thought I'd take him down a peg by telling him I was a lady welder. He merely found this intriguing. When I confessed that dancing was not my strongest suit, he — clearly adept at ballroom dancing — settled into an easy two-step. I thought this was quite gentlemanly of him.

Hal: She was smart and funny, and she didn't take any of my guff. I didn't care if she could dance — it was talk of her bridge club that made me wince. I liked playing gin or pinochle, but the thought of sitting around with a gossipy foursome in some clubby atmosphere made me nervous.

Lynn: *We made a deal that night. I promised never to ask Hal to play bridge if he would never ask me to dance the boogie-woogie. We shook hands on it very solemnly.*

The next night they met across the street from the Knicker-bocker at a cozy Russian restaurant called the Yar. They talked through dinner and missed both the concert they had planned to see and the last train to Libertyville. Hal insisted on seeing Lynn home in a taxi, which cost him a week's pay in those gas-rationing days, but he didn't mind. Having never met a "country hick," as she put it, he was intrigued by her no-nonsense ways.

Lynn: *I started working in the fields with my dad on our farm in Minnesota when I was ten. Raking hay was con-sidered woman's work, though there was nothing delicate about tramping in hay up to your waist in one-hundred-degree heat. Cultivating corn, where you straddle the seat and have a foot in each stirrup to guide the blades on each side of the row, was not pleasant with menstrual cramps. I remember stopping at the end of a row and bursting into tears in discomfort and self-pity. But not for long.*

For all his city ways, Hal had never heard anyone say the words "menstrual cramps" out loud. "Didn't you have any help on the farm?" he asked. "No money," she answered. "My brother John and I were the farmhands." In fact, they were both Depression kids, but Hal's childhood in East Orange, New Jersey, had made him resourceful in different ways. As a boy he learned to hop on buses and subways in New York to visit his grandparents on the Lower East Side, and he had a knack for selling ads in the school news-paper, learned at an early age from his father.

Hal: *My dad was a salesman from the old school — dig-nified and honorable. He worked for the Lion Match Com-pany and made a name for himself by inventing what they called the "feature match." This was a way of advertising* right on the matches — you put a picture of a car or radio across the matchstick rows, or shape individual matches into little cigars or tubes of toothpaste.

Dad was the first to teach me the tricks of door-to-door selling — or "trading," as he called it. "All right," he'd say. "So you go into the bakery. What's the first thing you do?"

"I ask for the owner," I'd say.

"Maybe not. The clerk may try to screen you first, so make the first impression right there. What do you say?"

" 'Hello, I'm here to sell — ' "

"Too abrupt. Introduce yourself first."

" 'Hello, I'm from East Orange High Sch—' "

"Your *name* first, make a personal connection."

" 'Hello, my name is Harold K. Lipset — ' "

"Skip the K. Too formal."

" 'Hello, my name is — ' "

How to shake hands, get right down to business, show the buyer you've done your homework, answer any resistance, and know when to close: these were techniques Dad knew backward and forward.

Hal took to selling with such industry that at age sixteen he launched his own business, a one-boy publishing company that produced the "official" game program for the 1936 high school football game in his hometown on Thanksgiving Day. For this, he sold over a thousand dollars worth of ads, pocketed a profit of six hundred dollars, and bought his first car. His father couldn't have been more proud.

A year later, Hal took on a partner and published a magazine called *The Suburban Student*. Selling ads as far afield as the Rainbow Room in New York City, he cleared an unheard-of three-thousand-dollar profit. But when, by the third issue, Hal's partner disappeared with the contents of both the cash box and bank account, the more conservative Louis Lipset gave his son a sympathetic clap on the back. "My father insisted there was a positive side," he told Lynn. " 'Count your blessings,' " he said. " 'If this magazine had taken off, you wouldn't have given a thought for college. Now you know you've got something to learn, even at your ripe old age of nineteen.' "

Lynn had never heard of such entrepreneurial ambitions:

The Mennonite way of life was one of extreme frugality. When my grandparents moved into a house with a bathroom, everyone was in awe. Of course, the city water wasn't connected until they got to be in their seventies, and then just in winter for the toilet only. Since they had their own well, they carried in all the water they needed. The bathtub was never used in the twenty years they lived in the house.

"Did they have electricity?" Hal asked.

"Oh, yes, they were very proud of their 'electric,' " Lynn said. "But the point was not to use it. The lights were never turned on until after dark. No more than the one-dollar monthly minimum charge could be used."

Lynn was prohibited by her father from reading books loaned by neighboring farmers because they had gone to college and were also considered "too worldly." She attended a one-room country school, but since her parents had never passed the fifth grade, she was allowed to attend high school only after making arrangements to move to town, where she worked at a family's home for room and board for the next four years. By the time she met Hal, Lynn had taken night classes at Northwestern and was halfway through business college.

On about the third date I could sense that Hal was trying to tell me something. "What is it?" I asked. "Please." He hesitated. "I'm not sure how you're going to feel about this," he said. "I'm Jewish." I almost laughed. "Oh, Hal," I said, "do you think something like that would bother me? Why, you could be a Muslim and it would make no difference. Besides, I can go you one better. I'm a Mennonite."

"A Mennonite?" He thought I was kidding. "Is that like being a lady riveter?"

"Sort of, only harder," I told him. "Mennonites are taught it's a sin to play cards or cut hair. They can't go

*to movies, dance, or take a drink. Women can't even wear
a dress with sleeves exposing the elbow."*

*"The elbow?" he asked. "What's the matter with your
elbow?"*

"Well," I said, "elbows are thought to be too worldly."

*He laughed. "Now I know why I asked you to dance. It
was the thought of one day getting a chance to look at
your elbow."*

There were positive aspects to a fear of worldly thoughts, Lynn
said. It kept Mennonites from associating with people who were
different from themselves. "We not only lack prejudice," she told
Hal, "we're *ignorant* of prejudice. The one Jew I ever heard of was
a merchant named Uhlberg who lived thirty miles away. The only
thing I recall Dad saying about him was that he ate at the table with
his hat on." Hal burst out laughing. "That's us, all right," he said.
"According to the Torah, hats aid in digestion."

Both their families, they discovered, were descendants of Russian immigrants who had fled to America to escape religious perse-
cution — Hal's Jewish grandparents from the pogroms of Minsk,
Lynn's German-Russian Mennonite ancestors from the steppes of
southern Russia. Even the ethnic languages spoken at home had
similar origins: Hal's family spoke Yiddish, Lynn's the Plattdeutsch
common among Mennonites with Prussian roots.

> *Hal:* My mother hated the full beards and heavy accents
> of my father's relatives on the Lower East Side. Dad wor-
> shipped her anyway from the moment they married. She
> convinced him to move into a Gentile neighborhood in New
> Jersey, and he willingly, though I think sadly, agreed. To
> my sister, Rosalind, and I, Mother was distant and a bit
> cold. She never wanted to hear anything negative, so
> whenever I had a problem, I went to Roz, who was six
> years older.

> Lynn: *My own mother was tragically burned in a stove fire
> one morning when I was nine. At the hospital I was too
> young to feel death settling in the room and did not realize
> she was gone until Dad whispered, "Sie es kalt" ("She is*

cold"). He never showed his grief to us, so perhaps as a consequence it took me a long time to realize that Ma was gone. I only knew that I was not a good Mennonite. I could not understand how God could take my mother away.

Such conversations drew Hal and Lynn into new confidences. When Hal left Chicago to finish the FBI course near Kalamazoo, Lynn visited him the next weekend. There he told her the whole story about his father.

Hal: After the fiasco with *The Suburban Student,* I decided to enroll at the University of California, because the tuition was cheap. This was still the Depression, and I wanted to show Dad I could give up the get-rich-quick schemes and help the family out. But soon after I got to Berkeley, somebody at a sorority asked me to help arrange a party. I hired an orchestra and got a 10 percent commission; I found a caterer and got another 10 percent commission. Pretty soon I was booking junior proms and big game dances at the big hotels, and they'd give me a 10 percent commission for those, too.

Dad wrote to me about the value of money, sometimes enclosing a check for five or ten dollars, while here I was making about four hundred a month and bluffing my way through with a "C" average. When I got another terrific idea — a monthly magazine I proposed to call *City Guide,* which I would pack with entertainment news and advertising and give away to people in taxis and hotels — I went home the summer of 1940 to tell my father about it.

He was conservative as always about money, but something else was troubling him, though he refused to discuss it. I did know part of the problem. My father had quit the Lion Match Company after twenty years when the owner had ordered him to fire his own brother. A series of investors backed him in his own company, Manhattan Match. As good a salesman as he was, he won several major accounts, but other manufacturers started freezing him out by selling below his prices. Apparently, they often did this to inhibit competition. Dad fought them as long as he could, but ultimately, Manhattan Match went broke and was bought by a third company, Universal.

In those days, if you went bankrupt, you could buy your company back for peanuts and not owe anything, even to your investors. My father wouldn't do that. He made a deal with Universal: He promised to stay away from the match business, and they promised to pay all outstanding debts of Manhattan Match, so his investors got their money back. Universal also hired him as a vice president in charge of one of their subsidiaries — with a salary of three thousand dollars, which was a lot of money in 1937.

Selling aspirin and cough drops turned out to be easy enough for Dad, but he was barred from seeing his business friends, and when his contract ran out, Universal did not renew it. He went to work for Gotham Tissue, the paper company that my mother's sister and nephew owned, but he felt his in-laws were making a job for him. We were all very proud of him for handling the Manhattan Match disaster so honorably, but he looked upon himself as a failure at fifty-five, mooching off relatives.

I was in Berkeley in November when my sister woke me up with a phone call at three A.M. "It's Dad," she said. Her voice was shaking. Early that morning he had locked himself in the garage and attached a vacuum-cleaner hose from the exhaust to the front window of the family car. He was dead by the time my mother arrived home from her bridge club.

I put the phone down and couldn't think of anything to do. Since Jewish law required the dead to be buried within twenty-four hours, I couldn't get home in time for the funeral. So I didn't do anything. Roz was married and had her own family to take care of, and my mother would take little comfort from me. I sat there in the room for the rest of the day, skipping classes and essentially never going back. I had promised Dad I would finish college, but now — well, to hell with it. And the *City Guide* — what a farce. If anything, I would kill those bastards at the competing match companies for using the system to ruin the things my father believed in. A man of his caliber.

A while later this guy who was flunking out told me he was going to join the National Guard, and why didn't I go with him. I said, great. Let's go peel potatoes with all the rest of the jerks. Maybe Hitler will march through Poland and kill us all.

Hal spent a year in the infantry as what he called a "sad sack grunt," doing exactly what he had predicted — peeling potatoes and picking up cigarette butts when not on guard duty. After Pearl Harbor, an officer told him he was too smart for the infantry and ought to apply to Officer Candidate School. "I had felt sorry for myself long enough," he told Lynn. "O.C.S. seemed right. So did the M.P.s and Purvis's school. I got lucky."

Lynn visited Hal when he was transferred from Kalamazoo to Mississippi. They talked of marriage, but neither was ready. Hal said he would be shipped overseas very soon, and Lynn was suddenly all too aware of the disadvantages of mixed marriages.

Lynn: *Many places in Chicago, including my bridge group, took pride in excluding Jews. "Gentleman's Agreement" was a best-seller then, and magazines ran articles on the fate of Jewish-Christian marriages. All of them said, "Don't do it." I chickened out with my friends and told them that Hal was half Jewish. This was almost true, since his mother had lived and traveled with Gentiles, but it was cowardly nevertheless.*

We both felt that children should be raised in the father's religion since they would bear his name, but that meant I would have to take instruction. Hal wanted the Conservative rabbi who had married his parents and his sister to marry him as well, but I felt a Conservative rabbi would never accept a Mennonite into the fold.

Hal: Our last long talk about marriage took place in South Carolina. We decided we were just not mature enough for marriage. We kept writing, though infrequently. I thought about Lynn a lot, then told myself to stop thinking about her. It was over.

Lynn: *I went back to Chicago and threw myself into work with a vengeance. Going out with the old crowd and listening to their bigoted jokes only made me irritated and cranky. I got another job, the most demanding I could conceive of, as business manager for the YWCAs of greater Chicago, which meant keeping charge of stock and real estate portfolios as well as accounting and payroll. I loved the work. It was the only thing I felt allowed to love.*

Hal: After the war I thought that I would try to see Lynn one more time. It was the end of 1945, and although I was staying with my sister in New Jersey, I wired Lynn and asked her if she would spend New Year's with me. She wired back, "Always glad to see you when you're passing through." Her sarcasm was sharp and delightful. If she sounded hurt, she must have missed me.

Ordinarily I would have hopped on the first train for Chicago, but in my haste I found a military transport plane that could take me from Newark straight to Chicago on New Year's Eve day. The weather looked fuzzy when we took off, and pretty soon we were in the middle of a snowstorm and lucky to make an emergency landing in Buffalo. Holed up there, I thought I'd never see her again. When the weather broke I got on the first plane out of there and made it to Chicago only three hours from New Year's.

Lynn: *By the time he reached me, I didn't care what day it was. I had missed him so terribly, there was nothing to do but stand there and hold on to him for the longest time. We had dinner at our old haunt, the Yar, and decided on marriage that night — two marriages: If Hal's Conservative rabbi would accept me, we could be married in his sister's house, then drive cross-country and be married by a Mennonite minister at my father's farm.*

Hal: The rabbi of course loved Lynn, and Roz and her husband, Joe, gave us a beautiful wedding. I knew driving up to her family's farm in Minnesota that Lynn's people would accept me — ethnic difference meant nothing to them. But most of all, I was really looking forward to the kind of farm cooking Lynn had told me so much about — homemade soups, bread, pies, and fresh produce. At the reception, however, the banquet table was loaded with packaged goods, including bread, cookies and cakes, and all sorts of store-bought vegetables, canned soups, and bakery-made pies. It turned out that Mennonites were so accustomed to country cooking that they bought packaged goods as gifts on the most special of occasions. And it was. I took my hat off every time I sat down at the table.

Chapter 6

The Detective as Salesman

I was an ex-cop, and the words came hard. I had to say them, though, if I didn't want to be stuck for the rest of my life with the old black-and-white picture, the idea that there were just good people and bad people, and everything would be hunky-dory if the good people locked up the bad ones.
— Ross Macdonald, *The Doomsters*

They never meant to go into business together — let alone operate the first mom-and-pop detective agency in American history. But when Hal and Lynn Lipset arrived in San Francisco after the war, other options disappeared.

Hal: I wanted to move back to San Francisco to see about finishing college and starting law school. Lynn planned to support us by working as an accountant, but she had been feeling poorly on our drive across country. So on our first day here, I came home from the admissions office at Cal to tell Lynn that I was accepted to law school, and she came home to tell me that she was pregnant.

We had not planned to have a child that soon and had gone to the expense of seeing a gynecologist who had inserted some kind of platinum ring, which was the IUD of its day. The amusing thing about it was that for some eight years after our son was born, we kept getting Christmas cards from the doctor. We never had the heart to tell him we had a child.

The result of Lynn's pregnancy was that we both went job-hunting. I did some investigations for the Office of Price Administration and Veterans' Hospitals, but government work was not for me. After the army, I resented law enforcement, with its phony value system and rigid pecking order.

We met a judge, Ed O'Day, who suggested that I go into business for myself as a private investigator. "What's that?" I said. I knew that private detectives were ex-policemen who had been thrown off the force for doing something shady, or at least that was the image at the time — but real detectives, I thought, worked only for law enforcement.

Judge O'Day had a vision. "I see professionally trained investigators coming out of the service," he said, "working directly for lawyers instead of the government and specializing in legal footwork — knowing the law and being the administrative right arm to the lawyer. I think you should be the first of your kind and go after it."

Lynn: *When we started our business on a shoestring — meaning very little money, a lot of energy, and even more gall — we decided the only way to be successful was to do a better job than anyone else. My ten-year-old portable typewriter, some stationery, and a cardboard box for a file drawer were all the equipment we needed. This was easily stowed in one corner of a bedroom.*

Furniture we did without. We had arrived in San Francisco with two thousand dollars in savings and from that bought a used stove, used refrigerator, used kitchen table and four chairs, and a used studio couch on which we both slept and sat. I covered orange crates with fabric to make end tables. We had one table lamp that we had received as a wedding gift, two pictures, some cooking pots, dishes, glasses, and a few linens. Any spare money went for used

*baby furnishings, and I made our clothing by hand, since
we had no sewing machine.*

Perhaps because the Lipsets had no other choice than to open
a detective agency, they were able to adapt more easily to unexpected trade-offs that even Judge O'Day couldn't have predicted.
Hal, a decorated veteran who wanted no part of government hierarchy, now had the freedom to operate exactly as he wanted, but
none of the power of law enforcement to back him up. What he
needed most, as his father once told him, was the power of persuasion.

Hal: I discovered almost immediately that doing a background check for an insurance company is much the same
as selling door-to-door. You have to sell people on talking
to you even though they probably don't want to. Since
you're not a cop — you don't have a uniform or a badge
to impress them — you've got to convince them to keep
talking. Part of the approach is instinctive, being able to
size up people when they open their door.

Insurance companies needed to know if potential poli-
cyholders were telling the truth when they filled out their
applications. When we first started out, my job was to talk
to the applicant's neighbors to verify statements so the insurance company could decide whether or not he had both
his arms and legs, didn't take unnecessary risks, hadn't
lied about a preexisting condition, and so forth.

The first thing I learned is that most people don't want
to talk about their neighbors or friends. They'd rather shut
the door on you than get involved. So before I ever rang
the doorbell I'd at least find out the names of the people
inside. When they answered the door, I'd say, "Mrs. Jones?
I'm from such-and-such insurance company, and we're
bringing our files up to date on Mr. Smith, your next-door
neighbor. Your name was given to us as a reference."

Now, the trick is that you don't then say, "Would you
mind speaking to me?," because they'll probably say no.
So I would start right in with innocuous questions: "How
long have you known the Smiths? Were they living here

when you moved in, or were you living here first?" I'm asking them these questions to make them think about their neighbor and not have time to decide whether they want to talk.

Normally you'd get the answer to your first question — yes, I lived here before the Smiths — without difficulty. But then you have to follow quickly with another bland question, say, "Do you know what kind of car they own?" You keep tossing out minor things for a few minutes. To get to a real question, you say, "I'm sorry to ask a silly question like this, but would you know if Mr. Smith flies his own plane?" They think, ha-ha, what a funny thing to ask. Usually they don't know, and they don't mind saying so.

From that point on, you can ask them anything. Do you know what church they go to, do they have loud parties, that sort of thing. You end with something you need to find out, like, "I know this is a ridiculous question, but does Mr. Smith have both his arms and legs?" Then you can get into questions about whether the guy walks with a limp, or has a back problem, or mows his lawn regularly (which may mean his back is OK), or drinks too much. The point is that once you get them going, they'll tell you anything.

What about the morality of the private investigator conning people into telling secrets about their neighbors? If they could see through your sales pitch, wouldn't they be right to shut the door in your face?

Hal: It's the insurance company's right we're talking about — the right to check on the validity of the statement made by the applicant. The neighbors are adults. They can shut the door if they want. I'm just making it easier for them to answer the questions.

Both Lipsets embraced the idea of the Detective as Salesman. Bringing accepted methods and standards of one field (sales) to another (investigations) could only help to upgrade the standards of their new field. While Hal was downtown selling law firms on the idea of hiring Lipset Service, Lynn, with their new baby, Louis, kept the business running at home.

> Lynn: *Hal is a tremendous salesman who gets the cases, creates the ideas on how to handle them, and keeps the clients happy. I'm in the rear echelon and see that the cases are assigned out with the approach Hal has in mind, that the work is satisfactorily done, and that no angles are overlooked. I never visit clients, but when they telephone the office, I take the calls and do whatever selling is required right there.*

The launching of Lipset Service was a matter of making every case a chance to start anew. The diplomacy of salesmanship was even effective in the seemingly routine side of detective work called process serving.

> *Hal:* Serving subpoenas is a good way to learn the detective business. You have to track the subject down, almost like a missing person if he's trying to hide from you. Then you plan your approach, nail him, and get out of there before he reacts.

> Lynn: *Most people gracefully accept service of a legal process. Those who have been trying to evade it often chuckle when we outsmart them. They're tired of playing cat and mouse and sometimes even feel relieved. Still, the wise thing for any investigator to do is to serve the papers and get lost. Sometimes if you wait a moment to see what remarks will be made, you'll find yourself dodging chairs, children's toys, or just about anything that is handy.*
>
> *That happened to me on what I thought would be a routine service. The subject yelled and cussed, kicking an old work shoe up and down the hallway that chipped paint off the wallboards. I wouldn't have been witness to this except that I had to stick around to serve his wife.*

> *Hal:* It's not true that the process server has to touch the subject to make the service legal. As long as you clearly

identify the person and explain that a legal document is being served, you can leave the paper in the street or shove it under the door. As far as the law is concerned, you've served him.

Lynn: *One woman was so mad she grabbed Hal's wrist and tried to bite him. He broke her hold and left as politely as he could. Her home was on a hillside, and it took a moment for him to get down about twenty stairs to the street level. He entered his car, where our client was seated, and was backing out when BANG! — through the windshield crashed a metal patio chair that she had heaved from her deck above. A leg of the chair went right through the shatterproof glass, depositing a shower of glass particles all over Hal and the client.*

Surveillance was another area of detective work that proved unexpectedly dangerous.

Hal: The key to stationary surveillance is that you always tell the police who'll be on the stakeout and what street you'll be watching. That way if a neighbor spots you sitting out there all night and calls the cops, a patrol car won't come along and blow your cover. Of course, I never tell the police why I'm going to be there or what the case is about — that's none of their business. And they don't tell the neighbor all they know. They say, "We know the car. It's on official business (they don't say 'police business'), and will be gone in a few days."

Mobile surveillance is another matter. In the early days we didn't have a set of cars to leapfrog each other behind the subject or track him by radio along side streets. Usually it was one car with me in it staying about three car lengths behind and a lane to the side of the subject.

Lynn: *People think surveillance work is boring. The fact is, chasing a subject in heavy traffic or running red traffic signals to keep up may not make an interesting story, but the operatives better not have weak hearts. If they lose the subject, they risk a possible chewing out from us.*

Hal: On one case I followed a gambler who had several bodyguards riding with him. I kept farther back than usual because they kept glancing around to check for cops. One night the gambler left his bar around two A.M., got in the car with his bodyguards, and pulled away. I followed. Pretty soon we were in the warehouse section of town, which at night was pretty isolated. I realized this too late, however — after we had turned into a dead-end street. In the rearview mirror, I could see a car moving in to block the path behind me. Before either car moved, I made a fast U-turn, drove up on the sidewalk between a utility pole and the side of a building, and raced out of there, leaving a lot of paint behind.

Lynn: *A sequel to that episode occurred a week later. Hal was out of town when late one night I became aware of a car slowing almost to a stop in front of our house, picking up speed, driving around the block, slowing in front of our house again, driving on, and repeating this routine many times. I got the license number and had it traced the next day — sure enough, it was the gambler's bodyguards trying to frighten us off the case.*

It took one more experience like that before we transferred our auto registrations so no one could trace a license number to our address. Hal had served papers on a very tough customer at a die-cutting plant. He had waited until the subject's employees were in view so there would be no trouble. As he left the plant, Hal saw the man watching him from the window. Two mornings later we discovered the radio aerial had been broken off the car. The next morning the paint was scratched, and the following morning a tire was slashed. That night we rigged up an alarm system, but we saw no more of him. I was grateful this six-three, 250-pound bully turned out to be a coward. He could have been waiting in the bushes some dark night for Hal to come home alone.

Hal: It soon became clear that we needed a radio system to keep tabs on each other. I was going up the stairs of an apartment building to a third-floor flat to serve papers on a man for the second time. Just as I got near the top of the stairs I heard the cock of a revolver and looked up into the barrel of a .45. I put my hands up and retreated backward down the stairs.

The next day we had a radio installed in the car and office, but the band used by civilians was so crowded we devised a code early on that only Lynn and I understood. She took the role of an anonymous dispatcher while I was one of her drivers "on location" (on surveillance), "picking up a passenger" (sighting the subject), "ready for delivery" (about to serve a subpoena), or "stopping for coffee" (locating a witness). People used to joke that I was one henpecked husband, since my wife knew where I was every second of the day. But that radio was our lifeline.

It was common for private detectives to hire cops who wanted to moonlight on surveillance or security jobs. But Hal was one of the first private eyes to build relationships with police officers in much the same way he cultivated informers. Waiters, news vendors, cabdrivers, porters, doormen, bartenders, clerks, messengers, *and* police officers learned that working for the avuncular Lipset could be as intriguing as it was lucrative. Downtown, Hal was so well known on the street that he couldn't walk half a block without being greeted by secret winks, waves, smiles, or nods. Still, little did his informers know, in those early years, how cash-poor he really was.

Hal: We got in the habit of keeping track of hours and income in our heads. Finding out if an insurance applicant had all his arms and legs paid four dollars. When things were really rolling, I could do five insurance jobs a day and put in a couple of hours on surveillance — that brought in maybe thirty dollars. When things weren't so good, we were lucky to make a hundred a month.

Lynn: We could go for a long stretch with a few personal injury or insurance jobs, but then the cases might come in one right after another. In one day, for example, I might enter and write up four cases such as these:

1. A nightclub entertainer's car is involved in a hit-and-run accident at two-thirty A.M., *but the car is left at the scene with the keys in it. A six-foot, two-hundred-pound man is seen fleeing the accident. The entertainer, who is about five eight or five nine and weighs 160 pounds, says he was so drunk the night in question that he spent the night with friends and can't recall what happened prior to his passing out. We are engaged to help this man trace his activities and find out who used his car.*

2. We are engaged to help a woman move her personal effects out of her apartment. Her husband has beaten her in the past, and she is now fearful for her life. She describes this man's pornographic collection, which we confiscate as possible evidence in a divorce action.

3. We are engaged by a warehouse owner who suspects his employees of stealing merchandise. The police say they can do nothing. The case is complicated by a hostile union and upcoming contract negotiations. Hal's surveillance leads him to suspect two of the senior drivers, then calls in the police to make the arrest.

4. We are engaged by a woman who says her husband has abducted one of their children. He has taken this child abroad and is not returning her. The two have instituted divorce proceedings, but decisions about child custody have yet to be made.

Learning to work with some of San Francisco's more flamboyant attorneys was another step in the Lipsets' launching period, Hal recalls.

Melvin Belli had developed a reputation as a lawyer who could handle personal injury cases better than most other attorneys. One time he took me to Arizona on a case involving a railroad and their insurance company.

Belli had gotten a call from the attorney representing the family of a man who was killed in a train accident in a small town about a hundred miles north of Phoenix. The railroad's insurance company was offering the small sum of $15,000, but the family lawyer felt they should receive more than that, maybe somewhere between $25,000 and $50,000.

The case was scheduled for trial on a Monday, so we got down there the Thursday before. The other lawyer had done very little investigating, and all we really had to work with was the story of the accident and the depositions of the railroad engineer and some of the railroad employees.

Belli was a very clever operator. The first thing he did when we got to the town was to call a press conference, introducing me as a veteran detective and himself as a great lawyer. Then he reached in his briefcase and pulled out a photograph of the accident scene that showed thirty people standing around. He said that I already identified many of the people in the photo who would testify the railroad was at fault. He made it sound as though this was going to be a serious exposé of the way railroads did things.

By that evening, as we had dinner with the local attorney, the railroad had upped their offer to $50,000. The lawyer was dying to take the cash, but Belli kept telling him to calm down. "They'll be offering you $75,000 by tomorrow morning, and Monday when we go in to start the trial, we'll settle for $90,000."

The next day, Friday, Belli spent his time in the law library preparing his case to present to the judge. I ran around all day trying to find some of the people from the picture of the accident, which in fact had happened three years earlier, so the trail was pretty cold. I had to be ready if we actually did have to try the case before a judge.

At about five P.M. that night, Belli and I met at our motel and had a drink. We decided we'd better find the other lawyer and go over the day's work. We left messages for the rest of the night, mystified that he would disappear at a crucial juncture.

We found out the next day that the railroad's lawyers had taken him back to Phoenix, poured a lot of booze down him, and offered to settle the case for $60,000. He accepted. Of course, Belli was furious because he knew if he had done the negotiating himself, he could have gotten the $90,000. That small-town lawyer was, I think, intimidated by so much money for one case. I, however, received full pay.

Once the Lipsets began working for law firms, Lipset Service built up a steady clientele, eventually employing a dozen full-time agents and independent operatives and handling over fifty cases at a time. Yet one stumbling block would always remain — the power of law enforcement to throw a criminal case off balance.

Hal: When we started taking on defense investigations, I found that key witnesses would refuse to speak to me. They would say they'd already talked to the police, so why should they talk to me? Or they'd say the police had told them not to talk to anybody else, especially a private investigator for the other side.

I knew if I could slow them down for half a second, I could get them talking. I might say, "You believe in the Constitution, don't you? Where it says a person is innocent until proven guilty?" They might say, "So?" Then I'd say, "Well, under our system, every defendant is entitled to have a lawyer, and every defendant's lawyer is entitled to all the pertinent information to establish a proper defense. It's just like *Perry Mason* on TV. I'm sure you believe in everybody having his day in court. That's the American way. It protects us all."

My agents used to tease me about my "American Flag speech," but it really did work. I felt that if most people understood the full measure of the American justice system, they would want to do the right thing. "An investigator is a fact finder," I'd say. "If I don't get the facts, my client could be convicted on lies. Don't you think it's right to give the defense the same information you gave the prosecution?"

I varied the approach depending on the witness — a conservative tone if I saw a Veterans of Foreign Wars sticker or National Rifle Association medallion in the front window; more liberal if the subject's car had a "Vote for

Helen Gahagan Douglas" bumper sticker — but they'd get the American Flag speech all the same.

It got so that I didn't regret not having the power of a cop. I didn't want to force people to talk to me. I wanted them to decide by themselves, because that meant they'd tell me more. They could trust me, not a uniform.

Hal got to be so good at the American Flag speech that he even used it in convincing a reluctant witness to whom the U.S. Constitution meant nothing and against whom the police had become virtual adversaries. In the Case of the Paralyzed Drunk, "a little flag waving" became an impressive weapon against police officers whose brutality made them, as far as Lipset was concerned, a formidable enemy.

Hal: Jeremy Davis had retired on disability from the navy and was attending night school college classes in an East Bay town. One of his teachers had decided to leave the school for another position, and a party was held in his honor. Davis went to the party, had several drinks, and headed home in his car, somewhat intoxicated.

On the way he hit a light pole in an oddly constructed intersection. According to the police, they were driving by and saw the broken light pole and while they were investigating it a black man, Davis, walked up to them and asked for directions. They realized that he was involved in the accident and checked his car, which was nearby, for damage. They were sure enough he had caused the accident to give him a sobriety test right there. Davis evidently didn't pass, so they arrested him for drunken driving.

Exactly what happened next we'll never really know, but an inordinate amount of time passed during which the man said he was handcuffed, which was standard police procedure, and thrown in the back of the squad car. Davis was left there by the police — he thought they went to a diner for coffee — and was eventually taken for a blood test at a lab where a technician was on call.

The technician was an Iranian awaiting citizenship and working in the lab in the meantime. He ended up being the witness I interviewed. He gave me a statement to the effect that when the police arrived, Davis was very cooperative, except he complained that the handcuffs were too tight and was begging the police to take them off. He wasn't fighting or screaming or even violently drunk.

The handcuffs were removed and he was taken into another room and given the blood test. After the blood was drawn he asked for and received permission to use the bathroom. The lab tech went into a back room and started to work on the test. He told me he heard a noise and came out to see the black man on the floor, facedown, one officer with his knee in his back handcuffing his hands together behind him again, and the other officer holding his legs down. He had heard some scuffling and banging noises before.

Our man, Davis, testified that he had come out of the bathroom and said, "Please don't handcuff me again — I'll do anything you want, but I don't want those handcuffs on, they're too tight. I have a diabetic condition, and they're cutting off my circulation."

The police insisted on putting the handcuffs back on him and got pretty rough, picking Davis up by his arms and legs and banging his head against the wall. The tech said Davis complained that he couldn't get up. The police then asked if the lab had a gurney, and he said no, there wasn't one there. The police then each took an arm and a leg and dragged Davis down a hallway (we later measured the distance — it was over a hundred feet), pulled him out the door, threw him back in their car, and drove away. That was all the technician saw.

Davis told us he was taken to the police station and thrown in a cell, where he lay on the floor for more than an hour until finally a police sergeant came back and asked him why he hadn't gotten up. Davis told him he couldn't move. The sergeant examined him, realized there was really something wrong, and told the arresting officers they had better take him to the hospital.

They called an ambulance to take him to the county

hospital. The attendants put him on a stretcher with sandbags packed around him to be sure he wouldn't move and drove to the hospital, where he was examined briefly and found to be paralyzed. At some point they determined that he was a navy veteran, so they put more sandbags around him and transported him to the naval hospital. When I first saw him he was totally paralyzed, both arms and legs. He subsequently did recover some use of his legs, but not his arms.

There was spinal cord damage, which a doctor later told us could only have been caused by a tremendous blow to the back of the head, in other words, from driving his head down into the spinal column. This made Davis's story pretty realistic. When he contacted the personal injury lawyer who eventually hired me, the decision was made to sue the police department and the city for undue force with damages totaling a million dollars — quite a bit of money in those days, but then, it's not often you get arrested for drunk driving and wind up paralyzed.

The police, of course, wouldn't talk to me as an investigator for the plaintiff, but I was able to get a detailed account from the Iranian technician. As a foreigner, he was afraid of becoming involved. He had just enrolled in citizenship classes and believed that going against authority would jeopardize his chances of becoming a full-fledged American. (By that time I thought the system was so corrupt, I agreed with him.)

My only hope was that he believed in telling the truth, and it was very clear to him what he had seen — and what the police wanted him to now say he had seen. He did not understand the Bill of Rights, due process, the adversary system of justice, being innocent until proven guilty, or benefit of the doubt. Maybe that was better: This man wanted so much to learn about our way of life that he soaked up everything I had to say — to a point. He would nod his head earnestly when I told him about the importance of equal representation, but when I got to the part where he would get on the stand to testify, he would nearly pass out from fear. After what he had seen of American police tactics, I didn't blame him.

He was our chief witness because everything else was a matter of timing. The jurors would have to know what time the police report was written, what time the blood test was taken, when Davis arrived at the county hospital, at the naval hospital, and so forth. That was the kind of information we used to piece together the case. Normally our presentation would have included charges of racism, but we didn't go in that direction because one of the officers was white, but the other was black. They didn't seem the type of police officers you could argue were bigots. They were following standard procedure for arresting an intoxicated person, which includes handcuffing to prevent additional incidents.

I think the police should have a little more latitude in their procedures, particularly when it comes to required use of handcuffs. Drunk or not (we never denied he was intoxicated), this man was a victim of an automobile accident; he wasn't involved in any violence and had no police record. He obviously wasn't a well man, and there was no need for handcuffs or any heavy-handed treatment.

We decided the best way to approach this case was on the premise that these cops had never been properly trained in how to cope with a situation like this.

I interviewed all the people at the party Davis had attended to establish what time he had left and how sober he was at that time. We tried to determine exactly when the police picked him up. I went to both hospitals and talked to the doctors, nurses, and attending staff people who were there when he was brought in. I tracked down the ambulance attendants who transported him, paramedics who might have seen him, jail prisoners who might have overheard him. I was looking for any statements made by the police officers or Davis, anything that could shed some light on how he got injured.

All we had was his recollection of what had happened, and he was admittedly somewhat intoxicated at the time.

Of course, the police denied they had picked him up by his arms and legs and swung him against the wall so his head would slam against his vertebrae. They claimed he was refusing to be handcuffed and that they had to use a "limited amount of force" to throw him down on the ground and get the cuffs on, but they said no one had hit his head against the wall. Our doctor testified that slamming him by the head against a stone wall was the only way his spinal injury could have happened; that no reasonable way of restraining someone and putting handcuffs on would result in this kind of paralysis.

The key to the case was that the Iranian was willing to talk. The police, who had a great deal invested in this case, tried to intimidate him, I'm sure, but he stuck to his guns. What was the use, he told me later, of becoming a naturalized citizen if you don't know anything about your rights as a citizen?

There's a great deal of law written on this type of lawsuit. If it had been found that the police officers exercised due care and diligence and had not exceeded the bounds of proper procedure, then we would have lost the case. But if a jury was convinced the cops had exceeded their right and acted in an improper manner, then the city is responsible. As it was, this case never went to court. It was settled for about $350,000, thanks in large part to one very brave Iranian immigrant. He disappeared after it was over — probably to get a job someplace else and enroll in naturalization classes without fear of retaliation.

Watching the structure and content of a case change before the investigator's eyes was to become a common theme in the investigations of Lipset Service, leading Hal to his most valuable insight, the Jigsaw Puzzle theory.

PART III

THE JIGSAW PUZZLE THEORY

Chapter 7

The Lying Client

Both as a scholar and as an astute criminologist he practiced deduction. Until he had assembled facts and impressions he would not particularize.
— Roy Winsor, *Three Motives for Murder*

He wasn't to speak publicly about it for forty years, but from the beginning of his career as a private detective, Hal based his approach to every case on a working concept he called his Jigsaw Puzzle theory. Ironically, he didn't come upon it until he noticed a strange phenomenon in the detective business — that none of his clients ever told the truth.

Hal: All clients lie to a degree. They lie because they want the private investigator to be on their side. They have this mistaken idea that if you believe in them emotionally, you will work harder; if you don't, your investigation will not be as thorough or reliable. So from the moment they walk in the door, clients try to sell you on the correctness of their side of the case. They want you to think they're the guy in the white hat.

The irony is that for the detective, exactly the reverse is true. A good investigator is more objective if the client tells him everything — the good and the bad side of the case. In fact, if the investigator does find himself emotionally involved in the client's side, he might not do as well, because his mind is on his feelings for the client rather than on the facts of the case.

It's a terrible trap for the investigator. From the first interview, your tendency is to trust the guy, take his word for things, find out what he wants, and go get it for him. But when you consider that he's probably concealing much of what you have to know, you have to grill him in that first interview as though he were the key witness in a murder — subtly, though, because he often doesn't know when he's lying. You can fill in many gaps by asking a lot of questions and triggering responses and insisting (without saying so) that all the facts come out.

After the interview, when you go out to conduct the investigation, you take what the client has told you as a kind of hypothesis. If what he has said is true, the new information you bring to the case will fit that picture, that hypothesis; if it isn't true, the stuff coming in isn't going to make any sense, and you have to alter the hypothesis to fit that stuff. Many detectives aren't good at this because they don't take the time or don't have the receptivity to deal with unexpected information.

The kinky husband in Chapter 2 who "forgot" to mention his peculiar sexual needs; a bereft father who didn't tell Hal his daughter had attempted suicide before she ran away from home; an embattled property owner who omitted the fact that her neighbor had granted her an easement only a year before; a heroic union-busting employer who never mentioned his affair with a union employee; a maligned dockworker who forgot to say he did time in prison — these are all examples of the Lying Client — people who never imagine that Hal will discover their secrets in the course of his investigations.

It isn't as though I would run back to the client every time I found a new piece of information and say, "Why didn't you tell me you were on death row for six years?" In fact, I wouldn't say anything for a while. I'd wait to see how the rest of the pieces fell. I would keep altering the original hypothesis until it fit all the new information.

Years of making adjustments to the Lying Client led Hal to view each case as a series of pieces in a puzzle that he, not the client, had to collect and put in order. This is how the Jigsaw Puzzle theory began.

The detective has to figure that the client gives you a picture of the puzzle that almost certainly will change, but you use it all the same at the beginning to set your direction and goals. You start out with that picture, that hypothesis, and every time you pick up a new piece of the puzzle, you see how it fits. As long as it does, you can make certain assumptions along the way that will keep things going in the right direction.

Many times these pieces won't fit the picture you started out with, and this is where we separate the bad detective from the good detective. The bad detective will try to change the pieces to fit his original conception of the case and how it's going to turn out — either because he's lazy or dishonest or just wants to collect his fee. But the good detective will keep the pieces intact and change *his own* picture as the pieces begin to fit together by themselves.

Of course, the jigsaw puzzle is everywhere in detective fiction. Agatha Christie's Miss Marple states it most succinctly when she points out, "Mystery is like a jigsaw. Until you've fitted the last piece into place, you cannot see the whole picture."

The jigsaw puzzle is the metaphor that mystery writers use to show how the logical mind of the detective brings order to chaos. At first, all we know is that a murder has been committed — that's one piece of the puzzle. Then witnesses and suspects are interviewed — more pieces come in. Then contradictions appear, new clues turn up — more and more pieces appear.

The test for the detective as he sorts through this jumble is to resist drawing conclusions until all the pieces of the puzzle have been collected. "It is a capital mistake to theorize before one has data," Sherlock Holmes tells Watson. "Insensibly, one begins to twist facts to suit theories, instead of theories to suit facts." That's what bad detectives do, Hal says.

The good detective waits until he has all the pieces of the puzzle before he deduces anything from them. This process, this art of deduction, forms the basis for all detective fiction from Edgar Allan Poe's "The Murders in the Rue Morgue," the first mystery in Western literature, to Angela Lansbury's TV series, *Murder, She Wrote*.

Poe called this way of thinking "ratiocination," but Arthur Conan Doyle is considered the great creator of the method of logic that has captivated generations of fans. Over and over, Sherlock Holmes demonstrates that logic and reason can overcome chaos and emotion. What Hal calls his hypothesis, Holmes calls his "provisional theory" — that early picture of the puzzle that temporarily "covers all the facts," as he tells Watson. "When new facts come to our knowledge which cannot be covered by it, there will be time enough to reconsider it."

Holmes also adjusts ("reconsiders") his picture of the puzzle with every new fact, but he uses his provisional theory as Hal uses his hypothesis, to make assumptions (Holmes calls them inferences) along the way.

The twist here is that Hal begins each case with an inductive method Holmes would abhor — by starting with a premise (given to him by the client) that is sure to bias his outlook, rather than waiting to collect data objectively. Only when the information coming in doesn't fit his idea of the overall picture (which, given his theory of the Lying Client, happens almost invariably), does he reject that premise and start over, using the deductive method Holmes idealizes.

How does the Jigsaw Puzzle theory apply to a murder case in real life? Let's begin with Lipset's account of the Case of the Reluctant Driver:

> An insurance company in Los Angeles retained a lawyer to look into a double idemnity case in which the insured, a woman, died under mysterious circumstances. The company was reluctant to pay off the policy, and the woman's husband, the beneficiary, threatened to sue unless payment was made. The lawyer called me in to handle the investigation.

I contacted the Los Angeles Police Department because it was a homicide — death by a bullet in the head — to see what kind of investigation the police had done. My job was to find evidence that would hold up in court showing why the insurance company had not immediately paid the husband, in the event he did file a civil action.

The police had investigated and could not charge anyone with the murder, but I was not really concerned with finding the killer. I was looking only for facts that might prove the information given by the insured had been false. That alone would invalidate the policy.

The victim, Kay, was a young woman in her twenties who had married an older man, Robert, in his late fifties. According to the police file, Kay had known Robert for only a couple weeks before their marriage. He had divorced his wife of seventeen years one day and married this young woman the next. The application for the insurance policy was made on their wedding day, and on the day the policy went into effect, about two months later, he got on a plane and left for Hawaii. Kay's death had occurred during the time the plane was in the air.

Robert's sister, Margaret, claimed that on the day he left, she drove to his home, picked up Kay, and together the two went shopping for Christmas-tree ornaments. They ate a Mexican dinner between six and seven o'clock and then drove to Margaret's home from the restaurant, arriving about five minutes after seven. There Margaret got out of her car with her packages and told Kay to take the car and return it early the next morning. They said good-bye, Kay drove off, and Margaret took her own purchases into her house.

Margaret said she then went inside, put away her packages, trimmed the tree for a while, and went to bed. About two A.M. she was awakened by a phone call from her brother in Hawaii. Robert said he had been trying to call Kay to tell her he had arrived safely, but there had been no answer. Since he knew she was expecting him to call, he had become concerned and asked Margaret to go over to their house in the morning and ask Kay to phone him.

Margaret said that after hanging up the telephone, she looked out the window and saw that her car had been returned. It was parked in her driveway. She didn't think anything more about it until morning, when she dialed Kay's number, and there was still no answer. She then called a neighbor and asked him to check on Kay and call her back. The neighbor phoned a few minutes later to report that he had gone into the house and found Kay dead on the sofa, apparently the victim of a single bullet through her left temple. He said there were no signs of violence or intrusion and no weapon that he could see. He had just called the police.

All of this had been investigated by the Los Angeles police. The coroner examined Kay's stomach contents and fixed the time of death to be around eight-thirty P.M., meaning that approximately an hour and a half had passed between the time Kay left Margaret's house and the time of her death.

The police looked into Robert's criminal history and discovered he had had several run-ins with the law, ranging from bad checks to petty theft and even a stay in Alcatraz many years ago. Nevertheless, his alibi was unshakable. The police had checked on Robert's alleged trip to Hawaii by consulting their counterparts in Honolulu, who verified his arrival at the hotel where he claimed to have stayed. A copy of his registration form was sent to the Los Angeles Police Department where a handwriting expert verified the signature as Robert's. Eventually, the police were convinced that Robert had been in Hawaii when his wife was murdered.

The police then turned to Margaret. To their minds the key question was how Margaret's car had gotten back to her house the night of the murder. Margaret guessed that Kay must have gone out later on an errand or something, met a friend unexpectedly, and dropped the car off that night, maybe so the friend could drive her home so she wouldn't have to get up early the next morning to return the car. Then maybe the two had gone into Kay's house, there had been an argument, and the "friend" had shot Kay and left. The police didn't believe Margaret, but they didn't have enough evidence to file charges against her. Since they couldn't charge Robert either, they felt they had run out of leads, and that ended their case.

Miss Marple would love this seemingly uncrackable case because Kay's murder is a perfect example of the Jigsaw Puzzle theory in action.

Consider the pieces the police have collected so far: There is Robert's haste in marrying Kay, his departure on the day her policy went into effect, Margaret's shopping trip with Kay on the same day Robert left for Hawaii, Robert's unshakable alibi, and the mysterious return of Margaret's car.

The police sense that the way the car got back to Margaret's house may be a missing key to the puzzle, but they don't know what it might mean or what happened to it during the night of the murder. Left with these questions, they find themselves pursuing dead ends, so their decision to close the case shouldn't surprise us. After all, "If a homicide isn't solved in the first forty-eight hours, solution probability drops off to a nit," Lawrence Sanders tells us in *The Second Deadly Sin*.

Enter Hal Lipset in the classic role of the fictional private eye: Hired by somebody outside of town to solve the case in his own way, he might very well review the department file and think, as has Sherlock Holmes, "The police are excellent at amassing facts, though they do not always use them to advantage." Lipset's job is to throw out the police hypothesis and start over, collecting facts without prejudgment, the time-honored first step in the art of deduction.

> I went at the investigation from my own angle, not to solve the murder but to get the information my client needed — that there had been enough foul play behind the application and approval of Kay's policy to prove the insurance company was right in not paying Robert.
>
> I started by interviewing the insurance sales representative, George, who originally sold the policy to Robert. It

turned out that George had been a friend of Margaret's for years, and that she had introduced him to Robert a year or so before. About two or three months earlier, George had tried to write a policy for Robert and some of Robert's children from a previous marriage. Robert wanted health and accident coverage for himself but was refused on medical grounds by the company. At that time, George said he talked with Robert about trying to get a life insurance policy.

A few months later, George said, he was talking on the phone with Margaret and asked, "Do you think Robert is still interested in taking out that life insurance policy?" She told him, "I think so. He just got married, so he's probably more interested now than before. Why don't you go over and see him. He's home right now."

So George said he had dropped by. It happened to be the same day that Robert and Kay were married. The two men sat down at the dining-room table. As they were talking, George said, "Since you've just gotten married, this would be a good time to take out that life insurance policy we talked about." Robert agreed. "I better do it right now." George then filled out the application, and Robert signed it. According to George, Kay came into the room at that moment, and he said to Robert, "Why don't you take out some insurance on your wife, too?" Robert turned to Kay and said, "Honey, would you like some insurance for yourself?" Kay answered, "If you think it's a good idea, sure. Go ahead." So George wrote out an application for her as well.

George's story didn't sound very plausible to me. He had to know his company wouldn't write that type of policy for Robert, because the company had refused to accept a similar application a few months before. George had the attitude that he was just a salesman and his sale to Robert was straightforward and legitimate. Since the company had approved the life insurance policy he had written for Kay, he couldn't understand why the company now refused to honor it. This was bad business, he said, because now word would get around town that his company would not pay when a legitimate claim was made.

I now wanted to see what the insurance company's own investigation had come up with on Robert and Kay.

As a general rule, when insurance companies write these sorts of policies they have a very brief, inexpensive investigation done by an in-house investigator, or they contract with a detective agency on the outside. The investigator simply reinterviews the policy applicant just to make sure that the person exists, knows the policy was taken out (it's improper for anyone to take an insurance policy out on other people without their knowledge and consent), and doesn't have a preexisting health condition not covered by the policy. Many years ago I used to make those investigations — it's a matter of making sure that a person has two legs and two arms and doesn't have a bad heart. By having it done, insurance companies feel they are safeguarding themselves against the possibility of fraudulent claims.

I read the investigations that were made about these policies by two independent companies. One report said that Robert had written a book, which I later found to be true, and that he had made $80,000 off it, which I doubted, and thought we might be able to prove was a lie. It also said he had other "investments," but I was pretty sure he was broke. Both reports quoted Robert extensively, but there was very little information about Kay. Robert told them that Kay had lived in Los Angeles for fifteen years and at her "present address" for five years. Well, I knew that was true for Robert, but probably not for Kay, because she had apparently moved in with Robert only two months before.

In fact, everything about Kay was very hazy. The policy application gave no information about her background, family, friends — anything that would take an investigator back to the time before she and Robert had met. The only thing I knew for sure was that she had come from Bakersfield, because the police had contacted her family there when they needed a relative to come to Los Angeles and identify her body.

I decided to go to Bakersfield and talk to any of Kay's relatives I could find. Kay's parents, brother, and sister were very cooperative in meeting with me and answering my questions. The consensus was that Kay had been an active young woman, but she had also been slightly retarded. She had never had a job other than baby-sitting and had never been outside of Bakersfield in her life until she had decided to go to Los Angeles.

Her family saw this as an attempt by Kay to finally get out on her own. They had been worried about her but felt she had a right to get away, and they hoped the experience would help her mature. When Kay got to Los Angeles, she never told anyone about her family, and Robert, who married her in such haste, never really knew her background. I think now that he assumed she was like so many young women who show up in cities like Los Angeles and have no family background, at least nobody who would really miss them if they were to disappear.

The key piece I picked up in Bakersfield was that everyone who knew her said Kay could not drive a car. Apparently she had been in an accident as a child and had developed a deep fear of cars. She didn't even like to ride as a passenger. If this were true, it would completely change my picture of what was going on.

This is the point where Ellery Queen might turn to readers and ask if they know why Kay's inability to drive changes Lipset's picture of the puzzle. The answer, as Holmes would say, is elementary: If Kay could not drive, she would not have driven the car back to Margaret's house, nor would she have borrowed it in the first place, which means that Margaret is lying and that Robert is supporting Margaret in that lie. It also means that if Kay didn't drive herself home, who did?

I went back to Los Angeles to find out if anyone there had actually seen Kay drive a car. I sat down with Robert and Margaret to go over what I told them were some "routine" questions. In the middle of the conversation, when I hoped they were least expecting it, I told them how extensively I had interviewed Kay's family, and how interesting it was for me to learn that she had been terrified of cars and did not drive. The shocked looks on their faces were very revealing. It was like a whole new piece of the puzzle. It satisfied me that Robert and Margaret had thought Kay was a little nobody with no relatives or friends who cared if she was never heard of again. A perfect victim. It never occurred to them that all people have a personal history that is unique to them; there is always somebody who knows and remembers in the background.

Robert and Margaret continued to claim that Kay was not only able to drive but was in fact "an expert driver." Margaret now remembered that she and Kay had gone to Las Vegas together and that Kay had driven most of the way. I asked them if they had taught Kay how to drive, and they both said no. I asked them if they could refer me to anyone who had seen Kay drive, and they suggested one man who later said he had seen Kay behind the wheel, but not actually driving the car.

I felt that this was one of those cases where people outsmarted themselves. Kay had a California identification card, which is issued by the Department of Motor Vehicles and looks just like a driver's license except that under the word "California," it says, "Identification Card" instead of "Driver's License." People who don't drive can get these cards so they can have a drink in a bar or cash a check. I think Robert and Margaret saw it enough times to think it was a license and assumed she could drive.

They were also unaware that a coroner could set the time of death by analyzing the stomach contents of the victim's body. If Kay had gone out again and run into a friend who had followed her back to Margaret's house so they could drive to Kay's home together, by the time Kay had returned it would have been much later than eight-thirty.

I concluded finally that Margaret had killed Kay —

that's the only way it all fit. She had driven Kay back to Kay's house after dinner, stayed around to help her unpack her purchases and hang the ornaments on the tree. Then, perhaps as Kay lay down on the couch to rest, Margaret shot her through the left temple. After waiting until dark so no one would see her, she drove the car home herself. Well, Margaret lucked out — no one saw a thing.

I also felt the insurance agent was in on it. How many people buy insurance on their wedding night? It was just too coincidental that George should call Margaret on the day Robert got married, that he should innocently suggest that Robert take out a policy just as Kay came through the room, and that he should write a policy on Robert that he knew wouldn't go through. That was all a line the three concocted to keep me at bay.

However, with no gun, no witnesses, and certainly no confession, my version of the puzzle was only conjecture, and the police concluded they still had no case, so no charges were brought against Margaret or Robert. On the other hand, when Robert did sue to get the double in-demnity payment, the insurance company had more than enough evidence to prove Robert guilty of fraud: he had lied about Kay's former residence, her background, and the length of their marriage. So they never paid him.

The outcome of this case is perhaps one of the most odious in the files of Lipset Service. First, the police are apparently ineffectual: Here they follow Hal on his investigation to see if he'll succeed where they failed; when he does by opening up a key piece of in-formation, they can't find any way to use it and close the case again. Second, Lipset doesn't seem to care if justice is done — he did his job for the client and will now go home to collect his fee. Third, the murderers get away scot-free; there isn't even a trial.

On the other hand, Sherlock Holmes would find the case both amusing and instructive. Watching Lipset discover the first missing piece (that Kay couldn't drive) and inferring from that data that Margaret was lying, Holmes would note happily that "one true in-ference invariably suggests others" and agree with Lipset that

Margaret murdered Kay — that, as Lipset says, this was "the only way it all fit."

Readers of *The Thin Man* will recall that Nora Charles never quite figures out how this line of reasoning works. She asks Nick, "Then you don't know positively that [the killer] was robbing Wynant?" Nick answers, "Sure we know. It doesn't click any other way." Later she says, "Then you're not sure he . . ." and Nick replies, "Stop saying that. Of course we're sure. That's the only way it clicks." When Nora still doesn't see enough hard evidence to justify Nick's conclusions, she asks, "But this is just a theory, isn't it?" Exasperated, Nick responds, "Call it any name you like, it's good enough for me."

Dashiell Hammett shows in this exchange how a good detective adjusts his picture of the puzzle as he moves through a case, constantly making sure all the pieces "click" in his mind whenever he accepts new information. Once all the pieces fit, that is the puzzle; the mystery is solved. There is no other answer.

This complete reliance on logic is so prevalent in detective fiction that you don't have to guess at its subtle message. "Detection is, or ought to be, an exact science and should be treated in the same cold and unemotional manner," says Holmes, and for Arthur Conan Doyle, that was the point: Appearing as he does at the end of the Age of Reason and the beginning of the Industrial Revolution, Holmes represents the ideals of a society seeking to control its environment with the new tools of science. Keep the brain working in its "cold and unemotional manner," says Holmes, and reason alone, like the tool of science it, too, was made to be, will resolve the chaos of the world.

In a sense, all mysteries are a celebration of the rational mind, a dismissal of "brute emotion" and an exercise in morality. The detective, always on the side of good, uses science as a sword in his unending battle against crime, cutting through the corruption of emotion that makes people fall prey to evil.

What does all this have to do with Lipset? Beyond recognizing the role of the deductive method, let's look at the larger symbolic picture of the puzzle: Holmes may solve case after case, but it is his personal nemesis, the evil Moriarity, against whom Holmes can never triumph, because good and evil will always exist in the world, and Moriarity will always return to test Holmes's powers of logic and deduction.

We could say that Robert and Margaret represent an impersonal Moriarity in this case because if there were ever two rotten evildoers, this brother-and-sister act is at the top of the list. Perhaps even more incomprehensible than their plan to find someone as young and vulnerable as Kay to kill is their stupidity: They never notice that Kay doesn't drive, yet their entire plan is based on Kay driving the car from Margaret's and returning it in the morning. The fact that Robert does not get the insurance money is less a last-ditch triumph of good over evil and more the terrifying prospect of the future. Like Moriarity, these two are going to try their own form of evil again, and if the police are as stumped as they were before, more vulnerable young victims will meet their deaths.

That Lipset shrugs off the outcome of this case should come as no surprise. As we will see in a future chapter on the adversary system of justice, Hal believes that every case is a test of that system; if the police (with whom he is sympathetic in this case) can't find enough proof to support a formal charge, their case is rightfully closed.

There is also evidence here that Lipset is smart to walk away from this case, knowing he can't walk away from it at all. As is true for Holmes, Moriarity really is everywhere — on those "mean streets" as well as in law-enforcement systems; in the idea of science as the savior of civilization; ingrained in the competition between female emotion and male logic; and in the concept of good versus evil itself. What the detective "owes" society is not situational heroics but situational ethics: In Chapter 17, for example, we will applaud, not criticize, Lipset for offering to let a killer get away.

This is the grid of fact and fiction that offers us insights into human nature and American society when placed against an episode such as the Case of the Reluctant Driver. Here the insight might be expressed in this way: Mysteries tell us the morality we should have; detective cases in real life tell us the morality we do have.

At least that's the theory that launches Lipset's chase in the Case of the Runaway Jewel Thieves.

Chapter 8

The Case of the Runaway Jewel Thieves

He could not help thinking what no detective ever wanted to think: that a man could make his moves without leaving a trace.
— Roderick Thorp, *The Detective*

Lynn: *From the beginning, we were amazed to learn that very few investigators operated their agencies on a businesslike basis, that is, clearly understanding the assignment, accumulating the evidence, and presenting it to the client in a concise written report, on time. To this day, when I read another agency's report, I am often embarrassed to see the grammatical errors, the rambling off into unnecessary details, and lack of organization.*

Lynn's attempt to upgrade the office standards of her new profession led her to devise a filing system that reflected almost exactly the Jigsaw Puzzle theory that Hal was formulating in his mind.

The steps involved in opening a new file were deceptively simple: Whenever a new client came in, Hal took preliminary notes on a yellow legal pad, gave the case a name, and established the initial fee. His "intake sheets" were stapled on the back cover of a manila file, which was labeled and tabbed, and an "activity sheet" was prepared for agents to use in monitoring the date, mileage, expenses, and billable time they spent on each assignment.

A case number was then taken from the heavy office log that Lynn had started on their first day, beginning with case number one. Her simple process of opening a file was as efficient and reliable then as it is accessible today through Lipset's IBM computer system.

The case file was the working bible for all agents assigned to any part of the investigation. Into it, Hal encouraged everyone to place anything remotely important — newspaper clippings; court records from a previous litigation; driver's license and voting record information; public records, such as property bought and sold; photographs; ideas for possible leads; and the expected "activity sheets" from the field, operative reports, transcriptions of interviews, statements by witnesses, and copies of bills sent to the client.

Years later you could open any file and see how the case had shaped itself as elements were collected, sorted, pared down, and shaped toward the end goal, which was to conclude the investigation as efficiently as possible. To Hal, closing the case was as important as closing a sale: From the moment you began it, you pushed yourself to finish it. "Otherwise, you'll work on the damn thing forever and we'll never get paid."

The brilliance of Lynn's filing system was that here, without being aware of it, she had constructed the first step in the process of deduction — the physical means of gathering facts without prejudgment. Then and now, the case file existed as an unbiased collector of information that eventually, under the keen eyes of the private detective, formed a picture of the completed puzzle. Until all facts were in the file, the case could not be solved.

Since the file never went out of the office, Hal always carried its contents in his head, acting very much in the tradition of "Mr. Bucket," the symbolic detective George Dilnot described in his book about true detectives, *Triumphs of Detection,* as far back as 1929. At the beginning of each case, Mr. Bucket turns himself into a receptacle for the unbiased holding and carrying of assorted facts. "Mr. Bucket pervades a vast number of houses," wrote Dilnot, "to outward appearances rather languishing for want of an 'object' as he secretly picks up and plunks bits and pieces of information in his bucketlike mind. As the bucket fills up, the case file thickens. The pieces come in, the hypothesis is adjusted, the puzzle takes shape, and inferences are made.

In the Case of the Runaway Jewel Thieves, inferences would either make Hal Lipset's career as an investigator or brand him a failure in front of a million or so San Francisco readers. The case began like this:

"SECRET AGENT STUFF: A busy week at the Swissair office on Post Street," wrote *San Francisco Chronicle* columnist Herb Caen one Monday morning.

> First, in came Grete and Jim Carson, who bought first-class tickets — paying cash — for Geneva (Switzerland). Hard on their heels trod Harold Lipset, the noted private investigator, who also bought a first-class ticket for Geneva.
>
> First clue: Grete, who worked at Bard Jewelers, is suspected of taking $100,000 worth of diamonds from that jewelry place; her husband, who managed a Jones-Abrams (men's clothing) branch store, is a bit short in his accounts, too.
>
> Second clue: Mr. Lipset is on their trail, and their paths should be crossing in mysterious Geneva any minute now. He is sure to return — empty-handed or otherwise — because he bought a round-trip ticket. Grete and Jim bought one-way passage only and may have to be returned at Gov't expense. Tourist class.

The gossip item couldn't have been more thrilling: a big-time jewelry heist (later estimated at a million dollars retail); a possible inside job; a husband and wife on the lam; a private eye hot on the trail.

No police, though? No FBI? So far, the elements are only the two "clues" mentioned above and a love affair at the jewelry store that even Herb Caen didn't know about. The case really started, as Lipset recalls it, a few years earlier:

> The president of a large retail jewelry business hired a young German woman, Grete, to assist him. At twenty-three, she was already knowledgeable in fine jewelry and diamonds and soon became his chief assistant. The president, Winton, worked closely with her, and in a while they

had an affair. He was married; she wasn't. Eventually they broke it off.

I got involved some years later, after Grete married a salesclerk from a local men's clothing store chain. Jim, her husband, was the kind of guy who felt that he was smarter than everybody else and that the world was passing him by. Even when he was made the manager of a branch store, he wanted a lot more money, so Grete devised a plan for the two of them to run what was known as a badger game on her boss and former lover, Winton.

One day at work, she confessed she was still in love with Winton, even though he was still married. When Winton reciprocated, she invited him to her apartment that afternoon to resume their affair.

A few hours later Jim came home with another salesclerk, who was not in on the plot. They walked into the apartment and found Grete and Winton in bed together. When the other salesclerk left, Winton offered to pay Jim to keep him from talking, and Jim accepted the bribe. Later Winton decided to go to his lawyer and tell him about the whole mess.

The lawyer hired me to investigate the matter, which I did. I confronted Grete and Jim with information from Winton that I believed could convict them of blackmail. This seemed to scare them. They said they were sorry and assured me they would return Winton's blackmail money and never bother him again. I advised Winton that as president of the jewelry company, he should fire this woman, but he believed she was genuinely sorry and felt that no matter what my investigation had uncovered, it had been Jim's idea, not hers, to pull this badger game on him.

About six weeks later Winton's lawyer called me early on a Monday morning. He said that Grete had not shown up for work and that a great deal of jewelry was missing from the store. I made contact with the police and found that Jim had taken the weekend's receipts from the men's clothing branch store he managed. It turned out the company had been dissatisfied with his work and was planning to demote him from manager to salesclerk.

The police went to Jim and Grete's apartment and found that two sets of luggage and some clothing were missing. They reported that the couple had cleaned out the place as though they did not intend to return. Meanwhile Winton was trying to compile an inventory of what was missing and within an hour gave me a list of ninety-nine pieces of jewelry, most of them diamond bracelets, necklaces, and rings, along with some plain stones, such as emeralds and rubies. The value of the theft, at first estimated at $100,000, kept increasing as Winton found out about more missing pieces. Eventually he figured the amount to be about a million dollars retail.

The police learned that Jim and Grete had purchased tickets the week before to fly from San Francisco to New York to Geneva, Switzerland. I called an associate — a member of the World Association of Detectives — whom I knew well in Zurich and commissioned him to go to Geneva and see if he could find any trace of them. Meanwhile, the lawyer and Winton agreed that I should pursue the matter as a private investigator rather than wait for the police or FBI or Interpol or other law-enforcement group to establish jurisdiction and get somebody on the case. Nobody could find a picture of the two, or of either one, which meant they covered their tracks pretty well on their way out of the country. The police did advise me that Interpol would soon know about the theft and that I should use its international network once I got to Europe.

I flew the fastest way I could to London and from there phoned my associate in Switzerland, who told me that Grete and Jim were not occupying hotel space in Geneva. I figured they had gone on from there, but I had no leads at this point.

Perhaps the most interesting aspect to the case so far is how quickly everyone turns to the private detective to chase after the runaway thieves. Here a million dollars worth of jewelry has been stolen, yet the San Francisco police, who themselves discover Grete and Jim's flight reservations, can't or won't get on the trail while it's still hot. Nor does the jewelry store's insurance company send its own agent. Nor does the FBI appear to be interested.

While in fiction the private detective is almost always capable of moving faster and more independently than law enforcement institutions, here Lipset gets to take things a step further — he has the blessings of the police, an introduction to Interpol, a paid retainer, and a blank check to hire anybody he wants along the way.

The trick is that the authorities not only want Lipset on the side of law enforcement, they want him to *be* law enforcement. They want him to think not as a private investigator who relies on jigsaw puzzle theories, but as a willing cog in the machinery who flatfoots it out according to the book. "It's all based on the theory," says the police detective in Octavus Roy Cohen's *Lost Lady,* "that if a crime has been committed, a trail has been left with an arrow pointing to the guilty person or persons. It's founded on the certainty that the criminal can't afford to make one single mistake; that if he does, he's hooked. It's based on the theory that the cops can make plenty of mistakes and that they've only got to do one right thing; the one right thing at the one right time will get them the man they're after."

Before he can marshal those law-enforcement personnel, however, Lipset is alone in the field with nothing but his Jigsaw Puzzle theory — and an empty bucket.

> At this time I had two pictures of the puzzle in mind. On the one hand, I had been thinking of Grete and Jim as accomplished criminals who pulled off their badger game and subsequent "confession" to me of blackmail almost too smoothly. These were people who had been caught yet had gotten away with their extortion scheme only to bring off a million-dollar jewelry theft a month and a half later. The fact that Grete was something of a jewelry expert led me to suspect that she might have been planning the crime all along and got her husband in on it after he had sort of proven himself in the badger game.
>
> On the other hand, a professional jewel thief just doesn't fool around with petty blackmail, for starters. It seemed to me that had Grete and Jim really planned this out, they would not have given the airline their real names. In those

days when you flew out of the country you had to show the airline your passport before you boarded, and I felt that true professionals would have had fake passports made up for them long beforehand.

It was important to know which direction to pursue, because if Grete and Jim turned out to be professional thieves, I was going to put their pictures in the international newspapers and offer a sizable reward for any knowledge of where they were going and what they were carrying. After Herb Caen ran that item in the paper at home, I realized the jewels would get very hot very soon; they were easily identifiable and by now they were for sale in quantity. The word about these two would get out in the European underworld, and I wanted to be in on it before the jewels were fenced and gone.

But if Grete and Jim were amateur thieves, putting their pictures in the papers would only tip off real professionals that here was a million bucks worth of stolen jewels somewhere in Europe waiting to be restolen, and that could be dangerous for everybody. I wasn't even sure some syndicate in San Francisco hadn't sent somebody to track me while I was tracking Grete and Jim down. But I did know that if professional thieves got to Grete and Jim before I did, they would kill both of them rather than leave any trace, then take the jewels.

Either direction I pursued, I needed a picture of Grete, which I didn't have, and more information about her, which nobody in San Francisco, including the president of the jewelry company, seemed to have. I did know that according to Winton, Grete once referred to her hometown as Cologne, Germany, and there was an outside chance she wasn't lying.

So my next stop was Cologne, a relatively small city with public records that are simple to investigate, and there I found her family's address. On the off chance she would make the mistake of bringing Jim home to meet her parents, I arranged a surveillance on the house and waited twenty-four hours. When neither thief was observed I continued to check bus and train stations in Cologne and eventually was satisfied neither Grete nor Jim were going to appear.

Hal has referred to this case as a "good old-fashioned international chase," but we can see in his constant juggling of jigsaw pieces and his fretting over Grete and Jim how complicated it soon became. Thinking of Grete especially — where her parents live, whether she lied, what her next move could be, how she might make a mistake, why she might bring Jim "home" — makes Lipset more an intimate than predator, a phenomenon we often see in fiction when the chase is on. Indeed, the hunter and the hunted become one in *Inspector Maigret Pursues,* as Georges Simenon tells us: "A curious intimacy has sprung up between follower and followed, between the man, whose face is now dark with stubble and whose clothes are crumpled, and Maigret, who never for a moment stops trailing him. There is even one rather comic point: they've both caught colds. Their noses are red; they pull out their handkerchiefs almost in time with one another."

Hal does not know Grete well enough yet, however, to infer that she is an amateur or a professional. Poised at another precipice with no leads at all, he knows the outcome of the case is going to depend on what Poe calls "the quality of observation," on "*what* to observe."

> During the Cologne house surveillance I observed several members of Grete's family and made contact with her brother, who spoke English. I explained that I was looking for Grete, at first without telling him why. It turned out he had applied to medical school in the States and was anxious to find out if I knew anything that might help him. When it was clear no one in the family had been contacted by Grete, I told him why I was there. It scared him. He thought if Grete were caught, no medical school in the States would take a chance on the brother of a known jewel thief. I told him the country was a pretty big place and that his medical school applications would probably not be judged on the basis of what his sister did.
>
> When I explained that all I wanted was to recover the

stolen merchandise, he was more cooperative. He gave me some photos of Grete and some information about jobs and friends she had had before leaving for the United States. He agreed that if she showed up, he would contact my office in San Francisco.

Her brother also gave me an address of a girls' school Grete had attended outside of Geneva some five years earlier. He said she had become very attached to the instructors there and had told him she missed the school after leaving it. That seemed to me another possibility. If she and Jim suspected the police had found out about their flight reservations, they might have thought a visit to the school would be a way of lying low.

I left Germany and stopped at the school on my way to Geneva to interview the headmaster and his mother, who ran it. They said that Grete and Jim had in fact visited the school and had talked for an hour with the headmaster. It was clear from the beginning that neither the headmaster nor his mother knew about the jewels or where Grete and Jim were going afterward.

At this point I decided to assume that Grete and Jim were not professionals. Accomplished jewel thieves would hardly take the time to make a nostalgic visit to somebody's former school. The way the headmaster talked, it had meant a lot to Grete to introduce her new husband to her former teachers, and as I looked at hotels in the area, I knew that this was the last place a former student returning with her husband could lie low. I stopped debating whether to put a notice in the European papers with pictures saying there was a reward out for Grete and Jim. I figured instead that I should keep the theft quiet and keep working confidentially with law enforcement agencies.

When I got to Geneva I took my copy of the San Francisco police warrant to the chief of police, and he helped me find the hotel where Grete and Jim had stayed while visiting the school. Then it was a matter of figuring out how they had left Geneva, which meant contacting every travel agent, train station, airline desk, and ticket counter in the city. In those days, this was a labor-intensive job that could take three days, so I left the search in the chief's hands and went to Paris, which is the headquarters of Interpol.

At that time [1966], I believed, as the police in San Francisco had told me, that Interpol was a kind of central intelligence bureau for all the police agencies in Europe, and that I could engage their assistance and maybe find Grete and Jim sooner than if I were to run all over Europe enlisting the help of individual police departments from city to city. About half this assumption turned out to be true.

First I went to the American embassy in Paris, talked to the people who were acting as liaison to the Paris police, and briefed them on the case in the event something might cross their desks that could help me. Then I went to see the head liaison man for Interpol. By now it was four days after I had left San Francisco and some eight days after the actual theft had taken place.

Interpol officers were surprised to see me. They said they knew nothing about this San Francisco jewel theft and could take no action without official word from the U.S. government. "But they *have* given you official word," I said. "No monsieur, we have no word," he told me.

I showed them my license, the newspaper clippings, the name of the chief of police in Geneva. I explained that the San Francisco police had gone through channels to get to Interpol the minute they learned that Grete and Jim had fled or were fleeing to Europe. They had turned the matter over to the U.S. Attorney, who as a federal agent had gone to Federal Court and sworn out a complaint stating that Grete and Jim were making "an unlawful flight to avoid prosecution." A federal warrant had been issued for their arrest, and Interpol had been contacted.

"No monsieur, we have no word." This is all I heard. Another conference took place, and I realized that the U.S. Attorney in San Francisco had filed the complaint with the Department of Justice, which was the federal department he worked under, when he should have filed it with the Secret Service, which operated under the Department of the Treasury, which was the U.S. arm to Interpol. "Well, let's call them and get it fixed," I said. It seemed a simple matter of moving a piece of paper from one building to another. But that would be impossible, they said. They did not have the authorization.

Finally I asked the Interpol agent, "Do you believe me when I tell you that this theft has taken place?"

"Oh yes, monsieur, we believe you," he said.

"And do you believe that I am representing the owner of the jewelry company and that I have the full support of the San Francisco Police Department, the insurance company, and the FBI?"

"Why, yes, monsieur," he said. He seemed happy to agree. "And that the San Francisco Police Department and the U.S. Attorney's office are trying to reach you about it in accordance with Interpol regulations?"

"Ah," he said, holding up his hand. "But you see, monsieur, we have not received the official letter from your government."

I walked over to the window. "You mean if I look out this window and there she is, carrying a bag under her arm and all the jewels in the bag, you would take no action?" He spread his hands out. "No, monsieur, we would take no action." I said, "Then what the *fuck* am I doing here?" and left.

We could understand the agents' position at Interpol if it were not for the fact that Interpol exists to cut through red tape for detectives chasing after crooks. Hal, already hostile to bureaucracies, stomps out of Interpol like Mike Hammer, a chip on his shoulder the size of France and a sense that he was a fool to waste all his time with the law enforcement "team."

Later he would discover that J. Edgar Hoover himself was responsible for stopping the official chain of command, since Hoover controlled the Department of Justice and hated Interpol, which he didn't control. Such was his power that Hoover would not allow the FBI or U.S. Attorney in San Francisco or the Attorney General in Washington to deal directly with Interpol, thus forcing the U.S. government to handle all its liaisons with Interpol through the Secret Service of the Treasury Department, a route unknown, of course, to the police in San Francisco. This intriguing aspect to Hoover's character was not known to many people outside Washington at the time, and learning of it only made Hal furious all over again. Bureacracies bred fascists like Hoover, as far as he was concerned.

> I went back to my hotel room in Paris and called the police chief in San Francisco to see if he could start the ball rolling with Interpol again by getting some kind of "official letter" to the Treasury Department. About nine o'clock that night the liaison officer of the Paris embassy called to say that he had just received word from the police in Geneva, who told him they had found out Grete and Jim had purchased tickets to fly from Geneva to Brussels, Brussels to Madrid, and Madrid to Las Palmas in the Canary Islands. They also told me the date and time the two had flown out of the city. This was some four days earlier, just about the time I had left San Francisco.
>
> I took a taxi to the airport and got the first plane to Madrid. There I contacted the head of the Spanish National Police and explained the situation. He advised me after searching his records that Grete and Jim were not in Madrid and had probably gone on to the Canary Islands. I went back to the airport and flew to Las Palmas, arriving about seven o'clock in the evening.
>
> I found the chief of police in Las Palmas and explained everything again. He started a search in Las Palmas and found out that the couple had stayed there one night — the night before — and had gone on to Tenerife, another island in the Grand Canaries. I was just twenty-four hours behind them. I got to the airport in time for the last plane from Las Palmas to Tenerife, arranging for the chief of police in Las Palmas to send a wire to the chief of police in Tenerife, notifying him that I was coming and would explain everything.

I arrived in Tenerife about ten o'clock that night and had a meeting with the chief of police there and again explained the situation. He started a search and said he would let me know what he found out. I found a hotel room and fell asleep. About five o'clock the next morning the chief awakened me to say he had located the place where Grete and Jim had stayed the night before. He said that they had made arrangements to go to Porta de la Cruz, a little town on the far side of the island.

At five-thirty the chief of police, four detectives, eight or nine police officers, and I rode in three cars across the island, over the mountains, and down into Porta de la Cruz, arriving there about seven o'clock. Again the chief arranged a search, and this time he found the hotel where Grete and Jim were staying. We surrounded the hotel and decided the best thing to do was not to break down the door but wait until they left the room.

Jim came down for coffee about nine o'clock and was arrested. Then we went upstairs and knocked on the door. When Grete opened it, we advised her that she was under arrest, and that she had to go to the police station. She took a few things, showed me where the jewels were, and was accompanied downstairs. Then the chief of police, the four detectives, the eight or nine police officers, Grete, Jim, and myself all went back in three cars to the police station in Tenerife.

On the way, Grete told us that she and Jim knew they had gone about the theft of the jewels all wrong. They had been trying to figure out how to return the jewelry, she said, when we arrested them. She was very cooperative. We got to the police station and laid all the jewels out on a table, and she went over the list of missing items with me. There were even some jewels unaccounted for on Winton's list.

Suddenly the chief of police decided to keep all the jewels in his safe. His position was that since I wasn't a police detective, I had no official standing, and that because the jewels had been smuggled into Spain, the Spanish government was entitled to levy taxes on them. Disgusted, I left on the next plane and a few days later returned with Winton's lawyer to have the jewelry moved from the chief's safe to a vault in the bank of Spain, where they were finally picked up by the San Francisco police.

Grete and Jim were extradited and got a public defender after they returned to San Francisco. They, too, decided I had no standing since I wasn't a police officer, and they wanted to sue me for illegal arrest. When they realized everybody had arrested them but me, Jim convinced himself, with Grete's help probably, to do the "gentlemanly thing" and say the crime was all his idea. He pled guilty, broke down and sobbed in court, and was sent to prison. Grete pled not guilty and was allowed to return to Germany.

The night before she left the country, Grete called and said she wanted "to meet the man who caught me." I thought she might be after something, but I met her at the St. Francis bar for a drink anyway, thinking I might get some answers to questions of my own.

Why, for example, had she gone back to her old girls' school? Was it really just nostalgia or did she figure the police were after them and thought it best to lie low? Nothing of the kind, Grete said. She had had an affair with the headmaster when she was a student there and wanted to show him her new husband. The jewels, the police, the chase, none of that entered into it — she had a personal mission to confront her former headmaster/lover, and that's what she did.

Why pick the Canary Islands, where an American and German traveling together would be easy to find? That was a mistake, she said. The travel agent in Geneva had misunderstood them when they said they wanted to go to Palma, Majorca, where they had friends. He had instead written down Las Palmas de Gran Canaria, without their knowing it. I had to smile at the fact I ever thought of them as professionals. "That must have been quite a moment on the airplane," I said, "when you and Jim realized you weren't going to Majorca but some island where you knew no one." She shrugged. "Oh, we knew we weren't going to get away with it long before that," she said.

A few days after she returned to Germany, Grete wrote to ask if I would help her get a divorce from Jim. This was before no-fault divorce, so I got her a good divorce attorney. There is some irony in the way he handled Grete's suit — as grounds for divorce he used the fact that Grete's husband had just been convicted of a felony in the state of California.

Alfred Hitchcock might have created the character of Grete, the kind of "sympathetic criminal" who appeared in so many of his movies. Grete, manipulating everyone, failing at everything, leaving a trail of men in her path, is somehow innocent throughout it all; wily and vulnerable at once, she comes through as sincere and almost chummy at the end. She even allows Hal to place the last pieces in the puzzle during a how-did-you, why-did-you conversation that sounds more like the last five minutes of the TV version of *Perry Mason* than the end of a case in real life.

In a way, though, the case could never have been an exercise in fiction: Grete and Jim seem to sleepwalk their way through it, stopping at the school, getting on the wrong plane, and halfheartedly planning to return the jewels, knowing they'll be caught eventually. Hal, inferring from their actions that they are amateurs, not professionals, deduces a pattern to their flight, confirms his picture of the puzzle, and makes the nab. If anybody deserves to be caught, it is this once-clever, now bumbling and ineffectual pair.

Yet their only real mistake lies in visiting the girls' school. It never occurs to them that a detective will learn enough about Grete's background to check out the school himself, and for Hal, considering all the possibilities facing him — running ads in the newspapers, finding Grete's old friends and employers — deciding to try the school first was a neat bit of deducing. Acting in the tradition of all fictional detectives who refuse to accept coincidence, Hal saw in the proximity of the school to Geneva, where Jim and Grete first landed when they flew to Europe, a "fit" of the two pieces in the puzzle rather than an irrelevant duplication.

But then: The sympathetic thief gets off while her dumb-but-not-so-guilty husband takes the rap. Where's the justice in that? On the one hand we could look at such classics as *The Postman Always Rings Twice, Double Idemnity,* or *Body Heat* and recall that in crimes of love and lust, it's always the man who ends up playing the patsy. That's his fate. Dames such as Grete get away because it's their fate to play out men's worst fear — that unleashed emotion and sexual appetite (the opposite of objectivity, logic, and the scientific method) will lead to ruin.

On the other hand, our grid of fact and fiction offers this observation: Mysteries show us the inevitability of justice; a real-life detective's cases show us a working system of justice with all its imperfections.

Just how imperfect it can be is Hal's next challenge in the Case of the Elusive Entrepreneur.

Chapter 9

The Case of the Elusive Entrepreneur

"There's only one thing about it I don't like — the fact that it's coincidental. And I detest coincidences."
— Ellery Queen, *The Chinese Orange*

Coincidence, the accidental and remarkable concurrence of events without apparent causal connection, has no place in the deductive method. Since the detective's job is to search for patterns in a seeming chaos of events, he automatically distrusts any connection that occurs without meaning.

Like coincidences, red herrings exist to seduce the detective away from the careful inferences of his deductive theory. The smart detective, testing each piece of the puzzle against his hypothesis, looks to coincidence not for what it adds to his picture of the puzzle, but for what it's trying to take away.

Taken as a sign that something's afoot in the Case of the Elusive Entrepreneur, coincidence creates one of the great tests of Hal's Jigsaw Puzzle theory. Here the investigation takes on a separate dimension when Hal, faced with a $5 million lawsuit, steps into the case as his own client, only to face coincidental information that he knows "couldn't happen in a million years."

With emotions running high, henchmen bullying his agent, secrets mired in U.S. Army records, and FBI operatives hovering in the background, Hal struggles to maintain his objectivity while the pieces of the puzzle fly around him in three-dimensional disorder.

Readers may have some fun with this case by recognizing the source of the coincidence that forms the key piece of the puzzle; this is a bit of information Lipset couldn't have known twenty years ago but is common knowledge today. Follow the clues he identifies along the way, and you should have an idea of the mystery's solution long before he does. (Hint: Another clue can be found in the Introduction.)

Hal: I was out of town when the office was contacted by a lawyer representing a company on the East Coast — call it Eastern Capital Company. This group was in the money-lending business and had loaned several million dollars to Paul Maris, a management consultant who had appeared on the San Francisco garment scene a few years before.

At that time, Maris had become friendly with Alvin Duskin, the owner of a successful dress manufacturing company. Initially, Maris was hired by Duskin as a consultant. He was a quick study and impressed Duskin with his ability to come up with new ideas for running the company. A year or so later, when Duskin started talking about retirement, Maris put together a package to buy Duskin out. He went to New York and made contact with Eastern Capital, which advanced $2.5 million to buy out Duskin and loaned Maris another $1 million for the personal stock that he would hold.

By the time the attorney contacted me, Maris had taken over the company and been running it for several years. He had a good advertising campaign going and had instituted new lines. He put in some hotshot sales representatives and was successfully building up the company's gross volume. He was also spending a lot of money doing it. He hired his wife, her brother, and her father at high salaries. He brought some friends in as executives and gave them all expensive cars — Mercedes, Maseratis, Ferraris, very fancy types.

In a few years, Maris started to slip on his commitments to Eastern Capital. He was growing too fast, and his decreasing cash flow began to eat up the profits. He was an arrogant CEO, especially to his board, and after many attempts at finding some middle ground, the moneylenders decided to oust him.

They flew to San Francisco, drove directly to the dress company, and tried to take it over. They thought they could walk in and say, "Mr. Maris, we just called a meeting of the board of directors and voted you out." But instead of replying, "Yes, sir! I'm leaving," Maris snarled at them. He not only refused to go, he threatened to punch one or two of them in the nose.

They didn't want any violence, so they decided to work out some kind of legal compromise. But they were suspicious of Maris because he was so volatile. That's when they got a local attorney and hired our company. David Fechheimer was running the office while I was away, so he conducted the first surveillance. He watched people walking out of the building with computer printouts and design process sheets that belonged to the company. He also saw Maris leaving the premises with the heads of various departments — the head seamstress, the head cutter, the head bookkeeper, and so forth.

By this time Eastern Capital had created a compromise and let Maris remain as president, but it was kind of an armed truce at the place. When I came home, there were head-to-head conferences going on in my office among the Eastern Capital people, who still wanted to get Maris out but didn't want any trouble. They had requested their lawyers to prepare a temporary restraining order so that Maris, his wife, his in-laws, and his executives would be restrained from taking anything out of the building and from talking to employees who were not part of management.

Our job was to physically remove the Maris contingent in the most efficient and least violent manner. As the attorneys prepared the restraining orders, we wrote letters to employees in English, Spanish, Chinese, and Tagalog telling them how we were going to effect the takeover. We hired twenty operatives and gave each of them written battle instructions for the day of the Maris oust. We provided Eastern Capital's chief executive officer, Glenn Stevens, with a full-time bodyguard, Ed Butler, a six-foot, six-inch licensed private investigator who used to be a narcotics law enforcement agent with the federal government.

The dress factory was a big building with half a dozen floors. We knew we would have to keep people from moving around and telephone calls from going out. It was the same as securing a whole building, as you would do in an army or a police action. We wanted to time it so everyone would be processed out of there within hours, and we wanted to do it on a Thursday so we could lock it down Friday and use the weekend to take it easy on security and keep Stevens's bill to a minimum.

Early on Thursday morning, the lawyers, Glenn Stevens, and I went downtown to court, only to find that the judge did not want to sign the temporary restraining order. He was not sure that Maris was really hurting the company. He felt that to have a man thrown out of his business before he had his day in court was not fair. We were stunned. To us, the board of directors had every right to get him out of there on any day they chose. The temporary restraining order was their legal means of getting him out; since it *was* temporary, he would have his day in court within a few days.

The judge finally got around to signing the order that afternoon — with the proviso that Eastern Capital would put up a $25,000 bond to protect Maris in case it cost him $25,000 to sue and he won. This took even more time. All the while I had my army standing by and ready to go, with the meter running.

We went back to the factory, got everyone organized, and marched in force into the building. I dispatched several agents to the parking area at the back of the building with instructions not to let employees get into their cars. I put a man on the front door, a man on the elevator, and a man on each stairwell to stop employees moving from floor to floor. We then went to the executive floor. I said to the switchboard operator, "We are temporarily replacing you. Sit down over there and let my employee here take your place. When a call comes in, tell him how to answer it." The whole thing was like a military coup.

I went through the offices, followed by Eastern Capital officers, each of whom was accompanied by one of my agents, who in turn were armed with court documents, to serve various officers in manufacturing, sales, processing, and other departments. Every time we dismissed a Maris executive, we put an Eastern Capital executive in his or her place, or locked the desk or office of that person. Then with Stevens accompanying me I went back into the CEO suite, deploying one man on the way to guard the computer systems room. We walked unannounced into Maris's office. He was sitting behind his desk. He didn't know anything was happening at this time.

"What is it?" he said.

"Paul Maris," I announced, "I'm here to serve papers on you."

He looked at Stevens and smiled. "Oh, you're trying to scare me. OK, go ahead. I've got the best law firm in San Francisco, so just try it."

"Mr. Maris," I said formally, "I'm serving these documents on you in addition to a complaint allowing Eastern Capital to take over this company. These papers specifically restrain you from removing any company property. You are not allowed to take your company car when you leave. You are not allowed to take business papers from this office. You are not allowed to take printouts from the computer room. You are not allowed to take plans from the designing room. You are not allowed to take any samples, and furthermore, according to paragraph sixteen of this order, you are restrained from discussing this matter with any employees until this case is heard in court."

He curled his lip in a way that wasn't friendly but wasn't

tough and said to me, "OK. What are you doing here?"

"I'm serving the papers."

"Oh yeah? Well, who's that big guy — what is he, six seven? — standing behind Glenn Stevens?"

"That's Mr. Stevens's personal bodyguard," I said. Then, trying to lighten the tension, I added, "I think he's a little afraid of you." Maris said, "Aw, I wouldn't hurt anybody. Just let me clean out my desk and I'll — "

"If you will just show us what it is you want to take," I said, "we'll make a list. We don't want to have to search you, but you're not allowed to take company property."

"Oh, the hell with it," he said, throwing down his pen. "I'll be back in a day or two. I'll leave it all here." He got up and left.

I accompanied Maris out of his office, where another of my agents took him to the first floor. It turned out we were having similar problems with other company officers. Once they were served, they insisted on taking things out of their desks. We wanted to get them out of the building so there would be no trouble. So we said, "You must leave right now. After you leave, we'll go through your desk, and anything that doesn't belong to the company we'll put in a box and deliver to your house." Some people tried to get to their company cars down in the parking lot, but we took their keys away from them. Some yelled at us, but everyone on our side remained businesslike and courteous.

We decided to reinstate a surveillance on Maris to be sure that he didn't violate the restraining order. We watched his apartment and found that he did meet with other people, most of whom we did not recognize. One day he went up to Nob Hill, where he appeared to be holding a conference in the lobby restaurant of the Stanford Court Hotel. I sent my operative, Sandra Sutherland, who had taken photographs of our factory takeover, to go to the hotel and photograph whoever met him so we could tell if he was contacting any of the key employees and violating the restraining order.

Sandra took one of the representatives from Eastern

Capital with her because he knew most of the factory people by their faces. He didn't want to be spotted by them while he was with Sandra, although she was unknown to these guys. So he went in with her, pointed them out from a distance, and then went back outside. He wasn't recognized, but a few minutes later they saw her with a camera and got suspicious. Before she knew it, they were coming toward her and grabbing hold of her wrists. Then they threatened to slap her around.

Maris or one of his cohorts said they were going to call the hotel management and say that she was a prostitute who tried to solicit their business. Sandra laughed and said, "Yeah, right, with a camera." She warned them, "If you do that, I'll sue you for slander. I have as much right to be in this lobby as you have." They pushed her up against a pillar in the lobby and tried to frighten her, but she wouldn't budge. They grabbed the camera and pulled out the film. She left without any pictures.

My client also wanted to know if Maris had taken company property to his home. David Fechheimer talked to the manager of the apartment house where Maris lived in the city and found out Maris had a country home in Sonoma County, about fifty miles north of San Francisco. He drove up there and talked to an employee on the property. Maris, it turned out, had a tractor and other equipment we knew had appeared on the company books. He had also thrown parties and entertained customers up there.

About three days after the big takeover coup, a sheriff's deputy walked in my office to serve papers on me. It was a countersuit by Maris against Eastern Capital, Glenn Stevens, myself, and Lipset Service, alleging that the takeover was improper and would do great damage to him financially and personally. The suit against each person was $5 million. It alleged that I had illegally tapped Maris's telephone and illegally entered his property, home, and ranch to conduct an illegal search.

I was upset for two reasons. First, my insurance costs me money when I'm sued because attorney fees eat up the deductible regardless of the outcome. Second, I don't like being accused of criminal acts because most people already think I do illegal things, and these accusations just reinforce that belief. I did not search his premises illegally; Maris knew that. But he also knew the judge's ruling would give him a $25,000 expense check if he won.

I drove to the dress factory, where Stevens was now running the show. We still had two or three guards there, one at the front door, one on the switchboard, and Stevens's bodyguard, Ed. I said to Stevens, "Just who is this Paul Maris?"

"Why?" he said.

"Haven't you been served yet?" I asked. "Sure," he replied offhandedly, "that's nothing new."

"Well, it may be nothing to you, but I'm named in here for five million dollars. I'm accused of committing crimes I've never done. That's why I want to know, who is this guy Maris?"

I had never been interested in who Maris was or where he came from because his background and identity had nothing to do with the case. We had been hired to aid in the takeover, nothing more.

Stevens went over to his filing cabinet and pulled out Maris's resume. "We had him checked out by a very well known detective agency in New York," he told me. "This firm is run by an ex–FBI agent, and he said everything in there is accurate. Somewhere around here I have a copy of their report. You'll see that Maris checks out one hundred percent."

I looked through the resume. It described Maris's army career, specifically that he had worked as an intelligence officer, but it gave no unit, which usually is put down as a matter of rote. There was a list of stocks that he owned, so many shares in this company and that company, but they were all privately held, and no addresses were given. I got these vibrations that something didn't fit.

Stevens gave me a copy of the ex–FBI agent's report, which explained that the investigator had checked with the registrar at the school Maris listed, and that some "confidential sources" in New Jersey had given Maris very high recommendations. But the registrar wasn't named, and there was no reason given for the sources being "confidential." I felt too many things didn't ring true and were worth verifying on my own.

I turned back to Stevens and said, "I've been doing background checks like this for a long time. I don't know how many years this New York agency has been in business or who this ex–FBI man is, but I will bet you this background story is false." Stevens shrugged and said I was just trying to get more business and make more money. I was furious. "I'll bet you Maris is a phony," I said, almost shouting, "and if he's not, you don't have to pay for this investigation. But if he is a fraud, you have to pay for all of it."

Stevens shouted back, "Fine! Go ahead!"

"All right!" I yelled, and walked out.

In detective fiction, this is a familiar scene: The private eye refuses to leave the case, decides to investigate on his own, and races out to discover the truth for himself, alienating the client and risking a lot of work for no pay. Now he is in trouble: His personal involvement removes all objectivity; he may lose money instead of earn it; he feels personally threatened and is acting almost entirely on the defensive. Yet as vulnerable as he may be at this stage in the case, to whatever villains are after him, he is also very "dangerous," as Hercule Poirot puts it, compelled as he is — obsessed as he is — by "a passion for the truth."

I got on the phone and called an investigator in Philadelphia where Maris claimed to have been born. I asked him to get me a copy of the birth certificate and confirm or disprove whether Maris went to the elementary and high schools listed on the resume. I called another investigator in Ohio and asked him to check on the college where Maris claimed to have graduated. I contacted an associate in Washington, D.C., and gave him Maris's military serial number and service record to investigate. Then I began to look through the company records to see what I could find out about Maris's background. Naturally enough, he had allowed nothing of his background in the office files.

Then things started coming back. The Philadelphia investigator said there was no record of birth for Paul Maris, and that Maris had never attended school there. The man in Ohio couldn't get to the college for a week or two, so I called him off and wrote a letter to the college requesting information about Maris's attendance. My associate in D.C. called back in twenty-four hours to say there was no such military serial number and no record of a Paul Maris in the army. He said, "You know, they're getting a little excited back here. It's a crime for anybody to represent himself as an ex–military person if he's not." That was interesting, but the point was that by now I knew Maris was not Maris.

Checking the payroll records in Maris's office, David and I noticed a funny thing: Maris's social security number was exactly one digit off the number of his wife's social security number, while her father's social security number was only one digit off hers, and her brother's social security number was only one digit off her father's. I looked at David and said, "Some coincidence. This couldn't happen in a million years."

In fact, consecutive social security numbers should have been a total impossibility. I can see a man and his wife having consecutive social security numbers if they started in life pretty much together with their first job, but Mrs. Maris's father was a great deal older than Paul and should have started work many years before he did.

Even as we worked on other cases, David and I could not get those social security numbers out of our minds. Pieces of the Maris puzzle would come in piecemeal and from different sources, and we would always go back to those numbers. David thought maybe the whole thing centered on Maris changing his name from, say, Mariscal or Markovich or Maresh. I felt we could operate on that theory for a while, because it did account for the lack of information we were getting on the name Maris, but it had no bearing on the four-digit sequence of the social security cards.

I decided to make a direct call to the detective agency in New York. When the ex–FBI agent came on the line, I said, "We represent the Eastern Capital Company, and we are in a lawsuit with Paul Maris. The company has turned over to us a copy of the report you made when you investigated Maris. Will you check your files and tell us who you talked to in making out this report?" It was a proper request — detective agencies verify information for each other all the time.

The ex–FBI agent said, "Sure, I remember Maris. We checked him out thoroughly, and everything was fine." I asked him, "Did you check out where he went to school?"

"Oh yes, we have a letter from the registrar of his university stating that he graduated from college in the year that he said he did, and with the degree that he said he had." I now had in my hand a letter from the registrar denying any such thing, but I didn't want to tip off the ex–FBI agent. "Good," I answered. "Will you get your file and read the letter to me and tell me who signed it?"

"Just a minute," the man said, and the phone was set down. He came back a minute later and told me the file was not there. It was out on Long Island. The agent who had handled the case had a branch office out there, and the ex–FBI man said he would get hold of that agent by phone and have him call me back. In a few minutes, we got a call from the Long Island detective saying the file was missing and at the moment he couldn't put his hands on it, but he would get back to us. The whole thing had a phony ring to it.

A couple of hours later, I got a phone call from Maris himself, who suggested that I meet with him. He said he heard I was doing a big investigation of him, and he wanted to talk to me about it. Except for a few legal proprieties that had to be observed, meeting with him sounded fine to me. I had already been advised by Glenn Stevens that Eastern Capital's lawyers had an answer to Maris's cross-complaint and subpoenas for depositions to serve on Maris and his executives and relatives. I had told Stevens what we now knew about Maris, and aside from being properly flabbergasted, he agreed we should keep everything quiet until the whole picture fell into place.

I told Maris I had some reservations about seeing him because he was represented by counsel and technically I wasn't allowed to talk directly to him. He dismissed this as so much pettiness on my part. The following morning he called and wanted me to come down to the hotel for breakfast.

"Well, I'll be glad to meet," I told him, "but you know that I'm working for the other side. If we're going to talk, we should have lawyers with us. But I will meet with you because I have papers to serve on you and on some of your men, too."

I was more than a little suspicious, but I knew the only way to find out what was going on was to meet him. So I drove to his hotel, serving the papers on him in the lobby. He called his other men over and I served them, too. We then sat down to have a cup of coffee.

"Mr. Maris," I said, "officially it's not proper for me to talk to you, because you're represented by a lawyer."

"That's the reason I wanted you down here," he said. "This whole lawsuit is ridiculous. The only people who'll make money out of it are lawyers. I want you to tell Stevens that the case is going to be settled. There's no reason to fight — it's just that I got upset when you folks threw me out of my own company."

"Yeah, well, I got upset about what you did to my employee, Sandra."

"That was a mistake," he said, "I'll have the man who roughed her up apologize. The important thing for you to know is that there's no point in continuing your investigation of me. I can tell you right now that the reason you can't find my military records is that I had a top-secret job in the army, and everything about it is classified. All reports were filed in such a way that nobody can ever find them — at least nobody who's talking to you."

I did not tell Maris that I knew he had not gone to the university he had claimed to, or anything else we had found out. I just said, "Look, why don't you stop all this business? I don't know who you are, but I do know you're not Paul Maris. You can tell me about your secret classification from now until doomsday, and I'm not going to believe you. You are out of the military, and when you're out, you're just another record in the files. They have a military record of me in Washington, and if you were ever in the army, they have a record on you."

"You want to see my record, Lipset?" His lip was curling again. "I'll show you the only record on me you'll ever see." He got his wallet and pulled out a card that identified him as a captain in the U.S. Army. It had the letters "ADJ" after his name, which I took to mean adjutant. The card did not look like any army ID I had ever seen. "It's not really correct," he said. "I've recently been promoted to major, and I haven't gotten my new ID yet."

I took out my pen and said, "Do you mind if I make some notes off this card?"

"Sure," he said, "go right ahead."

I copied down the serial number, the date the card had been issued, and some other information on the back of the ID and gave it to him. "As far as I'm concerned," I told him, "your name has been changed. There is no record of Paul Maris anywhere along the line. So tell me the truth. Tell me where you were born. Tell me where you went to school."

"I'll tell you this, Lipset," he said. "We are both investigators. I was an investigator in the service, and that's why you'll never find me. As one investigator to another, I am telling you that we should cooperate with each other. I just explained why your investigation is going nowhere. Now let me settle this lawsuit and walk away clean." Well, I had been conned before, and I knew a sales pitch when I heard it, but I couldn't figure what his scam was.

I think if I hadn't been so personally involved I would have realized that the only way Maris could have known I was investigating him was by word from that ex–FBI detective in New York. I mean, the school he never went to is not going to call him. The army that has no records is not going to call him. The company that's trying to oust him is not going to call him. But if he were somehow in league with this fancy-schmancy ex–FBI agency, that guy certainly would have called him — although to what purpose?

I put my pen away and said to Maris one more time, "Look, just tell me who you are. You say it's all going to be settled. You say quit the investigation. OK. But then you lie and tell me that the army keeps your identity secret. I don't believe it; it's bull. Just come clean now and I'll walk away — that'll be the end of it."

"Oh no," he said with his surly laugh. "No, I'm not going to make your work any easier, Lipset. You run along now and see how far you get."

Here's another familiar scene: The lone private eye, armed with his only weapon, the deductive method, confronts the lying crime boss in his lair. There Maris makes the perfect villain — with his curled lip and surly laugh, he is affable, defensive, and threatening at once. He begins the meeting arrogantly and closes it with a bluff, having given all his powerful chips to Lipset, who ironically doesn't know anything more by the end of the meeting than he did at the start. Meanwhile, the truth becomes a third character in the action, sitting between them, waiting to be recognized.

Back at the office I was more convinced than ever that I was on the right track. I telephoned my contact in Washington and said, "I just saw this guy's card. He's carrying ID that says he was a captain in the adjutant general's office. His serial number is such and such. He tells me he just got promoted to major. Now I don't want to say all of this is false if it's true, but I don't believe it. It's up to you to tell me. As far as I'm concerned you can tell the FBI out there that someone is impersonating an officer, and let's put an end to this one way or another."

A couple of hours later my colleague rather anxiously

called back. "There's something very mysterious about this," he said. "The army has no record of that card — it doesn't exist. I told the FBI about it, and they want to talk to you."

"If they want to talk to me, they know where I live."

"No, they want to talk to you here, in Washington."

Now, I know the FBI doesn't work this way. This agency operates under the Department of Justice, and if its agents wanted to see me, they would teletype their San Francisco office and send a couple of agents over to talk. Hell, they come around here once a month about something anyway.

"Well, that's a lot of baloney," I said. "I'm not flying to Washington at my expense because they want to talk to me about some guy impersonating an officer." This should have been the last clue, and eventually it was. But at that moment I had no way of fitting it in.

Meanwhile, Ed, the bodyguard that I had assigned to Stevens, was hearing all of this since he was asking casual questions about the case as he was driving Stevens around or walking along with him. When the two of them were in my office, Ed not only talked to Stevens about the case, he had easy access to the Maris file, which was usually open on David's or my desk. He knew we were trying to figure out who Maris was. He could see David's doodling — "MARKOWITZ," "MARESCA," "MARISCAL" — with the Maris name. Ed thus became the one, because of his background as a federal narcotics officer, who made the final link.

Unfortunately, Ed was broke and not too trustworthy. He told Stevens that he had special knowledge of the Maris case because of his connections with the federal government, and that he would sell this information, without my knowledge, to Stevens for a couple of thousand dollars. Stevens took Ed to his lawyer, and they were so anxious to uncover the identity of Maris that they paid him the money and didn't call me. Ed then swore them to secrecy: He said that he heard what he was about to tell them from a U.S. deputy marshal. Then he gave them the last piece of the puzzle.

Here Ellery Queen steps in again to ask readers in his condescending manner how they're doing. If you haven't figured out the answer by now, here's a review of the clues: (1) the consecutive social security numbers of Maris, his wife, her father and brother; (2) Maris's phony background and especially his phony army identification; (3) the distant but apparently real interest of the FBI in the case; (4) Lipset's inference that the ex–FBI agent in New York and Maris are in cahoots; (5) the fact that Ed with his background as a federal narcotics agent is the only one to solve the puzzle. You have the last piece of information in your knowledge of common practices existing today, but Lipset doesn't. Want a hint? How could a fake identity be known and possibly protected by the FBI?

As we had suspected, and as Ed told Stevens, Maris was not the Paul Maris we had all known. He was a "relocated" hoodlum from the East Coast who years ago had testified against the Mafia and had been offered a new identity as protection. Through the Department of Justice's witness relocation program, he and his family had been given new names, new social security cards, and new identification papers and were shipped West under heavy security to start out with a clean slate. That's why he had Sandra roughed up that day at the Stanford Court — he didn't care what side she was on; it was her camera that scared him. He knew that if his picture ever got passed around, his Mafia enemies would see it and come West to kill him.

Ed figured that David and I were about a step away from this knowledge because although Maris never allowed himself to be photographed, a decent picture had been taken almost by accident when Sam Webster, one of my operatives, spotted Maris on Third Street and grabbed a camera in time to take a shot without being seen. When Stevens heard about this he demanded thirty copies of the shot immediately. I got them to him, not knowing he was sending them East to federal agents and New York police departments. Eventually, the pictures found their way to a Manhattan police officer who said, "Oh, that's Gerald Zelmanowitz from New Jersey. He testified against two big Mafia guys and then disappeared. The Mafia's got a contract out on him."

By the time I got wind of this, congressional investigators had arrived in San Francisco to interrogate the U.S. marshals who had allegedly leaked the truth about Maris to Ed. It had been the marshals' job to protect relocated criminals like Maris, and if they were telling people like Ed who Maris really was, naturally the million-dollar investment of the witness protection program had been corrupted. I also heard that Maris/Zelmanowitz was now screaming at the government, "Lipset shouldn't have found out I wasn't Paul Maris! You should have had a degree from the university in the name of Paul Maris! You should have had a birth certificate in Philadelphia for Paul Maris!"

So the FBI was trying to protect itself by blaming the whole thing on the federal marshals. The marshals were trying to protect themselves by saying the case broke open because of my investigation. But everyone knew that if Maris hadn't wanted to play big-shot wheeler-dealer, Eastern Capital wouldn't have taken over the dress company, Maris wouldn't have countersued, and I wouldn't have started the investigation.

When Ed came to see me about all this, I recorded my conversation with him. He admitted he had done the wrong thing but said he was broke at the time. Not wanting to reveal that he had figured it out in my office, Ed said he lied about the marshals giving him a tip.

I didn't know which was true — if the marshals told him or if he really did steal the information from me — but I did know I couldn't believe anything Ed said. At the end of the conversation I explained that only once before had someone I hired tried to manipulate a client of Lipset Service for his own benefit, and that person never worked as a private investigator again. I advised Ed that he should retire as an investigator early because I didn't think this

kind of work suited him, and he agreed. No one in the
business heard from him again. Stevens was pragmatic
about it, though. He thought we had all done a brilliant
job and even congratulated me for investigating Maris
without his consent, for which I billed him as large a fee
as I could honestly charge.

We all now knew who Paul Maris was, and as soon as
we did, Maris brought a $12 million lawsuit against the
federal government for failure to protect his new identity.
At one point, ten lawyers took my deposition in the case,
but of course Maris lost. He disappeared with his family
again, presumably to go on to a new identity and, given
his nature, another big-shot scene where he would be
found out again.

Many years later I was called to testify as an expert
witness in a suit brought by another private investigator
against a client who refused to pay. When I got to court,
some kind of commotion took place on the defendant's side
of the courtroom. Quite abruptly I was told the case had
been settled, and I didn't have to testify.

That was great, I thought, but months afterward, my
private investigator friend called again to say the client still
hadn't paid, so he was resuming the suit. "By the way,"
he said, "the reason this guy tried to settle last time was
that he saw you walk in the courtroom and knew you'd
identify him — his real name is Gerald Zelmanowitz."

I couldn't believe it. Even with his new identity, he was
breaking his cover again, using the courts to beat somebody out of the money he owed in yet another scam. He
disappeared after losing that case, too, but in June of 1990
he was in the news again for evading service, parole, and
probation on several extortion, forgery, and theft charges.
I felt the new motto of the witness relocation program
should be that you can't keep a *bad* man down.

It seems inevitable that at some time after he was "enrolled"
in the government's witness relocation program, Maris would blow
his carefully contrived cover. In the Case of the Elusive Entrepre-

neur, however, had Hal not continued to adjust his picture of the puzzle to accept new information, Maris might have gotten away with duping them all.

While the case changed radically when Maris brought his lawsuit against Stevens, Eastern Capital, and Lipset Service, the key was the series of consecutive social security numbers of Maris and his family. This was the piece that made no sense, that "couldn't happen in a million years," that didn't fit because it was too coincidental. In fact, it stood out so far from all the other pieces that the puzzle had to be entirely reconstructed to fit around it. Ed Butler, on the other hand, could read the puzzle like the open book it had become on David's desk.

Considered another way, this is a case about the many disguises of truth. At the beginning, to find out the truth about Maris, Stevens ordered a thorough background check from the ex–FBI agent, who hid the truth by telling Stevens that Maris's claims about himself were true. Hal, who nearly got himself fired by insisting on finding out the truth about Maris, kept offering Maris a chance to clear himself. Just tell me the truth, Hal said, and whatever threat I pose to you will end. Maris, taking the classic criminal stance (believing that with his lies he could pull off any scam), said the opposite to Hal: Go along with the lie, and I'll drop the suit.

The biggest lie in the case — because it was a government lie — was the series of consecutive social security numbers issued to Maris and his family. A lot of agencies (the FBI, Social Security, and the U.S. Army, for starters) had to be in cahoots for the government to pull it off.

Readers of mysteries often find themselves forgiving weak characters who seem to be products of a ruined society, and in the Case of the Elusive Entrepreneur, there are plenty of players who could use our sympathy. We can forgive Maris, who seems constitutionally incapable of staying out of trouble, or Ed Butler, a two-bit narc agent turned hustler who got caught in his own scam, or Stevens, who innocently thought a former FBI agent would never lie, or even the ex–FBI agent himself, who felt that his first obligation was to the bureau and so became both an informant and a mole in falsifying his report on Maris.

But what about the FBI itself? Now that we have seen how

much lying it takes to keep a person like Maris and his family under wraps in the witness relocation program, let's look at what it means when a government agency goes into the business of institutional lying.

The FBI might say that the witness relocation program is itself a working lie to protect the greater good. The FBI couldn't have convinced Paul Maris to testify against his mob cohorts in the first place unless it promised to disguise the truth of his identity. The fact that Maris misbehaved in a public way is no reflection on the witness relocation program or the bureau, the FBI might argue. There is always going to be one "criminally minded" bad apple in the barrel, and you can't blame the system for its glitches.

The problem is that all lies require other lies to keep up a pretense of truth, and an agency such as the FBI, operating at one of the highest levels of government, sees itself as lying to protect the truth. What this really means is that any lie that makes the FBI's job easier is a sanctioned one and thus overrides the principles of a democracy whose constitution prohibits any one person or office from dictating "the truth" to the people. Since the FBI historically has set its agents up as "untouchable" heroes carrying the banner of good in their unending battle against crime, lying for the sake of expediency is both inappropriate and shameful.

In this case the result of all the lying for a greater good is to place the dress factory, its employees, Eastern Capital, Glenn Stevens, and Hal Lipset in jeopardy. Yet against the weight of Maris and his social security—numbered family, the ex—FBI agent, his agency, and the FBI itself, it is Lipset, the kind of investigator Stevens wouldn't have hired to do Maris's background check (because he wanted somebody with the spotless reputation of the FBI) who saves Stevens, the dress company, and Eastern Capital from certain disaster.

Ah, well: "The truth, when such extreme efforts are made to conceal it, develops a peculiar life of its own," as Thomas Kyd reflects in *Kyd for Hire*. In a sense, the entire body of fiction is an "extreme effort" of concealing the truth to find insights that are "truer" than reality.

That's what happens here. Crisscross these elements of fact and fiction and our grid appears with this message: Mysteries tell us that truth is absolute — that there is always one answer, one "who" in every whodunit, one clear, bell-ringing set of facts the good guys seek and the bad guys hide. But a private detective's cases in real life show us that truth is always relative — that it exists for some people but not for others; that it is meaningful one moment and meaningless the next; that the challenge for the detective is not simply to find and disclose the truth but to stand up for it as well.

In the Maris case, the truth is that Maris is a phony whose real name is Gerald Zelmanowitz. That would seem to be absolute, except that it's meaningful only for the moment Lipset needs it to stop the lies (and the lawsuit) aimed at himself and his client. In the next moment (after the Maris case ends), the truth is meaningless. If the FBI responds at all, it will use the Maris case as a lesson, perhaps to introduce plastic surgery to its next group of Mafia stoolies, the better to hide their true identities.

Other than that, the environment remains the same. Holmes's old nemesis, Moriarty, is alive and well, not only in individuals but in institutions where lying has become so commonplace that by the 1980s we even gave it a new name, "covert action."

What's the purpose, then, of saying the FBI's lying is "shameful" when nothing changes — when the CIA, Secret Service, army and navy intelligence, Treasury, Justice, and attorney general offices have become far better at manipulating the truth than ever before? It's to witness how powerful an individual can be when determined to find the truth. It's to show that a "passion for the truth" is also an exercise in free will. It's to demonstrate that institutional lying means nothing when confronted by personal integrity, that independent thought will surpass governmental newspeak any day and that the truth, as it says on the front of every library in the country, really can make you free.

If you think that's a lot of big talk for one case, turn to Part IV, where the Lipsets find the truth (and the fee) by breaking into motel rooms and chasing ambulances.

PART IV

MEAN STREETS

Chapter 10

Sexual Snooper

I mean in my day they used to be nasty little men in macs, sniffing round the registers in cheap hotels. They used to spy into bedrooms with field glasses, in the ever-present hope of seeing male and female clothing scattered around.
— John Mortimer, *Rumpole of the Bailey*

The Miss Marples and Hercule Poirots of British mysteries seemed innocent once the hard-boiled detectives of American fiction took over. With their cynicism, their arrogance, and their world-weary humanity, the Sam Spades and Philip Marlowes saw the American Dream eroding right along with the American city. Wanting no part in the building or acceptance of either, the hard-boiled detectives became outlaws in the true sense of the term: They created their own laws — their own codes — outside the system.

To them, the great experiment of Western civilization had failed. The promise made by Arthur Conan Doyle — that logic, objectivity, and the scientific method were all that agents of good needed in their unending battle against evil — was obsolete, gone the way of Edgar Allan Poe's beatific notions of ratiocination and Agatha Christie's tidy parlor-puzzle mysteries.

Walking through the foggy alleys and mean streets of urban America the hard-boiled private eye seemed to say, If you could see the world from the gutter up as I have, you would know that life isn't as simplistic as good battling evil, that human nature is vulnerable to corruption of all kinds. The criminal element is not "out there," as law enforcement will tell you; it exists in all of us, making all systems, including (and especially) law enforcement, susceptible to corruption from within. The only way to live honorably is for each individual to develop a moral code of personal responsibility.

Hal and Lynn Lipset founded their detective agency with none of these notions consciously in mind. Yet they created philosophic approaches (the Jigsaw Puzzle theory, the notions of the Lying Client and the Complicated Lie) that paralleled many of the working principles used by hard-boiled detectives in fiction.

While their style of operation was different — no shabby office, no whiskey bottle in the files, no sexy broad in bed ("Lynn would kill me if I had another broad in bed," Hal would joke, elbowing the kids) — they nevertheless accepted cases that were sleazier, their critics liked to say, than any found in the pulps: cases that even the most hard-boiled dick in fiction would have turned down.

Today, when Hal is introduced as the former chief investigator for the Senate Watergate Committee or the defense investigator for Angela Davis or Harry Bridges, he is seen as a crusading detective. But when it turns out that Hal used to chase ambulances and break down hotel doors to take photos of adulterous couples in bed, people actually move a few feet away.

Hal doesn't see this. He is as proud of his personal injury and divorce cases as he is of his work on Watergate. From the beginning, both he and Lynn believed that the content of the case is not the measure of the investigator; it's what happens to his integrity when he's down there in the gutter.

Still, sexual snooping for hire? Isn't that the lowest of the low?

Hal: Before divorce laws offered the "no-fault" concept most states use today, the fact that a spouse was having an extramarital affair had a major bearing on the size and kind of financial settlement made to one side or the other. Property was split up based on who was thought to be at fault, and infidelity was regarded as the only true grounds for divorce.

Most divorce cases required proof of infidelity, so

detectives were hired to get physical evidence in the form of photographs showing the two people actively engaged in their affair. Sometimes we ended up doing some pretty risky things. Breaking in a door to get photos of a couple in bed wasn't uncommon.

It would happen that during the surveillance of a client's spouse, my agent would learn that an affair was going on at, say, a hotel or the lover's apartment. Usually the agent would call me when he had the couple staked out, and I would meet him there with a photographer. Then the three of us would sneak in as quietly as possible, hoping the couple would be asleep by the time we got inside.

Generally we tried not to break the door down because we didn't want them to wake up and leap out of either side of the bed. The court required pictures that gave no doubt the two were having sex, and you'd be surprised how quickly they could untangle themselves from an embrace and stand on either side of the room with all their clothes on the moment we stepped in the room.

So I'd either pick the lock or try to find a window big enough for all three of us to crawl through without making any noise. If we did have to break the door in, I made sure my agent was always big and muscular enough to break through it in one slam of his body.

One time we were following the wife of a client and had gotten to the point where we knew she was having an affair. The client, Harry, wanted to go with us into the hotel, so there were four of us — Harry, me, my agent Mick, and Bruce, the photographer — in the hallway standing around the door before we went in. I put my ear to the door and heard a man snoring. "OK," I whispered to Harry. "Mick's going to hit the door at the count of three. Bruce goes in first to take the picture, with me behind. You can come in and look, but then you turn right around and go. We go in, we snap it, we get out. Got it?" They all nodded. "OK," I said, as Mick crossed to the other side of the hallway. "One, two, THREE."

Mick started running with his shoulder low and —

BAM! — he hit the door like a battering ram. The lock burst, the door flew open, and Mick fell to his knees from the momentum, then rolled away just in time for Bruce to rush in, focus, and take a perfect picture of two tousled, shocked, naked lovers sitting up in horror with their arms still around each other. I helped Mick to his feet and started to usher the client out of there. But then, without warning, Harry decided to announce his intentions right then. "I'm sorry, honey," he said. "I love you, but I'm going to file for a divorce."

His wife looked hurt. "For God's sake, Harry," she said, "you didn't have to do this" — she gestured to the four of us.

"Well, goddamn it, Louise, you hardly gave me a choice," he said, his voice rising.

"Look who's talking, you bastard." Now she was shouting. "What about that tart you were with last month?"

"Look, he's leaving," I said to her. "Look, you're leaving," I said to him, trying to push him back.

"TART?" he pushed me aside. "You want to see a tart? Go look in the mirror!"

That did it. His wife turned to her lover and said, "Get 'em, Spike!" The guy got out of bed, spoiling for a fight. He came over to me, saw that I wore glasses, and turned away. Then he looked at Mick, who was big but also not a heavyweight, and turned away from him, too. You had to hand it to Spike — here was a guy with orders to deck somebody, and he was taking his time to find a fair match. Then he got to Bruce, who happened to be a former boxer and obviously a guy who could take care of himself.

"Put 'em up," he said. The photographer handed me his camera, turned back to Spike, and said, "OK, Mr. Big Guy, you asked for it." Spike came over, fists up. Bruce stepped forward, head down. They sparred a couple of times, threw a couple of punches. Then the photographer really hit Spike with a good right cross. The big man went down. That's when my guy made his second mistake (his first was being there in the first place).

"Have you had enough?" Bruce said, leaning over Spike.

Spike got up off the floor and said, "No." By the time they got through, it cost our insurance company over five hundred dollars to replace the teeth the photographer lost. Harry felt terrible. He had wanted Spike to choose *him*.

Such cases were strangely elevated in the public's mind at the time. Private eyes who burst in on adulterous couples in bed were seen as agents for good — something like FBI or Secret Service operatives — whose business made them guardians of the family, democracy, and all that was right about America.

"If you wanted to, you could use a CROWN GRAPHIC SPECIAL the way Private Eye HAL LIPSET does," ran the first in a series of *Wall Street Journal* advertisements taken out by Brooks Camera of San Francisco. That ad showed a drawing of the hardworking private eye dressed in coat, tie, and hat, hidden behind his flashing camera after bursting into a room. It was followed by *Journal* ads showing the even more businesslike private eye inserting a camera between venetian blinds ("If you wanted to, you could use a BOLEX the way Private Eye HAL LIPSET does") and setting up a miniature camera at a keyhole ("If you wanted to, you could use a MINOX the way Private Eye HAL LIPSET does").

The message of these ads — that private detectives were businesspeople to emulate, just like bankers — seemed fitting and proper to Hal and Lynn. Every time private eyes were pictured as professionals, they felt, potential clients would understand that the standards of detective agencies such as Lipset Service were as high as the fees they charged.

Like lawyers and police officers, the Lipsets referred to "domestic" rather than "divorce" cases, thereby lending a legalistic air to the kind of investigations others might characterize as sexual snooping. Sensitive to the emotional battering that clients endured when informed of spouses' adulteries, they were often pressured to take the role of psychotherapists, ministers, social workers, parents, and best friends. Wrote Lynn in her diary in the mid-1950s:

> *Domestic cases are far from our largest volume of business,*
> *but they are often the most time-consuming because emo-*

tions, sexual problems, money, property, and children take such a strong hold in each of them. Many of these cases are typically stranger than fiction. I usually handle most of these calls and visits. We are not professionally trained in psychology or counseling, but our experience has taught us how to help people use resources they don't know they have. To us, theirs is one case in hundreds, so we can be objective about it. I have had women come over and cry their hearts out about how badly they have been treated by their husbands. Some have turned at the door to say, "I'm sorry to have upset you. I'm sure I've ruined your whole day with my problems." I assure them it's all right and close the door. They are so emotionally involved that they believe we are too. They don't realize this is just another case, and that after they leave, we go back to whatever case we were working on when they came in.

Nevertheless, what distinguished Lipset Service from other detective agencies at the time was the care that Hal and Lynn Lipset, a couple who seemed to have weathered their own marital storms, extended to clients suffering the pain of ugly divorce. Here Lynn's Mennonite upbringing surfaced with predictable authority. While she was capable of instructing clients to sleep with their boyfriends so that lovemaking sounds could be recorded on tape as evidence in an ensuing paternity trial, she couldn't stand the thought that divorce was becoming fashionable in the contemporary urban life of the fifties and sixties.

I spend a lot of time telling domestic clients that a divorce is a serious move and to consider it carefully. So many people get divorced these days that it's almost the thing to do. To women I say: "How are you going to like living alone? Can you handle the children's day-to-day problems? Do you realize how much you depend on your husband? Do you think you'll remarry and, if so, do you think your new husband will be better?"

To men I say: "Can you afford to support two households? Are you going to enjoy living alone and eating your

*meals out? Who is going to do your laundry? Aren't you
going to miss your children?"*

Hal took a more pragmatic view of divorce, but his fundamental belief in marriage as an institution that demanded certain responsibilities of each partner was aligned with Lynn's. This was perhaps the one time in the history of Lipset Service that he allowed personal and professional views to mix.

> *Hal:* By the time I tell the client that, yes, his wife is having
> an affair, I can then caution him to take a deep breath and
> assess the situation. Usually he'll ask very specific questions. What did she look like when she came out of the
> motel room? Was she smiling? Did she seem talkative?
> What he really means is, Does she love this guy more than
> she loves me? Of course I can't answer that.
>
> Some private eyes can be real jerks at this time. Knowing the client is emotionally exposed, they'll toy with him
> and say, yes, she looked ecstatic; she looked as though no
> one had ever made love to her as tenderly, beautifully, or
> attentively before. They think it's funny to hurt people that
> way and take their money. We think it's childish and hurtful to anyone in the profession.
>
> I almost always advise the client not to tell his wife that
> he hired a private investigator to have her followed. It only
> makes matters worse, because the thought will always be
> on her mind that you did this dastardly thing, you hired a
> stranger to spy on her. Ironically, it's easier for the client
> to get over the fact that the spouse has been cheating than
> it is for the spouse to get over the fact that the client hired
> me to follow her. It's the old stigma about private eyes —
> that we are "snoops for hire" who invade people's privacy
> and violate their civil rights.
>
> Lynn and I believed the opposite. We believed we were
> protecting the rights of our clients. Maybe it was because
> of the divorce laws at the time or our own old-fashioned
> views on marriage, but we felt that when two people get
> married, they become one entity. They owe something to
> each other. The husband has a right to know what the wife

is doing, and the wife has a right to know what the husband is doing.

If we're called in to help develop a case that will hold up in court, and the client decides because of our investigation not to pursue the case, so much the better. But if the laws are so primitive that they require physical evidence of infidelity as the only grounds to bring suit, then what is the person who wants a divorce supposed to do? Follow the spouse? Break the door down? Take the picture? Present it in court? We are private investigators. We get that evidence recorded. We don't pass judgment on the morals of the client *or* the morality of the laws in the meantime.

Personal counseling of clients is nothing new to the private eye in fact or fiction, nor is it uncommon that what seems sleazy today may have been considered accepted or even prestigious thirty years ago. Like their fictional counterparts, the Lipsets found themselves carving out their own moral code in the midst of changing laws and mores. Yet unlike any detectives in fiction, they were also raising children in a household of colorful clients — and colorful language.

> Lynn: *One day I heard our two boys use the word "transvestite" in conversation. I asked them if they knew what it meant. They confessed they did not, so I assumed they had picked it up from a case we had just concluded in which a female impersonator was mugged coming out of his nightclub. After I told them what the word meant, we heard them using it for days between themselves. I had told the boys about homosexuality and all its related terms when they were young. One day someone used the word "fairy" in conversation, and Larry, about eight, piped up, "You mean boy or book?"*
>
> *Such outbursts frequently astound Hal and me. Giving your children a standard of values is more difficult when you run a business such as ours from your home. They cannot help but overhear conversations from time to time, most of it in fragments, that they must puzzle over alone.*

Often, of course, they understand far more of our "secret language" than they let on.

One evening while we were having dinner, the telephone rang. It was one of our agents out on a domestic case checking in. Knowing the children could hear me, in language that I thought was beyond their understanding, I asked what had transpired so far. When I returned to the table, Louis, then eleven, put down his fork and asked, "So. Have they checked into a motel yet?"

Then there is the difference between right and wrong. We don't want to preach to them, but I often wonder if they are able to figure out the subtle differences between what's legal and what's right in many of our cases. Burglary is against the law, yet we may work on the burglar's defense. The same applies to people involved in narcotics, murder, gambling, or prostitution.

But if the boys were aware that people on the fringe of the law paid some of the mortgage at Lipset Service, they knew, too, that the reason Dad kept rushing out of the house in the middle of the night was his dedication to another lucrative client service — ambulance chasing. Is it true, people ask today: Did you really get in your car and follow any ambulance whose siren you heard to pick through the wreckage of victims in an attempt to find a client? Absolutely, Hal replies, and I was good at it, too.

Hal: When I started investigating, there were only a handful of lawyers in San Francisco who were considered capable of handling personal injury cases. By far, most of the lawyers doing trial work thought it was beneath them or not a good field to be in because it meant bucking insurance companies that were pretty powerful at the time.

Of course I had started out working for insurance companies, so I knew that most "investigations" of accidents were really sales efforts on the part of the insurance investigator to keep personal injury payments to a minimum. If the policyholder caused the accident, the investigator for his insurance company was trained to convince the victim not to get a lawyer or "worry about a thing," to put complete trust in the insurance company and wait for a fair and equitable check in the mail. If, in the meantime, the investigator was able to elicit a statement from the victim that might reveal some kind of discrepancy, something that later on would enable the insurance company to pay next to nothing, so much the better.

I stopped working for insurance companies about the same time I got disgusted with this practice. Victims of automobile accidents weren't being served by the system and were in fact hoodwinked out of fair and reasonable settlements by the very insurance companies that were supposed to cover their damages.

Suppose somebody blindsides you at an intersection, and you and your passenger are sitting on the curb testing your arms and limbs for broken bones. Your car needs a tow truck. The other guy has given you the name and address of his insurance company, and you're sitting there in shock, half grateful to be alive and half outraged this idiot slammed into your car.

If I found you in that situation, I'd come up to you and say, "I'm an investigator, and I wonder if you have anyone you can call to check out your case. I'm not saying you need a lawyer now, but you do need an investigator. The facts of this accident should be established, photographs should be taken, records should be obtained and held, witnesses should be interviewed, statements taken — in other words, everything should be preserved for the day you want to make a decision." I would offer to do this on a contingency basis at no charge, just as lawyers will handle some personal injury cases for people who have been hurt in an accident.

I'd say, "You certainly don't want to settle right away with the insurance company, but they'll be knocking on your door anyway, offering you a sum of money. You have up to a year before you have to do anything legal about this accident, and it's to your advantage to wait a while to see how severe your injuries are.

"Maybe you're not a lawyer — maybe you don't know

how to measure the possible value of your case. You surely don't know right now if your injury is going to be permanent or partial or how long you'll be out of work. But the insurance company's representative is going to ask how much you want. He will have investigated the accident immediately, while you have no one working on your behalf."

In those days, California law stated that if you were one percent wrong in the accident and the other party was 99 percent wrong, you couldn't collect anything. It was called "contributory negligence." Years later, this was changed to "comparable negligence," which was much fairer. At the time, I would be the first to explain to people that the insurance-company investigators would try to find that one percent culpability that would then ruin your case.

Most people in these situations had no knowledge of how insurance companies worked, and they probably didn't have the money to pay an investigator — or to be billed for two hundred dollars and later be told they didn't have a case. But they might be willing to sign a contingency contract with me and agree that if they did have a case, and I could help them by gathering evidence on their behalf, they would give me a percentage of their award, like 5 percent of whatever they got. Many people did know that if they went to a lawyer they'd pay 33.3 percent of their settlement if it didn't go to court, and 40 percent if it did, or even 50 percent in an extremely difficult case.

I would tell them that I would do the investigation for 5 percent of whatever they got if they'd sign a contract with me. I would then go and investigate the case, and as time went along, I'd coach them in their dealings with the insurance company as well. This was easy because insurance companies were notoriously foolish about working with accident victims, whom they thought were trustful and naive. They also so underpaid their investigators that important aspects of the investigation were almost always overlooked — witnesses would be missed, evidence would be missing, photographs badly taken.

Lawyers were not allowed to arrive at the scene of an

accident looking for victims, but since investigators could, whenever I heard that an accident had happened, I would try to get there before anyone else and sell the victim on becoming our client.

It got pretty amusing at times, because there were only certain ways of finding out where accidents had happened. Some investigators had friends in the police department who would let them know when an accident occurred; others made a business of driving around with a police radio on. They would hear about an accident and go to the scene to take pictures. Then they would call the participants and tell them they had photos of the wreck. "Would you like to see these photos?" they'd say. "You'll need them if your case ever goes to court, and I have some pretty clear pictures showing how the other guy was in the wrong."

I didn't ride around with a police radio on, but I had friends and informers all over the city. People would call me and say, hey, my neighbor got hurt, or my friend at work was injured, maybe you should go talk to him. I had contacts in the police department who would call and say, "There's a good accident at such-and-such a corner, and the driver of the Pontiac looks like he's got a solid case." It was like a salesman who gets a lead on a prospect.

Morally we felt that if people were left alone, the insurance company would give them a pittance of what they were owed. We were educating people about their rights and getting paid for it. Of course, I wouldn't have done it if the money hadn't been there, but they wouldn't have gotten the money if I hadn't been there.

The insurance companies thought investigators like me were terrible people for doing this because they were no longer able to settle claims as quickly and easily as they were used to doing, and because it cost them more money. They called it ambulance chasing, and society frowned on the practice, but so what? Society didn't know what I knew — that the primary duty of the insurance adjuster was to keep the injured person from getting proper representation.

Today society's changed its mind: Now it's an accepted

practice for lawyers to go on television soliciting business from accident victims, which is chasing ambulances via the mass media, as far as I'm concerned, and I'm all for it. We should *often* see lawyers up there asking for our business *and* proving they deserve it with statistics about how many cases they've handled, how many wins, how many losses they have, what kind of settlements they've gotten for what kinds of accidents, and so forth. Have they ever been reprimanded by a bar association? Have clients complained? Have they won verdicts that have set new precedents in the fields in which they specialize?

Now why shouldn't you, as the victim, have access to all that information, if your case is so important to these lawyers? I think we need more lawyers out there competing on their records alone. Let's make all the information about every court case they've ever conducted easily accessible to the average person.

Are private eyes really such saints when it comes to walking those mean streets? Let's see how it feels when Hal arrives to kidnap your children.

Chapter 11

The Kidnapper

"Carrying a gun, especially a very utilitarian one, has the bully-boy flavor of the ersatz male — the fellow with such a hollow sense of inadequacy, he has to bolster his sexual ego with a more specific symbol of gonadal prowess. Except for those whose job it is to kill folks, having to use a gun is the end product of stupid procedure."

  — John D. MacDonald, *Darker Than Amber*

Part of the fun of a good mystery is watching the lone detective solve the puzzle without help from anyone. Isolated by his moral code and rebellious nature, he becomes fiction's favorite protagonist: With few friends, no roots, and no family, he is one man against the system, one outlaw against an army of law-enforcement officials.

Marriage and children can play no part in the fictional private eye's destiny. As mystery writers tell us, the detective must be released from the constraints of family life so that he is free to roam, to engage in sexual conquests, to fall briefly and tragically in love, to suffer rejection, or to grieve over murdered lovers. Only then can he return to that battlefield of good versus evil and resist (or fall into) temptation as society's conscience again and again.

Besides, family life is simply too mundane for the romantic rebel. It would be irresponsible to expose himself to danger day after day if a wife and children were waiting at home. One of the few private eyes in fiction who is married yet remains dashing and private eyes in fiction who is married yet remains dashing and fearless as ever is Nick Charles of *The Thin Man* — and of course, he has to stay half plastered most of the time to pull it off. Constantly courting, teasing, cajoling, and making eyes at Nora, the rich and beautiful heiress who is won over time and time again, Nick is at once the loving husband and carefree bachelor, the stay-at-home father and debonair man-about-town.

But when the time comes to solve a mystery, it's Nick, not Nora, who's back on those mean streets, fitting the jigsaw pieces together. Nora can't come because she isn't taken seriously as an investigator. As everyone from Sherlock Holmes to Mike Hammer reminds us, detective fiction as a genre is too misogynist to accept women as equal partners in the art of detection. Those who do hold a respected position as deducers — Miss Marple, J. B. Fletcher — are less women than elderly, eccentric, or sexless like their male counterparts Nero Wolfe or Hercule Poirot.

Despite some excellent younger female sleuths created by modern mystery writers Sara Paretsky, Sue Grafton, Lia Matera, and others, women are traditionally portrayed in mysteries as too emotional, too sexual, too nurturing, or too motherly to be able to think objectively. They may have their place as sidekicks, secretaries, girlfriends, or clients, but they allegedly can't arrange their thoughts in the logical, linear order required by the deductive method.

In fact, women so badly entangle the deductive mind that male detectives not only stay away from women as life partners, they deny the female side of their own natures. Holmes himself is so distrustful of women or anything remotely female inside himself that he turns into "a brain without a heart," Watson says, "as deficient in human sympathy as he was preeminent in intelligence." Holmes's continuing "aversion to women" worries Watson because it's "typical of his unemotional character."

Yet that's exactly what Holmes wants. "Detection," he instructs Watson, "is, or ought to be, an exact science and should be treated in the same cold and unemotional manner." Since Holmes's function in literature is to show how the mind can equip itself with reason to bring order to chaos, he extols science — the quintessential model of man's rational powers — as civilization's only hope in controlling the wildness or primitive urges of nature. Without science, there would be no great bridges, no magnificent skyscrapers, no sanitation, no wheel. Without science, Holmes makes clear, man would be lost in the grip of base emotion.

In the view of most civilizations, women and nature are on one side of life's spectrum and men and science are on the other side. Women have power because they give life; men have power because they have built the weapons and technology to control life. Women are biological; men are rational. Women are emotional, men logical. In detective fiction, the difference is made most clearly when women know their place as noncombatants, while men go out to fight evil in the world with guns.

The connection between the private eye as sexual loner and the gun he uses to combat evil is demonstrated by almost every hard-boiled detective in fiction. Because the private eye is a sexual being without lasting relationships, his gun is an extension of both his sexuality and his power. The bigger or more destructive the gun — think of Clint Eastwood's magnum in the *Dirty Harry* movies — the more power he has over other men, and the more attractive he is supposed to be to women.

It's no accident in *Bonnie and Clyde,* for example, that Clyde, who is impotent, first attracts Bonnie by showing her his enormous revolver, which she strokes and pets with awe. In *Tango and Cash,* the two cops, each a different kind of loner, are best distinguished by their very different and very large guns. Members of a gang of boys in the old West are not called *Young Outlaws* or *Young Cowboys;* they are *Young Guns I and II.* Pistols, explosives, grenades, bazookas, assault rifles, bombs, plastique, bullets, blood, and gore so dominate detective fiction today that Spenser, the Boston private eye, seems relatively tame when he sticks it to the karate-trained bad guy in *Mortal Stakes:*

"I stood up. 'Lester, let me show you something,' I said, and brought my gun out and aimed it at his forehead. 'This is a .38-caliber Colt detective special. If I pull the trigger your mastery of the martial arts will be of very little use to you.' . . . Lester said, 'If you didn't have that gun.' 'But that's the point, Les-baby, I do have the gun. Wally Hogg has a gun. You don't have a gun. Professionals are the people with the guns who get them out first.' "

It is the contemporary message of mysteries featuring hard-boiled detectives that when the streets get mean enough, logic stops working and force must be used. When, however, force becomes the sole attraction and the mystery behind it of lesser value, the entire genre changes.

For people not accustomed to reading the kind of detective fiction that features such heroes as Mike Hammer or Matt Helm, or seeing the kind of movies in which Sylvester Stallone or Bruce Willis or Arnold Schwarzenegger star, reading a novel by, say, police procedural writer Ed McBain is like stepping onto another planet. Here the landscape is peopled by the kind of bogeymen one visits in nightmares — men who "fuck" evil women, then take out their big guns and shoot them in the stomach, men who must always prove themselves in the toughest arena of the streets, men who must be right, then use their guns and muscles to prove their righteousness, then make the test tougher and tougher until they alone come out the best.

If they can do all this while seeming to protect innocent women from a common enemy, so much the better. *Rambo, The Avenger, The Terminator,* and *The Penetrator* all depend on setting up a crime so vile and atrocious that the unleashing of brutally spectacular violence to stop it will seem perfectly warranted. Reminiscent of chivalric romance in which the knight wins the maiden's hand by defeating the dragon, detective fiction often depends on simplistic acts of courage to sustain itself as a proving ground for male courage and strength.

But as far as putting the gun or sword away, marrying the maiden, fathering her children, and sticking around to do the hard work of raising a family and quelling the dragon within oneself, detective stories, like all fairy tales, stop short of ordinary responsibility. That's something that private eyes just don't hang around long enough to do — they have to get back to those mean streets to fight evil with logic or force once again.

This brings us to the only real difference that separates Hal and Lynn Lipset from their hard-boiled counterparts: their belief in each other as equals, their love of family, and their hatred of guns.

As we have seen, for many years Hal's own "arsenal" of electronic surveillance equipment was considered as lethal as any fictional detective's cache of guns. People who unwittingly incriminated themselves on tape accused Hal of "holding a gun" to their heads, or of placing a "time bomb" in their lives. Hal and Lynn never used such terminology. To them, using a tape recorder to capture a person's words was a means of protecting their credibility, not demeaning it with a substitute for weapons of violence. In fact, except for the guns he used in security and bodyguard work, Hal stopped allowing the use of weapons at Lipset Service about the time he and Lynn started raising a family.

> *Hal:* It was relatively easy for private investigators to get a license to carry guns in the postwar years, but we learned early on that the risk of shooting yourself in the foot is greater than anyone realizes. In one union dispute, where both sides were getting pretty hot tempered and fights were breaking out all the time, many of my agents wanted handguns for what they called their own protection. I couldn't blame them — one of our agents, Jack Palladino, once came home from work to find a death threat on his answering machine. Still, I believed that if these men were armed, regardless of their training, they would shoot themselves or each other by accident just by loading the guns and having them around.
>
> The idea that you wear a gun for your own protection is a myth, anyway. As soon as you put the holster on, you've automatically escalated the conflict. It's like throwing down a gauntlet. Now the other guy has to get a gun to defend himself, and before you know it, you're walking into a lethal situation that could have been settled rationally before. Now if you see that the other guy has armed himself first, call the police. Chances are he hasn't got a license to carry the gun, and he's not going to take on a bunch of cops unless he's really nuts. Besides, what the cops do best is to stop violence by brute force.

Might versus reason. Wits versus guts. The classic tension between brain and fist has played itself out in many detective agencies of fact and fiction. But a new dimension was added in a household where the wife, mother, office manager, and partner — unlike Nora,

Della, Mrs. Columbo, or any other "minor half" — insisted upon total equality.

> Lynn: *In my set of friends, where most of the daughters attend or graduate from college, I am amazed to see these girls ten years later with an inability to converse about little beyond house, children, food, and clothing. Try switching the subject to local politics, the world situation, equality of man, or the creative arts and see what happens. They're lost. The only reason I can see is that since the day they were born, girls are taught that their goal in life is marriage and children. Many marriages flounder because the woman will not grow with her husband as he advances in his chosen field.*
>
> *By the same token, young boys are trained, from infancy, that girls are weak, stupid, or inferior. This is often done by inferences more than direct statements, but the message takes hold. It is the young professional man who, during his struggling years, shuts his wife out from his problems when he says, "You're a woman. You wouldn't understand." She buries herself in the home and children as he rises in the world, leaving her behind, and then he is embarrassed to have her among his peers.*
>
> *My husband will argue this point because he does not feel that women are mentally inferior. This is a quality that endeared him to me back in our courting days, though sometimes it blinds him. Often I will tell Hal that with a certain attorney, I act dumb because the attorney does not appreciate intelligence in a woman. Hal is amazed and frequently doubts that I am correct, since he has no occasion to observe my behavior in front of the attorney. I tell him to watch this man with his women clients. When he does, Hal always expresses surprise that the attorney has such a low opinion of women.*

A few years after they opened their detective agency, the Lipsets formed Hal-Lyn, a limited partnership (and later corporation) that invested profits, set up pension plans, and gave equal responsibility to both partners. As children arrived and business increased, people who visited Lipset Service came to regard the Lipset family, agency, and corporation as a single entity.

Lynn loved it that way: When you walked in the door, she wanted you to smell her homemade soup, to feel at home enough to say hello to her children, and perhaps to gape in awe, as she did day after day, at the noisy and colorful clients, investigators, cops, attorneys, witnesses, and visitors who bustled in and out at all hours.

Guns certainly could have no place in such a household — it was too engaged in real life, too family-based, and too dependent on the equality of its founding partners. Although the Lipset marriage might be considered old-fashioned today — Lynn stayed at home and raised the children while Hal went out to earn money — it was visionary for its time, combining qualities that would seem contradictory in fiction: logic and emotion, morality and outlaw ethics, loner and parent, man and woman as equal partners.

> *Hal:* We've had a number of cases where a woman wants to break up with the man she has been dating but can't seem to get rid of him. He keeps showing up at her house, or calling her, or following her to work. Sometimes it's a man she barely knows, just an acquaintance or even a stranger who's got some obsessive idea that she'll fall in love with him if he can get her to notice him.
>
> Usually the police can't help her unless he makes a clear threat to her safety, and most of the time what she faces is an *unstated* threat that he's capable of violence if she doesn't do what he wants. Often the man creates a complex fantasy life around his "romance" with this woman, so that everything she does to reject him is interpreted as acceptance. Her life becomes a nightmare and she hires us to intercede.
>
> These men are often cowards when confronted by other men, but it does no good if we just go out and beat the hell out of him or threaten to beat him up if he continues to harass our client. Cowards can also be conniving and seek revenge, and as soon as we're out of the picture, he might come back and really hurt her.
>
> So instead of sending a couple of bruisers over there to

bust his head, I want to convince him that the long arm of justice is going to stand in his way the next time he thinks of calling up or visiting our client. I show him photos we've taken of him following her, or make him listen to tapes of his phone calls. I bring out requests for restraining orders, court injunctions, search warrants, criminal charges, and civil suits to show him we've got all the "ammunition," so to speak, to harass him in reverse — but we'll do it with the legal system, which takes longer, costs money, and makes him look bad. I talk to him about finding his mother, or a wife, or children whose child support he's forgotten to pay, or hometown friends and family who would hate to hear he's turned into the kind of man who preys on women.

Of course I sometimes do all this by sending one or two pretty hefty agents who look as though they *will* beat the hell out of him, but that's rarely necessary. These men are like children who need to be educated: If you want your little boy to do his homework, are you going to hold a gun to his head? No, you're going to convince him so that *he* knows the right thing to do when you're not around. That's the difference between violence and intelligence, it seems to me.

Hal's sensitivity to the daily existence of kids at home — and, more important, to the meaning of raising a family in the tough environment of contemporary American culture — was to come into greater play when he stopped snooping on the sex life of adulterers and took his turn as a full-fledged kidnapper. Here the idea of using force, even with children, had its merits for some investigators.

Hal: As divorce laws stopped placing blame for the breakup of a marriage and established no-fault dissolutions, divorce lost its place as a forum for jealousy and revenge. The reason child-custody battles have become so ugly today is that the old forum — what could be more deliciously vindictive than to take pictures of the fornicating spouse in bed with the person who wrecked your home? — was created anew. Now the focus for revenge was the children.

Take a man who hates his wife for no longer loving him — and who hates the courts because they don't care if she loves somebody else. He figures he's lost a round, so he's going to try a custody battle. He goes to a lawyer to have her declared an unfit mother. He drags his kids through depositions and court battles. If he doesn't win custody over his children, he decides to steal them. He waits until it's his turn for visitation rights, pretends he's taking them on a camping trip, picks up the kids with all the tents and sleeping bags in the back of the station wagon, and disappears.

Today the law takes a stronger position, but at the time custody battles first broke out in number, the father could correctly believe that as long as he and the kids stay disappeared, he's got custody. What can the mother do? The police won't help her — they'll say it's a civil matter. Days and weeks and years may go by, and she won't get even a phone call telling her that the children are safe. Her only option is to hire a private investigator to find the kids and steal them back.

For some private detectives, the most efficient way to handle a case was to find the children, kidnap them by force, sometimes against their will, and bring them to the client, who would be waiting in a hotel room or car to make a quick getaway before the other spouse found out and came after them. The children would be completely traumatized — how were they supposed to know this kidnapper was on their side, if indeed the children ever have a side — and the spouse with custody would be left to figure out how to get the kids away without running into local police or investigators hired by the other spouse.

I felt that using force in this kind of situation was all wrong. In the first place, the investigator might misidentify the subject and steal the wrong child. Second, no matter who had custody, the child's own rights and feelings had to be recognized or you'd end up with a mess of screaming kids in the car or at the border or airport who wouldn't go anywhere. Third, since I was going to set up the retrieval of the child as an out-and-out kidnap, I had to have the parent with custody accompany me as my partner in the investigation.

In other words, I wouldn't get involved unless there was sufficient evidence that the child would *want* to go with my client, the parent with custody, when we got into a kidnap position. By that time, the child wasn't necessarily unhappy, having been scurried off with the parent who didn't have custody. What you'd see instead was confusion and bewilderment because usually the child hadn't been given any explanation as to why this ongoing battle between the parents had resulted in all this running and hiding with no communication with the parent left behind. After some time had elapsed, most children were happy to see the parent they hadn't been able to talk to for a while, and that was the moment that we tried to use to the client's benefit.

When I say we mounted these cases like kidnappings, I mean that we did a full-fledged missing-persons investigation to find the parent without custody, then established a round-the-clock surveillance on the household to watch the children come and go, then zeroed in on patterns, such as the times the children were most vulnerable — on their way to school, or at a playground in the afternoon — then created a schedule of optimum moments in which the snatch could be made.

The more detailed the plan, the better it worked. If we figured that at 4:47 P.M. we had three pure minutes in which no one — not a parent, parent companion, babysitter, tutor, nursemaid, or bodyguard — would be with the child or children, we could plan the takeover with precision. I would coach the parent on the exact way our car would drive up, how the parent was to get out and approach the child or children, how the kids would (we hoped) get in the car with us, how the parent could keep them calm, how we would either take off for the airport or change cars at a later destination and go to a different airport, how the other parent might try to re-snatch the kids at a border or security station along the way, how toys, dolls, or stuffed animals might keep the children occupied if we had to take a different route and drive all night, and so forth.

All along I would repeat to the parent that taking the child would work only if the parent followed my instructions and if the child would come willingly. As a client, the parent had to rely on my experience. I've had parents ask me if it wouldn't be better if they weren't there during the kidnapping, so the child wouldn't be mad at them. I don't do it that way, I tell them.

Why not have the police come with us? they ask. Generally, I never tell the police about a kidnapping until just before or just afterward. If you go to them early on, they'll tell you not to do it. Then no matter how many court documents you have to show it's all legal, if you proceed, you're working against an admonition from the police. They will always tell you not to break the law (even if they don't know exactly which side of the law we're on), to inform the spouse who originally stole them, to go to a lawyer, to kidnap them somewhere else, and so on.

If I feel the spouse without custody may call the police after we get the kids and tell them we're kidnappers, I'll have a message delivered to that police department the moment we get the kids in our custody. The message will say we're at the school or playground or street picking up these children, that we're acting under court order for the parent with custody and are removing the child with full legal authority. That usually keeps the cops at bay.

The police did give chase to us in a case that was already complicated by the fact that the father wanted to use force at the last minute. The client was a doctor from South America whose wife had left him for another man and without his knowledge had brought their two young boys with her to the United States. We found that she was living in Palo Alto, a half hour south of San Francisco, and had yet to file for divorce. The doctor won custody in a U.S. court and wanted to take the children back to South America.

We began our surveillance and found that, unfortunately, the two boys did not come home from school at the same time. We decided to pick them up at different times, which is dangerous because it gives the spouse without custody time to find out about us and call the police or mount a counterassault. Nevertheless, the doctor was in a hurry, so at three-thirty in the afternoon we drove to the location of the younger boy, Chico, who was on his bicycle a block away from the woman's house.

"OK," I said to the father as we eased the car as close to the boy as possible. "Now's the time." The father got out of the car and went over to the youngster, who seemed glad to see him and was easily convinced to get in the car and come back to South America with him. Then we waited for the second boy, Juanito, to pass by the same spot, which he usually did at three forty-five. When we saw Juanito walk down the street looking for Chico, the doctor got out of the car and approached him with the same affectionate manner, talking to him about going back to South America. Juanito, however, wasn't willing to say that he'd come with us and told his father instead that he was going to go home to talk with his mother.

I saw the father pause, then reach for the boy as if he wanted to pull him forcibly into the car. This was strictly against my instructions, and the client knew it. I gave the horn a little beep and motioned to the father to get in the car. We couldn't risk staying in the neighborhood any longer, and I would not let the father use force to get Juanito in the car. Chico was now worrying that maybe he shouldn't go, either, so we had to get going or lose them both.

The doctor came back to us without Juanito, who backed away, waving. I drove as quickly as I could out of the neighborhood, because I was certain Juanito was going to tell his mother everything, and she might call the police.

I found out later the Palo Alto cops almost immediately started a search, looking for two "kidnappers" of our description.

I abandoned my escape plan, which was to take the doctor and his son to the San Francisco airport, where I was afraid the police may be waiting, and ended up driving back through San Francisco and on to Sacramento. There they took a plane to Los Angeles, then another flight to San Diego, and a taxi into Mexico so they could go to Mexico City and then on to South America.

The parents' relationship with their kids was always the key factor. In one case the mother and I were looking out a window, waiting for her two children. Suddenly she said, "There's my boy! Come on, let's get him." I said, "Wait, we want to get both children at once. We have to be patient." Ten minutes later another little boy came by, and she said, "Oh, my God, I made a mistake — the first boy wasn't my son! *This* is my son — let's get him." "Great," I said. "Suppose we had gone and kidnapped the wrong boy. When would you have found out?"

You tend to wonder, with someone like that, maybe this boy would be better off with the father who stole him. Maybe this woman is crazy, or drunk, or a lousy mother if she can't even identify her own son the first time. But then you aren't there to judge the right or the wrong. If the police won't help her and she hasn't seen her son for more than a year, who could blame her if she's overwrought or took a drink before coming out to do this terrifying business of kidnapping him back?

And, then, who are we as private investigators to ask these questions? She's got custody; that's what the courts have decided. If she needs help enforcing that court order and the system won't supply that help, we do it. That's what a private eye is there for.

But if I was going to run the show, there had to be no force, and the decision had to stay with the child. One woman, a native of the Philippines, came to me and said her husband had taken her five children over a year before.

She knew where they were living but had no idea how to
get them back. I told her that to kidnap five children all
at once would be impossible if the children wouldn't come
with her willingly. If she was sure they would follow her
(absolutely, she said), and if we could time it for during
the period of time after school, between, say, three-fifteen
and three forty-five, when all five would be coming home
together, we just might be able to get them all at once. I
asked her several times if we should maybe try for just one
or two children, but she was adamant; she wanted all five
at the same time.

We planned it all out, escape route and all, and on the
appointed day I took the client in my car to the Mission
district of San Francisco, where the kids were living. Down
the street we see them all walking toward us, arm in arm,
at exactly three-fifteen. I said, "Look, what a glorious opportunity. If you can get them now, we'll be out of here in
less than five minutes." "Certainly," the mother said. She
jumped out of the car as they approached and ran up to
them, saying "Children, children!" Those five kids took
one look at her and split in five directions. That was the
end of the case.

Sometimes a child-custody case can be more a comedy
of errors than a dangerous kidnapping. One time I had to
go to Germany and kidnap a boy whose father, a general
in the U.S. Air Force, was holding him as a means of getting his estranged wife to sign a property settlement before
divorcing him.

The mother of the boy had had an argument with her
husband and gone back to the United States, with the understanding that when school recessed at Easter vacation
the boy, aged fourteen, would be sent home to her. Instead,
the father kept him in Germany and insisted she sign an
agreement.

In the meantime, her mother, the boy's grandmother,
had gone to Germany herself to take care of the boy because the father was busy being a general much of the
time. The father had gone so far as to say to his wife that

if she came back to Germany and tried to take the child home to the United States on a commercial airliner, he would have air force planes force the commercial jet down, even if it meant shooting the plane out of the sky.

Well, I didn't believe that, but she did, and it was enough to keep her upset even when she hired me to plan the kidnapping on her behalf. I took the case on the condition that her lawyer, Lucille Athearn, would come with us and keep everyone, especially the mother, calm. So she, Lucille, and I flew to Germany, with them counting on me to handle the kidnapping. It was assumed the son would want to come home, but of course, you never know for sure what the child will do until you get into the kidnap position.

We didn't fly directly into Germany because I felt there was a small chance that a man in such a high-ranking position could get hold of the passenger lists or check with passport control and find out the names of any Americans entering the country direct from the United States. So we flew to Zurich, Switzerland, where I arranged with a Swiss investigator named Dolf Schenkel to drive us in his fancy Jaguar across the border into Germany. This way we knew we wouldn't have to show passports and nobody would have our names, so we could arrive without anybody finding out about us.

Our plan was to get the boy, drive back to Switzerland, and fly home from there. We spent the first two days observing his daily patterns — when he went and came home from school, when he played with friends, when he walked his dog. We managed to make contact with the grandmother, who was with him much of the time, and told her of our plans to kidnap the boy. She had expected this and planned to move out immediately to get away from the boy's father. We told her to stash herself in a beauty parlor so he wouldn't consider her an accomplice.

I changed our plan to escape across the border with Dolf when I discovered that a TWA flight left from a nearby airport about half an hour after we planned to pick up the son. I told our client the father could never mobilize his air force fighters to shoot us down in time, and I felt her son would appreciate the fast getaway. She agreed but was still quite anxious as I drove our rented car up to the boy the minute he left his school and started walking home. "Stay calm, now," I said to the mother. "This is it." She got out of the car and started talking to him. He ran up and hugged her with a big whoop and agreed immediately that he would leave with her to return to the United States. All he wanted was five minutes to get some of his things.

Oh-oh, I thought. We had only minutes to spare to get to the airport, but he insisted on going home, and I thought it best to let him go back in the house. To my complete surprise, he came out carrying his dog, a poodle he had kept with him throughout the turmoil of leaving his mother and staying with his father. He was adamant that the dog come with him or he wouldn't leave.

I had no idea if I could get the dog on the airplane, but we drove to the airport in a cloud of dust and managed to get on the plane without standing in line. The dog, thanks to Lucille, who made a very big deal about being a San Francisco lawyer in Germany "with important contacts with the military," which I guess was true, rode along with the boy in first class.

Then at the last minute the boy's mother got very upset about leaving *her* mother behind to bear the brunt of the father's wrath. So Lucille, harrumphing and acquiescing at the same time, got off the plane and stayed behind to later accompany the grandmother, who had long ago left the beauty parlor and headed for the airport on her own. We all arranged to meet in New York.

Of course I knew that no air force plane was going to shoot down a TWA plane with innocent citizens on it. But as we took off, I sat there looking out the window and feeling increasingly nervous. All in all we were in Germany less than seventy-two hours. The more time you take in these situations the greater the risk. We even had the boy's mother in a wig, because she could have been recognized by any of the father's acquaintances in the area. I was certain that I had covered every possible detail, but it wasn't until we were several hours away from Germany and no U.S. Air Force fighters were in sight that I began to relax.

I think the most traumatic kidnapping case I ever had took place when a woman came to me and said she wanted to get her two children back from her ex-husband, who had abducted the children some years before, after she'd been granted custody. She and her new husband came to me after seeing a couple of investigators with no success. They had looked everywhere and couldn't find any trace of the kids.

I found the husband had left a trail: His mother lived in Canada and he had mentioned to a colleague he might be going to visit her soon. I contacted a colleague in Canada named Jack Forrest who discovered that the husband had entered the country but had not said his children were with him. However, once we got the mother's address, Jack did find one of the children — the boy. When I flew there with the client to establish surveillance, I discovered the child rarely went anywhere without adult escort, and that he was never alone at any set time. The pattern was too irregular for us to continue.

So we flew back home after I asked Jack to put a man on the surveillance of the apartment and watch the father's actions to see if he could advise me of a pattern and tell us where the other child was. I finally got a report, about two months later, that the little girl had been sick and in the hospital. She was back with her grandmother and attending school. There seemed to be a routine we could follow.

I flew back up there with the client and met with Jack and his chief investigator, Duncan Stewart. The first day of our surveillance, as we watched the apartment, we saw that both children were alone with the grandmother. Every so often they would come outside for some fresh air after the father had gone to work. This was one of those times when you just make a decision and act on it. There we had both children out in front of the apartment house with only grandmother around, and no one else. So we moved swiftly. We had a rented car parked close by to use for our getaway, and the car of the Canadian investigators parked several blocks away.

I prepared a note to the chief of police in the town that said, "You may get a report of a kidnapping of these two children, but in fact we are here legally to return them to their rightful home. The mother, who has custody, as you can see by the enclosed copy of the court order, has come from the United States to take her children back with her. The father here in Canada with whom they have been living has no legal right to them." The only effect a note like this would have is to say, this isn't a crime, it's a civil matter. They would, I hoped, see the snatch as a domestic problem out of their jurisdiction.

We then hurried down to the street where the children were still playing. As soon as they saw their mother, they ran toward her, so she grabbed her daughter and headed for the car. Her husband grabbed the boy, but the grandmother ran out at that moment and took hold of one of the boy's arms. There was a very traumatic scene with them struggling and pulling, and I got out of the car to add my weight, which I don't like to do, but it seemed to me the boy did want to go with the mother's husband.

As it happened, I kind of took the little boy's hand out of his grandmother's, and she sort of sat down on the grass in shock. She later claimed I had knocked her down, which I hadn't done. We rushed the children over to the car and drove off.

The kids were crying. They didn't understand what was going on. They had just barely recognized the husband and hadn't seen their mother in two years. But she was able to calm them down as we drove to the other car, abandoned our rental, and drove on to a nearby town where we had arranged to rent a couple of hotel rooms so everyone could simmer down for a few days before going home. After we checked in under false names, the mother and her husband and children went to their room, and my investigator friends and I went out to have a beer.

We were sitting in a bar, feeling good that we had successfully tracked down and retrieved these kids, when a radio news report came on to say that the girl we had just kidnapped had leukemia and without her special medicine she would die. At first we were pretty cynical, thinking this was just a lot of baloney to get us to come out of hiding.

But by the time we had another beer, the report seemed plausible. I said, "You know, they could tell a lot of stories about the girl, but I don't think they'd dare make something like that up." Jack and Duncan nodded and drank their beer. "Did she look sick to you?" I asked. They shook their heads and stared at me. "Of course, how could we tell? We're not doctors." More shaking of heads, more staring.

There was a simple way of finding out. I telephoned San Francisco and got hold of the girl's grandfather on the client's side. I explained the situation and told him to get his family doctor to call the doctor in Canada whose name was mentioned in the radio report. I said, "Tell your doctor that when he calls this man in Canada to make it sound like we're already back in the States. Find out if it's true about the leukemia, and if so, what is the right medicine. Get a prescription over the phone for it and we'll try to get it here."

I told him I'd call him back on a pay phone, in case the police were trying to trace our whereabouts and had called San Francisco police to bug his phone. In an hour I got him back on the phone, and he said yes, the little girl had contracted leukemia soon after her arrival in Canada. He gave me the information for the prescription. Now I had to go back and break the news to the family, who were just getting reacquainted with each other. I thought the mother would fall apart, but she held up all right.

We decided then that there was no point in staying static — it was important to get the girl back to the States and to a specialist. Jack Forrest was able to get a doctor to prescribe the medicine, and we left town in a hurry.

We had to make a dash across the back roads of Canada that night, not knowing if the Royal Canadian Mounted Police were looking for us. We drove all night, with Duncan Stewart behind the wheel. The little girl sat in back with her mother describing how the doctor had told her that in her blood, the white corpuscles were fighting with the red corpuscles and the whites were winning, and that's why she was sick and had to take medicine. The previous month when we hadn't seen her, she'd been in the hospital for treatment. We drove along all night with tears streaming down our faces listening to her. She knew she was dying and had already accepted it. So had her brother. It was the adults who couldn't handle it that night.

The next day we secretly crossed the border by driving to one of the Great Lakes, where Jack had a motorboat. We sent the mother and her husband and the two children across the lake with Jack, while Duncan drove me through the Windsor Tunnel into the United States, then around to meet them at the prearranged drop-off point on the shore in Michigan. Duncan then drove us all to the airport, where we made connections to fly back to San Francisco. The little girl died a few months later.

If there is such a thing as a civilized kidnapping — or bringing a civilized approach to a kidnapping that won't work — Hal figured it out in Spain one afternoon while literally going around in circles.

A Mexican woman's husband, a native of Spain, left her in Mexico and took their three children with him to his estate in the Pyrenees. He used forged passports and traveled through the United States to elude her, but she knew an El Paso policeman who had picked up the trail. The cop called me into the case, and the mother, her cousin, and I flew to France.

The mother had been unable to get a passport to Spain because of some diplomatic problems between the two countries, so she stayed in France while the rest of us went to Spain to find the children. Once we arrived, I went to see some friends in the Spanish government in an attempt to get her in. They offered a specially authorized visa for her, so she could at least see the children. But they also told me that if I used the visa to kidnap the children and got caught at the border, it would create a big problem for them, because they would have signed the visa and vouched for my integrity. I didn't want to put them in that position, so the mother stayed behind.

I established surveillance on the father's house but realized that this kidnapping was almost hopeless from the start. The father owned a large country property with a high white wall running around the outside and servants who took the kids to school every day. These children did not play in a public playground, walk in public streets, or even pray in public churches. Every day the mother's cousin and I drove around that wall talking about how well she knew the kids herself and how important it was that the children understand what it meant to go with her, should we ever get in a kidnap position. And every day we saw absolutely no opportunity to approach them.

One afternoon as we were driving, the cousin mentioned that she thought the mother might be "emotionally a bit slow," which I took to mean not completely committed to raising these children, and I stopped the car. "You don't want to do this, do you?" I said. "I thought it was the right thing at first," she replied. "But now I'm thinking how the kids always loved their father, and how Maria [the mother] might be persuaded to give them up. She loves Jose [the father] and maybe she was so shocked when he took the children from her that she acted too hastily rushing over here to get them back."

We drove around again, talking about it, and then I pulled up in front of a telephone office. "I'm going to go in there to call Jose and tell him exactly what we're doing here," I told the cousin. She looked at me. "But that means you'll ruin everything we've set up," she said. "After all this secrecy and surveillance, he'll double the bodyguards and we'll never get to the kids."

I shrugged. "Under the best of circumstances we'll never

get them," I said. "You know that. So we go to plan B. If we think the children are being well taken care of, why not find out for sure? I could be the first of many private investigators Maria may hire to kidnap the kids. If he loves them, he won't want to worry about their safety for years and years. Besides, I bet they all miss Maria. Come on, let's try it." The cousin agreed.

Once I got Jose on the phone — and he got over his shock at who I was — we had a very cordial conversation. He invited me to lunch to meet the children and see for myself how they felt about Maria — they did miss her but didn't want to go to Mexico — and afterward we all got on his phone and called Maria in France. She desperately wanted to see them, but she couldn't get into Spain, and Jose was still too nervous to let me take the children to France. He did end up taking the kids with me to France, where he tried to talk Maria into coming back to Spain. She was considering the offer when I got on a plane back to the United States.

I have no way of knowing who was right or wrong in this situation. But if I had kidnapped those kids for the mother, it would have been a very traumatic thing for them, not to mention the risk in getting them across the border out of Spain. Sometimes you end up making these decisions.

He may think kidnapping children had its justification, but what about working for such cult leaders as Jim Jones of the People's Temple? Hal offers some surprising views on religious groups and their leaders in our next chapter.

Chapter 12

The Cult Detective

"This state is chockful of religions. You can find any kind you're looking for. There's some that'll take you to Guyana and teach you to raise oranges and how to kill yourself quick.... People are hunting around for something to believe in these days. All the stuff people used to believe in is kind of lettin' down hard."
— John D. MacDonald, *The Green Ripper*

There could be no meaner street in American life than that walked by such cult figures as Jim Jones of the People's Temple, the Reverend Sun Yung Moon of the Unification Church, Charles Dederich of Synanon, Werner Erhard of est, John Maher of Delancey Street, and other charismatic leaders of political-spiritual groups — all of which have hired Lipset Service.

The potential for mind control in these groups has long been acknowledged, yet at one time in their history, Synanon and the People's Temple were applauded (Delancey Street still is) for transforming "incorrigible" drug addicts, rapists, thieves, murderers, and other criminals into model citizens.

Exactly how they did this, few Americans wanted to know. But scholars who studied the groups in depth discovered a break-down-and-build-up process not unlike methods used by the U.S. Marines. The only difference they noted between, say, the Moonies and the military, was a form of psychological pressure that might be called leader loyalty and group love, applied most persuasively by mass meetings and relentless hugs — group hugs, leader hugs, sponsor hugs, teacher hugs, personal hugs, and more group hugs.

The world got its first look at the destructive side of group mind control, hippie-style, when followers of Charles Manson killed Sharon Tate and her friends "on direct orders from Charlie," though Manson still denies that he personally took part in the killings. Synanon's breakdown went public when members allegedly stuffed a live snake into the mailbox of an alleged enemy. Delancey Street seems to have survived the loss of its leader to alcoholism and suicide, and the Moonies and Hare Krishna members continue to appear "brainwashed" to their critics, and especially to parents who believe their children have been mentally kidnapped.

Certainly the worst example of mental lock-step in a twentieth-century cult occurred in Guyana in 1978, when more than nine hundred members of the People's Temple took their own lives by drinking poisoned Kool-Aid on orders from a clearly insane Hitlerian megalomaniac, Jim Jones.

How could a private eye of any integrity take money from cult leaders such as these? The hard-boiled detectives of fiction would laugh at such a notion. Their ideal is to forge one's own code of ethics in an increasingly corrupt society, and cult leaders would surely epitomize corruption of power and manipulation of individual autonomy.

More important perhaps is the existential nature of twentieth-century detective fiction. The reason the Philip Marlowes and Sam Spades are called "hard-boiled" to begin with is their rejection of the "soft" philosophic cushions, such as religion, that make life bearable, and their acceptance of the "hard" realities of life — that there is no God, no soul, no essence to a person other than individual action.

These modern-day existentialists believe that life begins with a clean slate. A person doesn't come into the world "damned" or "blessed"; there is no preordained destiny, no heaven or hell, no afterlife to make death any easier. The universe cares little about *who* you think you are, they might say; it's *what* you do, based on your present acts, that counts.

From Sophocles to Jean-Paul Sartre, to Dashiell Hammett and Raymond Chandler, the existentialists offer a philosophy of complete freedom and complete responsibility. On the one hand, life is easy: With no system to tell us right from wrong (since all systems are corrupt), we are free to act however we please.

On the other hand, life is hard: With that freedom comes the burden of responsibility for each of those acts. You can go out and kill somebody if you want to — no God will punish you, no system will damn your (nonexistent) soul. But now you must live with the awesome knowledge that someone died by your hand, that no father confessor, no court of law, no divine right can relieve you of that responsibility. Until your own death you will know that the universe has been unalterably changed by your act, and you must live with that burden.

But the existentialists get even tougher: Since you have the freedom to forge your own moral code in the midst of a corrupt society, you are essentially alone in the universe as judge and jury of the acts you perform. This means every act determines your integrity (or lack of it), and that you can never fall back on past acts or reputation as a measure of your worth. You are only as good as your next act, and the act after that, and the act after that, but you are always as bad as the last bad act you performed, because you must always bear the responsibility of whatever evil you unleashed upon the world.

The hard-boiled detectives are self-admitted pragmatists, focusing on acts, practical matters, and physical needs, such as getting up in the morning, making money, or solving crimes, rather than vague philosophies, doctrines, or religious precepts. Even their language is geared to the practical: They tell us every detail they observe upon walking into a room or meeting a client or driving into a neighborhood. For them, gathering information without prejudgment is the first step in the process of deduction, and they never know when the next puzzle will be placed before them to solve.

But if detectives don't prejudge information at the beginning of the case, they don't prejudge people, either. They may consort with Mafia kings, prostitutes, casino bosses, ex-cons, bookies, and drug addicts without preconception. Until an act is committed that the detective deduces from existing facts is wrong or evil, he will not judge anyone. To him, the acts people perform are a surer measure of character than the things they say, the things they are rumored to have done, or the things they may be capable of in the future.

Hal Lipset is both puzzled and offended when anyone suggests that Lipset Service follows in the tradition of "hard-boiled" existentialism, because he has never known what the term "existentialism" means and doesn't listen if you try to explain it to him. In yet another interesting parallel, like his fictional counterparts, he considers two-bit words such as "existentialism" to be some sort of vague philosophy that has nothing to do with real life.

Ask Hal if he stands for anything beyond making money, and he will point to the rows of cabinets in the basement of Lipset Service where thousands of case files are stored. "If I stand for anything, it would be those," he says. "You want to know what I stand for now?" He picks up the file of a current case. "Wait until I finish this." Of course, the idea that the detective is only as good as his last case is a beautiful existential concept.

But if the hard-boiled detectives would have rejected the idea of working with cults out of hand, Hal not only gladly accepted such cases, he also had the audacity to believe he contributed to the autonomy and moral choice of everyone concerned, the cult members especially.

At the same time, sounding very much like the "hard-boiled" existentialists, he will always say that he took these cases only for the money, which was considerable, and that he did not allow himself to become involved in the destiny of people inside the cults.

"We are not social workers," Hal likes to say, but the world must ask what he means by such a statement. Does he not care that cults rob people of freedom and responsibility, or is he really the ultimate pragmatist — in it only for the money? Let's go back to the first time Hal met Jim Jones and do what the existentialists do — judge him by his acts alone. Let's also do what the press would love to do — play devil's advocate and put Hal Lipset on the spot.

Hal: In the late 1960s I got a call from William Dean, an assistant district attorney in a small town north of San Francisco named Ukiah. Dean was a member of a church called the People's Temple that he said had started in Indianapolis some years before and had migrated to Northern California by a caravan of buses under the leadership of its minister, Jim Jones.

Dean told me that in recent weeks, shots had been fired at the church by unknown assailants, and that one of the bullets had narrowly missed hitting Jones. Nobody knew if an assassination had been attempted, but it would not be the first time there had been a backlash against the church in Ukiah, which Dean characterized as a "rather conservative" community.

Although many people in town had welcomed the church — witness the acceptance of Dean, both a People's Temple member and an assistant D.A. — others felt threatened by the many black and Hispanic people in the congregation. Hate mail, acts of vandalism, and other forms of harassment aimed at the People's Temple by unknown perpetrators had become almost routine, but there had been no gunshots until now. Dean said the police had investigated the shooting but "may not have done all they could." He wanted me to come up and consult with him and the church's management on security measures.

In those days Jones's entire operation was housed outside Ukiah in several buildings the members had either purchased or seemed to have constructed themselves. Dean walked me through the church, which was very modern and expansive, and showed me its altar, prayer chapel, meeting rooms, kitchen, and publications office. There I saw a lot of industrious church members running printing presses, collating materials, and stuffing envelopes.

Dean said Jones believed that people should have a say in political matters no matter how disenfranchised or racially mixed they were. So the publications office was in charge of sending mailings out about such things as the church's position on various political issues and Jones's thoughts on racism in society. It also handled a great many letters written by individual members to politicians, thanking them for voting one way or encouraging them to vote another.

It seemed to me that the church was becoming visible

in ways that invited attack, so I looked for specific areas of vulnerability. I noticed, for example, that there seemed to be a lot of unprotected moving about on buses by the whole congregation when Jones delivered sermons out of town. A caravan of buses following Jones's car, taking the same route over and over again, was, I thought, an obvious target.

I examined the residences, eating halls, buses, and grounds, found the bullet holes in the trunk of a tree where Dean said Jones had almost been shot, and met with Dean and Jones's security staff for a long talk about setting up what in the army we used to call a "defensive perimeter."

"The idea is to place a barrier of protection between the world and the thing you're guarding," I told them, "so that if an attack happens, you've either got it stopped by that barrier or you know how to mobilize against the threat the instant something happens." Jones's people thought I meant a ring of bodyguards around Jones wherever he went, but that, I felt, should be their last resort.

"No, I'm talking about very few bodyguards," I said. "It's the *unseen* perimeter of defense you have to start building." That took up the bulk of the case — teaching them how to think about that perimeter of defense. "If you think of it like a moat — and of Jim Jones or the church or the publications office as the castle — you'll always have the security ideal in the back of the mind. First, you want to set up a system on the grounds that will keep unwanted or unscreened visitors out and Jones and the church in — that's your moat," I said.

"Now, the moment Jones steps off the grounds and into a car, for example, you've got to ask yourselves, 'Where is our moat, and what is the possible breach? Is there a bushy area where somebody could hide with a rifle?' If so, get rid of it, make it an open area where nobody can hide. When Jones goes to another town to make a sermon, vary the route of travel so that no one can predict where the target will be. Now you've got a floating moat. Once he gets there and walks from the car into the church, have each of his security people responsible for watching a certain space around him. Say, security man A watches noon to three o'clock (noon being the way Jones is facing), B watches three to six o'clock, C watches six to nine o'clock, and so on. That's your moat.

"Inside the church, you can stand along the sides, but you don't want to disrupt people's concentration. Each security man should face the congregation and keep one eye on that part of the audience he's been assigned to — again, it could be noon to three, three to six, or whatever. You've got it covered; if anything out of the ordinary happens, you'll be prepared to act immediately."

I felt an aggressive defensive posture would secure the threatened area without need for guns. This surprised Jones's staff, because they thought the next time somebody took a shot at Jones or the church, they should return the fire. I described all the preventive measures they should use — screening unknown visitors, controlling exits and entrances, monitoring the actions of the audience, using metal detectors, if necessary — and made it very clear how dangerous it could be if a shoot-out were to erupt with parishioners in the middle of a crossfire that would inevitably go out of control. They seemed to listen intently.

Jones — a tall, big-shouldered man with sunglasses obscuring his eyes and a voice so soft I could barely hear him — was both gracious and full of himself when I met him. Like most group leaders who drive their security people to frustration, he dismissed concerns over his own safety as foolish, thinking he was protected by God, and moved confidently through crowds as if nothing could harm him. Everyone smiled when he came into the room, and he appeared to be particularly good with children, who ran up to him when he walked outside, showing him things or pulling at his sleeve so they could talk to him.

Jones did not seem crazy then. He impressed me as the kind of minister who was cropping up all over California at the time — more politically active and committed to civil rights than ministers before him, and already gaining fame for working wonders, or seeming to, with people who had been chronically unemployed, or illiterate, or addicted to drugs, or in and out of prison. I didn't know or care what his methods were. That wasn't my business.

Why not?

Because if I'm hired to consult on the security of a jewelry store, a computer company, a union, the U.S. Army, or a warehouse, I'm not going to say, "Well, I can't work for you until I know your workers are happy and are being treated well." I assume the workers are adults and have made their own choices.

What if you knew those people inside had lost their ability to make choices?

It's a matter of degree. I see people giving up their choices every day. If you work an assembly line or in a department store or for a fire department, you automatically give up some kind of freedom — that's a choice you made when you took the job. If you're a soldier in the army, you give up even more freedom — that's because you wanted to when you joined up. You made that decision. That's your business. It's certainly none of *my* business.

Surely you'd draw the line somewhere. Would you have worked for Hitler setting up security at Auschwitz if you didn't know what was happening to the Jews?

Of course I would have known what was happening. Jews weren't deciding to give up their homes, their incomes, and their families so they could crowd themselves into cattle cars and end up in the camps. They didn't know what was in those showers when they turned on the faucets. Hitler forced them to act against their will from the beginning. I would never condone or contribute to anyone's use of force.

There is now documentation that at the time you worked for the People's Temple, members were being *psychologically* forced to have sex with Jones, to work without food or sleep for days, to undergo all-night sessions in which they were beaten, whipped, or publicly castigated by Jones and members of his elite "planning commission." If you had known that, would you still have worked for the People's Temple?

> I don't turn down a job just because I think the client's way of life is distasteful to me, and I don't know what the term "psychologically forced" means when it comes to the question of individual choice. Jeannie Mills, in her book, *Six Years with God*, writes about her family (her husband, Al, and three children) giving up all their property and money to Jones, undergoing all-night humiliations, witnessing whippings, and suffering sleep and food deprivation for six years with Jones, and every time they doubted that he was something akin to a Second Coming, they decided all over again to stay. Every day for six years they made that decision.
>
> Now these were not stupid or insane people, and Mills never says they were "psychologically forced" to do anything. I think, in fact, it's awfully condescending to say that anyone who followed Jones in the early years had to be some kind of walking zombie. People have their reasons for doing any number of things that may not make sense to you. If you interfere with their choice, you become the dictator.

Do you not believe there is such a thing as mind control?

Let me put it this way. If the Catholic church wanted to hire me as a security consultant, I would take the case, even though I'd know going in that young men and women who become priests and nuns give up all their money and possessions, agree not to have sex for the rest of their lives, participate in symbolic acts such as self-flagellation or lying prostrate on the floor as a sign of submission, and sometimes never speak a word out loud for years. I don't know to what degree "mind control" has been worked on these people, but I do know the Catholic church has been around for a long time and is accepted, while new cults can be very threatening for the same kind of practices. To me the point is that people should have the freedom to choose any institution or alternative they want to believe in. That's our way of life.

Hal was later linked with Jones at occasional political gatherings after Jones brought the People's Temple to the cavernous, medieval-looking church that was to be its home in the Fillmore district of San Francisco. There Jones began to build an image of vast political clout: The letter-writing campaigns of his church members made politicians believe Jones had considerable pull with poor people and minorities on voting day, and his apparent rescue of drug addicts and felons from a life of crime made Jones seem actually heroic.

A white man with a nearly all black and Hispanic congregation who wasn't afraid to attack American policymakers for using minorities as cannon fodder in the illegal war in Vietnam, Jones soon became a power to be reckoned with, highly touted on the San Francisco sociopolitical scene and a familiar presence at public ceremonies. Standing with other civic leaders behind San Francisco mayor George Moscone, for example, at the signing of yet another bill to fight poverty, racial discrimination, and drug abuse, Jones seemed the perfect white liberal, a long-needed (and possibly exploitable) bridge between downtrodden people of color and prestigious people of power.

It is difficult for anyone who did not live in the Bay Area at the time to realize how many loving quotes and visitations were extended to Jones from the mayor, state assemblymen (Willie L. Brown, Jr., who later would become speaker of the house in California, called Jones "a leader with tremendous character and integrity"), Ralph Nader, AIM (American Indian Movement) leader Dennis Banks, black newspaper editor Carlton Goodlett ("Jim is a highly sensitive man, one who is completely dedicated to the cause of social justice"), the former president of the local bar association, First Lady Rosalyn Carter, California governor Jerry Brown, and others.

In an advertisement listing supporters of the People's Temple,

Jones named Jane Fonda, Tom Hayden, Harvey Milk, Vincent Hallinan, future San Francisco mayor Art Agnos, Monsignor James Flynn, Charles Garry (Jones's lawyer), and dozens of other famous people and civic leaders, who in a collective statement commended "Jim Jones and the People's Temple for their example in setting a high standard of ethics and morality in the community and also for providing enormous material assistance to poor, minority, and disadvantaged people in every area of human need."

Invitations were showered on Jones to exclusive dinners of trial lawyers, public advocates, civil rights commissions, and grants-making foundations. But the problem for the hosts of these elitist gatherings, often attended by as many patriarchs from San Francisco's old money set as working lawyers and social-climbing politicians, was what to do with Jones if he showed up.

Since he looked more like a Mafia hit man than a religious minister and was usually accompanied by at least one burly bodyguard and his nice but relentlessly closemouthed wife, Marcelline, Jones could be counted on to gloom up the chatter of every table in the room. His "friends" in politics, after all, wanted only to visit with Jones as they table-hopped their way around the hall making quick deals between courses.

The answer then: Put him next to Lipset, who also looked like a mug of sorts and who was rumored to have done some detective work for Jones that had made the two quasi-friendly, if not convivial. Assigned to a prominent table, always near enough to the speaker's dais to make him feel legitimately pompous, Jones, in his cream-colored suit and dark glasses, would sit, impassive and silent, except for a whisper to his bodyguard now and then and a nod to politicians who came by to pay homage.

At Jones's right the bodyguard would wolf the food down while glaring at everyone, while Marcelline would barely lift her eyes off her plate. Hal, salesman to the end, would chatter on about events in the news to all at the table except Jones, who, sphinxlike, might grunt every hour or so at one of Hal's jokes. If a photographer came by, Hal and Jim would lean toward each other as if to confer for a brief moment — Hal because Jones had been a client of his and might bring him more business, Jones because Hal was famous and might make him look good. The others, as Jones would tell his planning commission upon his return that night, were "a bunch of phonies."

Jones invited Hal to attend People's Temple services a few times but gave up after Hal begged off or made a joke about wearing his yarmulke to a Christian sermon. (He was afraid Jones would want him to work for the temple for free if he ever showed up.) One top-level People's Temple leader, Mike Prokes, began accompanying Jones to various dinners before the congregation moved to Guyana and tried to convince Hal to visit the church as a gesture of support for all of Jones's "community service."

A former journalist, Prokes said he had been assigned by CBS News to interview Jones but was so impressed by the "good work" of the People's Temple that he gave up his career and joined the Temple, and then found himself the head of Jones's press-relations staff. "Don't all those good works include getting enough sleep?" Hal asked a clearly exhausted Prokes on several occasions. "You don't understand," Prokes said with pride. "We are taking on the whole world."

It was Prokes who, having survived the mass suicide at Guyana, called a press conference a short time later, excused himself to go into the bathroom, and blew his head off with a Jonestown gun.

> *Hal:* By the mid-1970s the whole area of security work for cults took on a new dimension. A leader of a spiritual group, or a New Age group, or even a business manage-ment group would hit a nerve or get a lot of press and find himself or herself starting to get very popular. The hope for these people was to be at the forefront of a new move-ment that would sweep across the nation. Somebody who might be doing seminars in his living room one day would suddenly be filling the civic auditorium with thousands of followers the next.
>
> In the process there would be a lot of gaps in security. Staff workers were spending so much energy building up the operation of their leader that they didn't have time to worry about defensive perimeters or areas of vulnerability or that sort of thing.
>
> One group with whom we had many high-level confer-ences had encouraged their guru to develop a crowd-

pleasing ritual whenever he appeared publicly. When the hall where he was scheduled to speak filled up with people, he would enter from the back, walk slowly down the middle aisle so that the audience would start to see him and begin clapping, climb the steps to the stage as the cheering got louder, and slowly remove his coat, fold it, and place it on a stool. All this with the fans going nuts before he said a word.

The group was very proud of this theatrical entrance because they thought it showed the adoration of the crowd. Our job was to point out the vulnerability of such a show: As David Fechheimer said, "What if somebody chooses the moment he takes off his coat to throw a rotten apple? How will you guard against that?" The group was astonished. It had never occurred to them that anyone would feel negatively about their leader in any way.

We expected a certain naïveté from these clients because they felt they were creating great new changes in the world through the gifts and the vision of their leaders. We were professional investigators, free from that kind of devotion, so they listened to us more than to each other. We also worked with people who were worried about "enemy penetration," as one group called it, meaning unfavorable stories about their leader in the media, or infiltrators from competing groups stealing secrets, or "imitative leaders" copying the look and language of a guru to create a spin-off cult or movement.

One leader who was rising to prominence realized he might not know the extent of the protection he needed, so he came to me himself. "I want to hire an investigator to tell me just how 'bad' I am," he said, "so I'll know how to prevent an unfavorable media exposé, if it ever comes. I want you to be the reporter: I'm going to tell you as much as I know about myself, but I may be deliberately hiding something from you, or I may be subconsciously overlooking something that I don't want to have publicized. Then if you uncover some secret in your own investigation of me, I'll know how to protect myself."

So he told me the story of his life, his spiritual beliefs,

his business concerns, his personal investments, his closest colleagues and friends, his staff, and what he planned for the future. I interrogated him to see if I could learn more, didn't get much, left him, and began planning my strategy. Because the investigation had to cover a large number of sources, I hired several outside agents to complete it.

I checked out every detail he had given me — facts about his hometown, schools, employers, financial situation. I got on the phone with every person he had mentioned, plus as many acquaintances I could find whom he hadn't mentioned, plus anyone who had ever spoken negatively about him (to the press or otherwise), plus any of his ex-followers who were willing to talk about why they left him.

I had one agent working undercover who got into this leader's organization to see if he could find disgruntled employees, hidden office records, or peculiar back-room practices. I had a team secretly pick up his garbage and replace it with some of our own on the morning his garbage collectors were due. I had a financial consultant get into his bank accounts and stock portfolios. I had him followed. I had his top confidants followed. I did everything an investigative reporter or competing group might do to see if they could discredit him.

What we uncovered was nothing really damaging — some rather sad personal letters to the leader from his sister, which he realized should have been burned when we showed them to him, and some staff memos he had written that sounded too authoritarian and could have, in the hands of a *National Enquirer* type of reporter, made him look like a fascist.

Unfortunately, when I showed the memos to the client, he dismissed them as "no problem." This man felt that he, after all, was the head of his organization and like any corporate CEO or government head could "dictate" to his staff if he wanted to. "Of course you can," I told him, "but we're talking about what might be used against you in the press if somebody wanted to do a hatchet job. I think you should either write these memos a different way or make sure they're destroyed as soon as people read them."

That would be impossible, he said. His trademark, his image, his "central core," as he put it, depended upon a straightforward kind of honesty that cut through the bullshit of your usual bureaucracy or social interaction. If he pretended not to be as direct or "morally engaging," he said, he might as well take down his shingle.

I sat back and said, "OK. It's your choice, of course," and pretended to let it go at that. But I felt I hadn't done my job. He was so emotionally committed to his position as a leader that he couldn't see what he had hired me to see — too many of these memos would indeed make him look bad if they got into the wrong hands.

I mulled the problem over for a while and decided to have his garbage picked up a second time without his knowledge. He just wasn't getting the big picture, I felt. Our team went out again, and in the next pickup we found a dozen more memos, all written with what he called the same "directness of heart" that sounded more totalitarian than managerial. I went back to him with a sheaf of memos, placed them in front of him, and said, "This could be 'proof' that you're a dictator. Is that what you want?" He wasn't prepared for that. He sat at a conference table covered with half-crumpled memos that we had almost ironed flat and said to his next-in-command, "So be it. I'll cool it with the memos."

The leader came away congratulating Hal on a good job, but the case remains an embarrassment to Hal personally. It was one of the two occasions that an agent of Lipset Service violated a confidence of the client. The first time occurred during the Paul Maris case (see Chapter 9), when a bodyguard went behind Hal's back and sold a piece of information to the client. This time, the undercover agent who had infiltrated the leader's organization took some secret letters to the press and wrote the much-feared "exposé" himself.

Hal: It was nothing of any real importance to the client, but I was ashamed that my own judgment had been clouded in hiring somebody who could have been capable of exploiting the case for personal reasons. It seemed the undercover agent decided that he did not believe in the group leader, so he felt he had the right to divulge the very information we had been hired to find and keep secret. He leaked the fact that we had picked up some garbage and found some letters and ended up writing a derogatory article. Fortunately, the magazine later folded and few people ever saw the story or regarded it seriously.

The leader took it very well. He pointed out that we had been hired not to prevent an embarrassing article but to forewarn him of something "bad" that could be turned against him in the press. Now that he had seen how easily such secrets could be divulged and how quickly unfavorable articles could be written, he would take the whole problem as a "heart and head thing," an object lesson, and turn it to his advantage in the future. Then he gave me a big hug.

After firing the undercover investigator turned writer and assuring him I would see to it personally that he would upgrade the standards of my profession by never being hired as a detective again, I told the leader I would use the case as an object lesson myself.

How dictatorial were those memos?

They were stern, tough, sometimes accusatory. He was telling people how to think and act when they dealt with the press or with fund-raisers or with each other. He wanted things done one way — his way — and he didn't want any variation. If his name had been Lee Iacocca or Donald Trump, nobody would have blinked.

Word soon got out that Hal Lipset had "connections" among cult leaders. If you wanted to find a missing person who might have joined up with the Moonies, the Hare Krishnas, Synanon, or other closed organizations, Lipset Service was the place to go.

Hal: Many times distraught parents would say their child had found one of these movements, had gotten all wrapped up in it, left home, and wouldn't come back. I would tell them the same thing I told parents of teenagers who ran away to the Haight-Ashbury: I may find your son or daughter, but I can't guarantee your child will want to come back to you, and there's no way either of us can force your boy or girl to see you again.

Often they would disagree vehemently: "Our daughter has been brainwashed," they'd say. "We want you to kidnap her out of there, it's the only way. Just bring her to this motel. We'll have professional 'deprogrammers' there to brainwash her back the way she used to be."

"Let's stick with the way she is now," I would say. "We have to assume she joined this movement of her own volition, and that she has certain rights about deciding to stay with them if she wants to."

"What rights?" they would say. "What volition? Those cult people took all that away from her. Besides, she's underage. She has no rights. She's ours to take back."

"Now suppose you get her back," I would say, "and she accuses *you* of having brainwashed her in the first place. You may think she's spouting movement jargon, but what difference does that make if she believes it? Programming a person is not a simple thing; she does have a choice in the matter, and she can exercise it any way she wants."

We would go around and around about it, and sometimes the parents would just walk out in a huff. Those who stayed to hire me at least recognized there had to be more understanding on both sides before any reunion could occur.

I did do a locate job for members of a family who had previously tried and succeeded in kidnapping their son from a particularly strident religious order. Although they had kept him away from the group for three or four days, he refused to be "deprogrammed" and steadfastly maintained that he had been kidnapped by his own parents. He was over the age of consent, and by the time he got back to the religious order, he was bitterly opposed to everseeing his parents again. That's when they contacted me.

My strategy in these situations is to approach everyone with a plan that will work only if there's cooperation on all sides. In other words, the leaders of the religious order had to let me talk to the boy; the boy had to understand why his parents were so desperate to get him back; the parents had to believe their boy was acting on his own behalf. Only then could we even discuss a meeting, and only after everyone agreed there could be no recriminations could each person even consider forgiving the other.

I was the voice for all this, and as a result I sometimes ended up the bad guy. One time a husband and wife came in who were Holocaust survivors. They had known each other as teenagers, were sent to different concentration camps, found each other again after the war, and married. Their daughter, Victoria, was born after they immigrated to the United States.

Victoria was an extremely bright and enthusiastic young woman, they said. She had finished her third year at Northwestern University with straight A's and had looked forward all summer to returning for her senior year. A month after she had gone back, Victoria had suddenly become disenchanted and had walked away from everything — school, family, friends, temple, future.

The parents said they had been devastated by her disappearance and had hired a private investigator in Chicago who had traced Victoria to the Haight-Ashbury district in San Francisco. They assumed she was addicted to drugs because she looked and acted "completely unlike herself," so with their investigator they had tried to kidnap her off the streets. The attempt failed when other "flower children" in the neighborhood came to Victoria's aid and she fled. The parents had lost all trace of her since then.

I told this couple that I had contacts in the Haight-Ashbury who would work with me only if I guaranteed never to use force. "I think I can find your daughter," I said, "but after that all I can promise you is that I'll try to open a dialogue. Nothing else. I can't take the case otherwise." They took a long time to decide, but finally came back and said they'd do it my way.

When I located Victoria, I secretly photographed her walking down Haight with the hippie mailman she was living with in a nearby apartment on Cole Street. My clients, who had gone back to their home in Chicago, positively identified the young woman in the photograph and flew back to San Francisco immediately, wanting me to break my promise and try another kidnap. I refused, and we went around and around about the problem again. "Just give us her address," they said. "We'll take it from there."

"I'm sorry," I said. "We made a deal, and we have to follow it through."

The next day I waited until Victoria's lover left the apartment and then knocked on the door. She opened it, heard about two words from me, and slammed it shut. I went across the street and waited for her to leave. When she did, I followed her up the hill and approached her in a grocery store. "I wouldn't be talking to you if any kind of force were going to be used," I said. "All I want is a few minutes of your time." She dropped her groceries on the counter and left.

The next day I sat down next to Victoria at a local coffeehouse. When she started to leave, I said, "I'll just keep showing up, you know." She shook her head and walked out. It was the first time she had communicated to me, which I thought was a good sign. That afternoon she put on some elaborate robes and joined a group of young people in the financial district who were trying to sell religious trinkets to businesspeople. When I went up to her to buy one, she took my money and turned away. Clearly she wasn't afraid of me, which I took to be another good sign.

The next morning I waited until she came out of the house. I followed her until she turned around, looking for me. "Hello," I said. "Fancy meeting you here." She sat down on a bus-stop bench, and we had our talk.

It turned out that Victoria was deeply angry with her parents. They had told her too many times she was all they had in the world. She felt guilty because they had gone through the death camps and she hadn't. She had excelled at school for them, had been popular for them, got bat-mitzvahed for them, and it wasn't enough. They still wanted more, and she was suffocating. Now she was doing what *she* wanted for the first time in her life.

That first time, I just listened, nodding. Most kids feel that way at one time or another, but this one had the entire Holocaust weighing her down. I didn't push things. I had asked for only a few minutes, and after that, I left her.

The next day I stopped by her apartment and met Kent, her lover, who said he was also concerned. The rift between Victoria and her parents was tearing them all apart, he said.

We had a lot of conversations. I gradually got a little tough on her, pointing out that her parents *had* gone through the Holocaust, that they *had* given her a wonderful upbringing and perhaps she owed it to them just to have one more meeting. I said, "This is something between you three, Victoria. You have to see them and put it behind you. You can't just walk away."

When I talked to the parents, I tried to speak from my own experience as a private investigator and as a parent. "Sometimes people love their kids so much," I said, "that they tend to live their lives through their children." This did not go over too well — in fact, it infuriated them that I would insinuate they had been overbearing parents. I talked about the Haight-Ashbury, the religious cult Victoria had joined, the need for alternatives in a democracy, the reason so many young people like their daughter were giving up their "beautiful lives," as the parents called them, to change the world — and they just got madder and madder. "What kind of a lecture is this?" the father said. "Is she going to meet us or not?" Still, I felt they were ready to let go a bit.

Victoria did meet with her parents, and I think I was such a bad guy in all of their minds that they put aside their anger at each other and had a good time. They agreed to write, which was a start, and the last I heard, Victoria had married Kent, gone back to school, become a professor, and moved to Oklahoma City to teach. Her parents may retire there one day.

Didn't it bother you to work both sides of the fence — to have cults as your clients one day and parents who hated the cults the next day?

Why would that bother me? I'm a private investigator. Anybody can hire me.

What about client loyalty? Or are you in it only for the money?

Exactly. I'm in it for the money. Have contacts, will travel. My business is to get hired by anyone who needs my services. If the parents can be served by the contacts I made while I was working for a spiritual group, and if the group can be served while I'm working for the parents, what's the problem?

You mean you're loyal only so long as the client pays you.

Well, it's like kidnapping; it has to be done on my terms. One time, for example, the leaders of a spiritual group called late one night to say that one of their members, a nineteen-year-old named Simon who had been with the group for a year, had been kidnapped against his will by deprogrammers who worked for his parents. The leaders asked me if I would try to find him. I took the case, saying that if I did find him, it would be Simon's choice where to go from there.

Beginning with a witness's description, I traced the deprogrammers' van to Carmel (about a seventy-mile drive south of San Francisco) where I met with another investigator and began checking out motels and RV lots in the area. The deprogrammers must have smelled us coming, however, because they disappeared from the lot they had rented a day before I got there.

A gas-station operator identified the van as going south on Highway 1, but that was the only lead we had. I contacted several investigators along various routes south and waited. The van was distinctive and, I was sure, outfitted inside with all the tools of persuasion deprogrammers used — ropes, buckets for ice water, bright lights — so I thought it unlikely they'd get rid of it to throw us off the trail.

But Simon himself provided the next lead. Late the next night, he somehow untied himself, wiggled through a screened window, ran through some fields, and hid until sunrise, when he found a pay phone on a country road. He called my clients collect but did not have the slightest idea where he was. All he could tell them was the area code of the pay-phone number — 209, which is the Central Valley, where Fresno is located — and what he could see from the phone-booth window: an intersection with only one sign that said "Star Route," a Nehi root beer sign, some kind of silo or water tower in the distance, and fields in every direction (he couldn't tell what was growing there).

When my clients called me with Simon's information, I contacted an investigator in Fresno and flew down to meet him as fast as I could. The boy had been instructed to hide in the fields near the phone booth and to come out only when a man answering my description got out of a car, went into the phone booth, turned around, and walked back to stand by his car. We all knew the programmers were already looking for him, so every second counted.

By the time I got to Fresno, my colleague had figured out several possible locations where the Nehi billboard might be located, and on the third try, we found the boy. He was dehydrated and exhausted but in good condition. Once we got out of there and were on the plane back to San Francisco, I said, "Simon, this is your call. My instructions are to take you home. It could be your parents', it could be the group, it could be college or an apartment of your own or Timbuktu. Just tell me where you want to go, and I'll get you there." He answered without hesitation — "Back to the group."

If the parents of the boy had asked you to find him, would you have?

Only if they understood I was going to let Simon call the shots. I doubt they would have hired me under those circumstances.

Suppose a cult member's parents ask you to go undercover to investigate the cult. Would you do it?

Certainly. I once had a child-custody case in which we kidnapped a small child from a commune in Northern California for a client who was living in New York. The client was planning to sue the child's mother for custody and wanted to know if the commune was a Manson type of cult or just a group of hippies living together in the country. The wife had written glowing letters about the place to her husband and had apparently been living with the man who was the head of it. When she went to New York for the divorce hearing, we decided to take a look at the place.

This wasn't the kind of investigation where we could just walk in and take pictures of cult members — all we'd get in that manner was whatever facade they wanted to present. We had to find a way to infiltrate the commune and get an in-depth idea of the living conditions, how the child had been looked after, and whether the mother and cult leader were doing anything that might have threatened the child's welfare.

First we went to a nearby town where we found a local investigator who had a relative who lived on the edge of the commune. He bought eggs and vegetables from the commune's road stand and over time built up some rapport with a few of the members. Using that as a base, we were able to get some idea of how the place was structured. It turned out that there weren't enough women in the commune at the time and that they probably wouldn't accept another man coming in.

I decided that my operative Sandra Sutherland would be ideal fitting into a situation like that because she had a daughter herself and was very open-minded and independent. She dressed like an itinerant hippie and spent two days trying to get in, looking in the neighborhood for someone whose name she could use as a reference. Then a man across the road rented her a small room for a night and suggested she try the commune if she wanted larger quarters and more people.

The members of the commune were very cold to Sandra at first. They said she could stay one night only, but they warmed up a bit the next day when she did some cooking and engaged them in conversation. By the following morning, they apologized for being unfriendly and explained that a custody suit was going on and that the husband in the case, who lived in New York, was "so weird he's capable of anything, like hiring a private detective to snoop on us."

They said they now trusted Sandra and gave her the bedroom where the client's wife had been sleeping with the commune leader. He warmed up to Sandra too, saying he so missed the woman that he couldn't bear to sleep in their room until she came back. He kept some guns on a rack above the bed and told Sandra, "I'll kill anyone who comes between me and that woman." It made Sandra nervous to go to sleep every night gazing at his guns, but she was a professional and kept her cool.

In a few days, Sandra decided that the place was not a Manson-style cult or violent group. The people there grew and sold organic vegetables; the children were in a school where they played out in the sun; there was no TV (nor any need for one); and the environment seemed both healthy and convivial. Sandra did discover that the mother and cult leader had smoked marijuana occasionally, and that the daughter, who slept in the same room with them, must have been in that room while they were having sex. She sent all this information to us from notes she made during daily visits to the small library in town and dropped them in a mailbox with postcards to her children.

The husband's lawyer felt he needed documented proof about commune life-style because he didn't want to rely on Sandra's word alone. A camera was the last thing you could bring into the situation, so Sandra smuggled a very small tape recorder in her purse. When she sat around having tea with the cult leader, she engaged him in conversation and gradually became his confidante. There was some talk about marijuana, some talk about sex, but nothing especially revealing, just enough to document her report so it wouldn't be questioned.

The commune leader did mention to Sandra on the tape that he would be going back to New York as a character witness for the client's wife. Of course, Sandra knew that *she* would be testifying that the man was sleeping with the woman in the same room where the daughter had slept, and she asked him if he didn't think it would be revealed that he was having a personal relationship with the woman. He told her he had a Ph.D. in psychology and felt it wouldn't be a problem — nobody would know, anyway, he said.

Meanwhile, at the hearing in New York, our client blew it — possibly deliberately. Talking with his wife outside the courtroom he became outraged and said, "Don't think you've got a leg to stand on in this divorce. I've had you under investigation from the start. Did you think you could smoke dope or screw your boyfriend in front of my daughter? Just wait and see."

The wife was terrified when she heard that and ran to a phone to call her lover at the commune. When he heard what the husband had said, he lost his temper and stomped around in a rage. He told Sandra he wanted to take her photograph and check on her identity. Sandra felt the atmosphere in the commune changing drastically. She waited until the next day, when everyone had gone to work, then left a note saying that she had just received a phone call that her son had broken his leg and she had to go home. "Shouldn't take long — back in a week," she wrote nervously, then took a cab to the airport. She got out in the nick of time — the commune leader figured out she was the culprit a few hours later.

Sandra was not at all happy with the case. She had never worried about endangering herself, but she felt that her job — to give an accurate statement of events in the commune — was being misused. The fact that marijuana was smoked and that there might have been sex in front of the child were both things that the courts would heavily frown on, as Sandra knew. But to her, in all other ways the commune was a very healthy place for any child. If the husband won custody of the little girl, he would put her in his apartment in the city, have a housemaid watch her during the day, and maybe spend a few hours or so with her at night. Sandra believed the girl had been happy at the commune, had made many good friends, and was learning to read and write faster at the commune than she would at any city school.

Sandra knew that all of this was conjecture and that it's not up to us to make these sorts of decisions. Our report to the client should list only the facts we knew for sure: that the school taught reading and writing; that the food was organic and vegetarian; that the mother and leader were lovers; that they smoked marijuana, and so forth. We were not there to make recommendations or to give our opinions or interpretations.

I sympathized with Sandra, of course. Maybe our client was using the custody battle to get back at the mother and didn't really care about having his daughter come live with him. Maybe the mother's relationship with the cult leader wasn't as healthy as it looked and the child could be damaged in the long run. These kinds of thoughts run through any investigator's mind. But when there is just not sufficient evidence there to get a finding, you have to let it go.

In the end, the commune turned out to have been a way station for the wife, because after a time she left the cult leader and went back to the husband, possibly to be with her daughter. That too was none of our business. The point is that when things get ugly, or seem to, someone has to go in and see what is really going on, and that someone is almost always the undercover investigator.

Don't you feel that Sandra's presence in that commune was an invasion of privacy?

How? The commune members themselves invited her in. If they were worried she was there on a pretext, they could have checked her out. More important, what about the father's rights? His daughter had been taken to a place that sounded pretty weird to him. How was he going to know if there was sufficient evidence to take to court?

How do you feel about asking your agents to enter a situation where they might risk their own safety just to bill a client?

Well, risk comes with the territory. You can't be a private investigator for long without jeopardizing your own safety — hell, you could get killed following another car through a red light. I don't order my agents on these assignments. They're adults; they make their own choices.

Have you tried to go into a cult yourself to contact a member — ever risked your life working with cult leaders?

Most of the time going undercover in a cult would have been ridiculous — I was too old and obviously establishment to ever look as though I fit in. But there was one time, after Jim Jones moved the People's Temple to Guyana, that I got a call from a man in Ukiah who said he thought his daughter was being held prisoner in Jonestown.

This man did not tell me that his daughter was really Jones's second-in-command in the accounting/bookkeeping area and that she'd been a mistress of Jones's for some years. He only told me that she couldn't get out and that he wanted her to be able to meet with him so he'd know she was safe.

I said I couldn't guarantee that I could get her out of Jonestown, but that I knew Jones and some of the people in his security and administration. My thought was that if I flew down to Venezuela or somewhere nearby, I might be able to make contact with someone in Jonestown and get in there myself. Then I could at least see what was going on, meet with some people, maybe talk to Jones and take a message from the father in Ukiah to his daughter.

This was long before the whole thing blew up, obviously,

although I'd read all the articles calling Jones a fraud, which was the reason he had fled to Guyana in the first place. But Jones knew the way I operated — if I said I wanted to come for a visit, he knew I wasn't going to arrive with an army. So did his planning commission people, who I understood were his chief decision makers. They all knew, too, that if I came for a "visit," I'd be working for somebody on the outside, probably somebody wanting me to do a locate job on a People's Temple member.

The father said he'd think about it and call me back, but when he returned the call a few days later, he had decided to hire me only if I could guarantee to get his daughter out of there and over to Georgetown where maybe we could all have lunch together. I couldn't make that promise, so he said he'd do it some other way, and I'm glad. If I'd gone down there and said to the daughter, "I'm really here secretly because of your father," and she told Reverend Jones, he might have seen that I got my Kool-Aid on the early side.

Chapter 13

Dirty Money

"He was an ex-Scientologist who wanted the electronic bugs removed from his ten-dollar-a-day hotel room because buzzing in the wires gave him headaches. He was a guy who knew who really killed Robert Kennedy and wanted to sell me the secret. Most depressing of all, he was a guy who had to be a flake because flakes was almost all I ever got."
—Timothy Harris, *Good Night and Good-Bye*

In fiction and real life, private eyes are routinely criticized for taking dirty money. It doesn't matter who gives it to them, or how they earn it. Money appears to be, as Hal often says, the "great equalizer," turning bums into paying clients and making lies sound like truth.

" 'We didn't exactly believe your story,' " Sam Spade tells Brigid O'Shaughnessy, one of the great Lying Clients in fiction, in *The Maltese Falcon*. " 'We believed your two hundred dollars . . .' "

" 'You mean — ?' She seemed to not know what he meant.

" 'I mean that you paid us more than if you'd been telling the truth,' he explained blandly, 'and enough more to make it all right.' "

Such glib exchanges create moral tension in fiction, causing us to ponder what really motivates the private-eye antihero. "You've never been bought," a prospective client says to Lew Archer in *Find the Woman*. "Is that right?"

"Not outright," Archer responds. "You can take an option on a piece of me, though. A hundred dollars would do for a starter."

What is money to the private eye? More than a means to pay the rent, it is a measure of whatever game is under way out there on those mean streets. It is the way people put themselves in play. Money regulates strategy, establishes rules, and leads to the exchange of power that shows who wins.

But the game must be played on several levels. If the private eye chases after money, it turns dirty in his hands; if he plays the game by his own rules, he can't lose. "Don't be too sure I'm as crooked as I'm supposed to be," Spade tells O'Shaughnessy. "That kind of reputation might be good business — bringing in high-priced jobs and making it easier to deal with the enemy." For Spade, the enemy is anyone who cheats at the game.

Hal has seemingly made a career out of chasing dirty money. Any detective who works for cult leaders, snoops on people's sex lives, chases ambulances, or kidnaps children for a living would seem not to care if the money he makes is clean.

But Hal poses the problem in a different way: If you're going to be a detective in a general agency, he says, you better be prepared to take every case that comes in. To him, any detective who refuses a case because certain aspects are distasteful should have his license revoked. "If I'm a full-service detective, I'm going to charge for that service," he says. "The money gets dirty only if I accept it without doing the job. That would be sleazy."

But what could be sleazier, Hal's critics want to know, than the private eye who takes money from people who have lost their minds, who believe the Martians are after them, who insist the CIA has bugged their bathrooms, who watch for UFOs flying by their homes, who listen to voices talking to them day and night? These are the unfortunates of society who turn to detective agencies for legitimacy, hoping to find evidence to show psychiatrists, social workers, police, family, and friends that they aren't insane. Hal has not only taken money from these people, he has encouraged some of them to put Lipset Service on retainer.

Hal: From the beginning I could tell when people were mentally ill. Their stories didn't follow any logical sequence or pattern. I thought I could help them by conducting a quick investigation and telling them their problem didn't exist, that nothing was the matter. Hearing this, they would be insulted and say that I was on the side of their enemies, or I had sold out, or I was just incompetent.

I could see that I couldn't satisfy them with the truth, so I thought I would be very clever. I would go to someone's house to investigate voices or something along those lines, and I'd stomp around upstairs, downstairs, all over, then reappear with a microphone I'd brought in my pocket and say, "It's OK, I've found it. Those voices will stop now. You have nothing to worry about anymore." I thought this would take away their fears and give them some peace. But they would be back in a month or two with the same story.

One time a fairly well-to-do woman came to me complaining that she was being attacked by radio beams. She mentioned that she and her husband wanted to move from their present flat, and since I owned a small interest in an apartment building that had a vacancy, I thought it would be simple to put her there. That way I could say, "This building is under my control. No one will bother you there."

It didn't work. She wrote me dozens of letters and called me over there numerous times. At first she thought that someone across the street was beaming messages at her, and the light switches in her apartment contained the receivers. We would go over there and examine loose wires and the switches, but we would find nothing. After we left, she would decide we hadn't checked thoroughly enough, so she'd pull out the wires herself and mail them to me. I would receive boxes of light switches, too. Eventually she tore out the walls and destroyed the wiring.

Obviously, I wasn't doing something right, so I went to a friend who was a psychiatrist, Murray Persky, and told him how I had been handling these investigations. He laughed. "When they ring your doorbell and ask to talk to you," he said, "you've already lost the game. Once you talk to them, you can't win. If you don't take the case, they'll believe you are conspiring with the enemy. If you take it and don't find anything, they'll think you're negligent and *also* conspiring with their enemy. But if you pretend to find something, all you're doing is feeding their fantasies and aiding their illness — they'll feel their paranoia is justified and only get worse."

He told me the only way to really help them was to try to get them to a doctor. So I changed my approach. I developed a new sales pitch, where I said, "I am the best detective in the world. If you have a problem as you say, I will find it for you. But if I investigate and find nothing, it's not because I'm with your enemies and it's not because you're crazy, it just may mean that you may have an illness, like a broken arm or the flu. The proper doctor can help you get better."

Then I would tell them, "I want to make a pact with you. If I investigate your case and find nothing wrong, then you must promise me to see a doctor." I must admit that out of fifty or sixty people, I've only been able to get two to see a doctor, but at least those two got some treatment.

Lynn Lipset kindly called these clients "neurotics" from the beginning. As she noted in her diary, it was often not easy to tell the crazies from the sane.

Lynn: *A desire to help people is a necessity in this business. And it follows that a substantial number of people with neurotic problems call on a private investigator. Often they belong on the psychiatrist's couch rather than in our office, but since people become involved in events that are out of the ordinary, an investigator would lose a lot of cases if he turned away all those that sounded fantastic.*

On a case that appears to be based on a client's hallucinations, we do a minimal investigation. It does not take very long to determine if the claims are real or imagined. By the time we have had more than one meeting with the client plus innumerable telephone conversations, if it all appears to be a fantasy, we recommend they seek professional help. We are not always successful in having them follow this suggestion, and often they'll try another investigator. But many times they're back in six months with the request that we work on the case again.

To cite an example, one lady was recommended to us by her lawyer. She was in her early fifties and married to a prominent professional man in the cultural entertainment field. She told us they had separate bedrooms and that she always locked her bedroom door at night. Yet she frequently awoke in the morning to find scratches on her throat and red marks on her arms. She thought that someone was doing something to her as she slept.

I asked her how anyone could do physical harm to her under the circumstances she described. She looked at me as though I were an idiot and said, "Many things are possible when hypnosis is employed." She added that mysterious scratches appeared on her furniture, and she found chips in her dishes. She wanted a guard to stand and watch over her while she was asleep.

We sent two men, whom she admitted to her room after her husband went to sleep. It turned out this woman had nightmares and in the course of the dreams scratched herself and squeezed her wrists, but did not awaken on her own accord. When our operatives woke her up and told her what they had observed, she accused them of being asleep when the real culprit, her husband, had been in the room.

We did not profit by sending two men on this case but felt it was necessary to avoid the client claiming later that the guard had committed these acts, or worse. We refused to do any more work for her. I saw her five years later in the supermarket, arm in arm with her husband.

Another time we had a woman, again referred by her attorney, who claimed that whenever she left her two-year-old baby with a sitter, her child was exchanged for another. This had happened many times. Yes, the children looked alike, she admitted. We recommended that she have

*a prominent pediatrician examine the child, take finger-
and footprints, type his blood, and give him a thorough
physical. She did this.*

*The next time the client went out, we had operatives
conduct a surveillance of her home to establish that no one
entered while she was away. The woman returned and
took the baby immediately to the doctor for an identical
examination. The doctor gave the baby the same thorough
physical, checked finger- and footprints and type of blood,
and gave her his report. Naturally, no one had switched
babies, and no one had even come near her home while
she was gone. But did she believe the doctor, her attorney,
or us? Of course not.*

*The problem is that cases we would automatically turn
down if the disturbed person came to us off the street are
cases we feel compelled to take because the client is an
attorney we have worked with for years — and is clearly
turning the disturbed person over to us because he doesn't
know what else to do.*

*One attorney called us to say that a woman claimed her
ex-husband was giving her and her teenage child a bad
time. He asked that we check her flat for possible bugs or
microphones planted by her ex-husband. The lawyer then
had her telephone us, and I elicited some details from her.
She did not actually think that there were microphones in
her flat, but that there were some kind of electronic devices
used by someone observing her place. These not only kept
an electronic eye on her but broadcast messages to her as
well.*

*For example, if she were taking a bath, she would hear,
"So you're taking a bath. Be sure to wash nice and clean."
Further, she said, these individuals must have some device
whereby they could see through the walls, or how would
they know she was taking a bath? She never heard these
voices if someone was visiting her, only when she was
alone. She wanted to give our investigator her key and
have him inspect the flat without her there so he would be
sure to hear the voices.*

I refused to accept this assignment, but the next day she came to the office. She said that on her way home on the bus the day before, someone kept saying to her, "So you're going to see Lipset. What do you think he'll be able to do for you? He can't help you." As she walked in the door, she saw a telephone-company truck parked across the street. She called me and said, "Come over and take a good look at him. He's following me." I bluntly told this lady that she did not need us, she needed a psychiatrist.

Her reply was that obviously we were working for her ex-husband, and she was certainly happy she found this out before she paid us any money. As I gently pushed her out the door, she kept muttering, "You don't believe me. Nobody believes me." How true. Her attorney laughed when I told him the details. He had never seen her before and had not bothered to get a lot of information from her, merely referring her to us. I was sorry he found the case so amusing.

Sometimes there is a tiny fragment of truth behind people's preposterous claims. A lady from a suburban community said she had been awakened at four A.M. by a noise in her garage. Her husband worked nights. She was a very brave woman and opened her garage door to see a police officer in uniform in the act of unbolting a large saw. When he saw her, she said he pulled his gun out, leveled it at her, backed out of the garage, got in his police car, which had the red light blinking on, and drove off.

She was very upset and said the next morning she called the local chief of police, who had come to see her in person. After she had related her story to him, the chief told her the officer was twenty-six years old, married, and had two young children. He said to her, wouldn't it be better just to forget the whole thing since she hadn't lost any property?

At this point we were called into the case. This lady felt that a dishonest officer should be punished along with the chief. She told her story with great conviction and in minute detail. Hal suggested that we install recording equipment in her home and that she call the chief back to her house and get him to repeat his recommendation to her. She said this sounded great, but she would like to get her husband's approval since they had discussed this matter in great detail. She later called back and said her husband refused to permit this.

The climax to this story we learned by accident about a month later when, by coincidence, we met her next-door neighbor. He just happened to mention to us our client's nocturnal visitors. He said one night he got up about four A.M. and glanced out the window just in time to see the lady's garage door open and a man leave. The man got into a car and drove off.

He knew her husband worked nights but was minding his own business until the husband told him about the police officer prowling in his garage in the middle of the night. It turned out that the iota of truth in this client's story was that she did have a "prowler"; what she didn't tell us was that this "prowler" was actually her lover. Why she had gone to the trouble of reporting him to the chief of police and an independent detective agency, we'll never know. Maybe she and her lover had had a spat. Maybe she was just a nut.

After Hal made his "bug in the martini olive" speech before the Senate subcommittee in Washington, word got out that he was an expert in electronic surveillance and could "sweep" anything that might have been implanted with hidden microphones or transmitters. Soon people began showing up at Lipset Service with pillows, potted plants, casseroles, bedposts, and dentures asking if Mr. Lipset could please debug these possessions so they could get some rest. Secretaries and agents learned quickly how to turn obvious kooks away politely, but some got through by virtue of their own sales pitches.

Hal: Some of these people are quite intelligent in their own way. I had a man come in one day who knew more about electronics than I did. He was positive that someone was beaming radio waves at him to drive him out of his mind, but unlike most people with that kind of story, he didn't want to find out who was doing this to him. What he wanted was total protection from these beams.

He said he knew it was possible to make some kind of protective shield in which he could move around freely but keep the radio beams out. After talking to him for a while, I found that he was already under a psychiatrist's care. I called this doctor and told him what the man was saying, and the doctor, in contrast to my friend Murray, said, "Please, go ahead and do anything you can to satisfy him. He is more eccentric than mentally ill, and I think this contraption may do him some good." I then called the man's father, who lived in another state, and he agreed with the doctor. He said he would pay whatever it cost.

So I brought in my engineer, Ralph Bertsche, and we took detailed measurements of the guy. We devised a helmet, similar to what a deep-sea diver would wear, out of lightweight plastic. We used two sheets of plastic and in between put a copper screen. We made a clear plastic covering for his facial area and put another screen behind that, so he could open it and eat or smoke. Then we attached this helmet to a long plastic coat with an embedded copper screen that covered most of his body. This was important because many people who believe they are being attacked by radio beams also think their sexual organs are being affected.

We put this getup on him and then demonstrated how it shielded out all radio signals. It weighed about twenty-five pounds and the guy left wearing it, completely happy. That would be the end of that story, except occasionally as I'm driving down the highway, I think of that guy. I wonder what would happen if a car passed me and I looked out the window to see him wearing his shield and waving at me. I'm sure I would have an accident right there.

Would any of the hard-boiled detectives ever work with known kooks? Surely *The Maltese Falcon* must inspire us to say yes: Confronting a wildly implausible story about a statue filled with jewels no one has ever seen, Sam Spade finds himself working with a megalomaniac Fat Man, a perfumed paranoid, a retarded fanatic, and a seductive, lying, vicious, sultry client. They are all nuts, rushing off (without Brigid) at the end to chase a statue that probably doesn't exist, leaving Spade shaking his head and counting his money. He does come out two hundred dollars richer, so the case was worth it.

PART V

THE ADVERSARY
SYSTEM OF JUSTICE

Chapter 14

Perry Mason and Paul Drake

"I am the prosecutor. I represent the state. . . . I am a functionary of our only universally recognized system of telling wrong from right, a bureaucrat of good and evil. . . ."
— Scott Turow, *Presumed Innocent*

There's nothing like a good courtroom drama to renew our belief in the adversary system of justice.

From *Perry Mason* to *L.A. Law*, from *Anatomy of a Murder* to *Presumed Innocent*, the image of two equally represented sides battling it out in a court of law appeals to the American spirit of fair competition.

Add to this the democratic concept of a jury of one's peers and that ingrained Judeo-Christian ethic that the truth shall set you free (plus a little suspense for good measure), and we have the perfect crucible of justice.

Like the deductive process itself, the courtroom trial exists to bring order to chaos. Justice with her scales of objectivity seeks this balance because she is blind to disorder and emotional bias. With her vision, the jury — the heart of any free and fair inquiry — sorts through evidence and testimony to determine the truth. For "if we cannot find the truth," says prosecutor Rusty Sabitch in *Presumed Innocent*, "what is our hope of justice?"

At least that's the theory. In civil cases, where one side sues another, and both sides can afford to go to court, the system appears to function as an imperfect (albeit expensive, backlogged, and sometimes corrupt) model of the adversarial ideal.

In criminal cases, however, it is generally conceded that the prosecution has an unfair advantage. With its massive resources of detectives, prosecutors, police officers, jails, guards, laboratories, fingerprint experts, medical examiners, forensic psychiatrists, computer records, and law-enforcement bureaucracy (plus a closing argument to which the defense cannot respond), the prosecution has far more weight on its side of the scales than does the defense. The lone defendant must pay for every service the prosecution receives for free, unless he uses someone from the overworked, understaffed, and underpaid public defender's office. More often, his defense "team" consists of one lawyer and one private eye.

Because of that imbalance, an attempt is made to throw some of the advantage back to the defense by giving the defendant the *presumption of innocence* and making the prosecution bear the *burden of proof* in assessing guilt. Throughout the trial, the defense need only point out that the defendant's innocence is not at stake in this case, that the jury's decision will be "guilty" or "not guilty" (never "innocent"), and that if jurors have even the slightest *reasonable doubt* that the defendant committed the crime, they must vote not guilty.

With such balance restored, is justice served? Some who work on the defense side believe that too often the prosecution attempts — often illegally — to tip the scales back in its favor.

> *Hal:* It's frustrating to be a police detective. You think you've built a strong case, but the judge springs your perpetrator, a criminal you know is selling cocaine to fourteen-year-olds, on a technicality. There's always a backlog of cases that will never be solved and too many new cases coming in, so when an arrest is made that looks like it should stick, the tendency is to put a little English on it. Not all cops do this by a long shot, but all cops are pressured to do it.
>
> When I started investigating for the defense, veterans of the court took it for granted that the prosecution might

commit a few improprieties to make its case look stronger in court. They sort of shrugged it off, and still do. I never could.

Early on I had a client in jail awaiting trial for robbing a bank. When the police marched him out of his cell to stand with five other men in a lineup, he noticed he was the only person in line with red hair. A witness positively identified him as the bank robber.

Earlier, we found out, the witness had told police that the only thing she could remember about the robber was his red hair. The police had picked up the first red-haired suspect they could find and used the lineup to "coach" their witness into making an easy identification. If they had placed other redheads in the lineup, she might not have been able to positively identify any of them as the robber.

These kinds of tricks are small but highly effective. One key witness in a rape case used to call me every night and say, "Look, do I really have to testify? I think I better not. The cops are showing up every day." It turned out police detectives were appearing at her job to intimidate and embarrass her in front of her colleagues. They irritated her employers by making a big deal of standing at her desk or by taking her into a glass-enclosed conference room where everyone could see her being interrogated.

Sometimes police detectives will say they just want to "ask a few questions," but that may take over an hour and sound like threats. They'll say, "Do you know what the penalty for perjury is in this state? Testifying could get you into real trouble." This is harassment, but what's the witness supposed to do? Who is there to complain to?

Hal and Lynn learned firsthand how the prosecution may apply undue pressure on defendants when Lynn became seriously ill shortly after the birth of their first son, Louis.

Lynn: *By the time I got to the hospital, I weighed about ninety-five pounds and felt like hell. The doctors said I was a severe diabetic and would have to use insulin for the rest of my life. I was twenty-eight at the time. The nurses gave me a shot before each meal, and after a few days the doctors said I was to give my own injections. This I found terrifying. My hand shook when I tried to jab that needle into my leg.*

Hal: When Lynn got home, we were both sort of paralyzed at the sight of those needles. The only thing I could do was to wait outside the bathroom trying to encourage Lynn or bring magazines for her to look at while she got up enough nerve to give herself the shot.

That lasted maybe three weeks. Once she got the hang of it, Lynn was so blasé about taking injections that she forgot other people might be a little queasy about it. Agents coming in at nine A.M. would see her racing down the stairs from our bedroom to answer the phone and pull open a drawer for her insulin kit in one motion. Somehow she could make notes on the call and fill the needle at the same time, hike up her skirt and plunge the thing in her thigh while talking to the client or opening a new case. By this time anybody watching her had turned a little green.

Lynn: Being a diabetic is one of the easiest disabilities to have, if you must have one. You look well, you feel well, and all you have to do is watch what you eat and take an injection once a day. My only problem was that both the internist and obstetrician were on the fence as to whether I should bear another child. When they finally suggested I wait — what else? — I found out I was pregnant again.

Hal: Lynn tried to carry on with the pregnancy, but her health started to deteriorate as before. After weeks of examinations and tests, the doctors said that the baby might be diabetic and that the ordeal would place a great strain on her system. Although abortions were illegal and "therapeutic abortions" very rare at the time, a panel of doctors said the pregnancy could have severe complications. Lynn decided to have the abortion.

Lynn: After my recovery, it took a while for me to believe that I was still a worthwhile person in spite of my barrenness. We certainly were open to adoption, but the prospects were not good. Doctors suggested we get on "the list" at adoption agencies, but what a joke that was. The experts at the time believed that a couple in an intermarriage should adopt a child with a like combination of the parents' religions. You tell me where you're going to find an out-of-wedlock child of a Jewish father and Mennonite mother.

Hal: We spent the next four years trying to adopt a baby, finally reconciling ourselves that if public agencies couldn't deal with our different religious backgrounds, we would seek out someone who was pregnant and who wanted to give the baby up — in other words, buy a baby on the "open" market (it wasn't so open). Fortunately, a lawyer told us about a young woman who was about to have a child she couldn't keep. We made the proper inquiries.

Lynn: The mother was pregnant by a serviceman. We asked her to consult our own obstetrician so there was a second person to sort of screen her. We met the mother and by chance saw the father in the hospital lobby the day we picked up our new baby, aged four days. He had the same physical build as my father — tall and lanky.

Hal: Now it was a matter of filing the papers and going through the courts to make the adoption official. The waiting period often took about six months, and in the meantime, our four-day-old baby, whom we named Larry, would live with us. We knew that Lynn's diabetes, our different religious backgrounds, and my work as a private investigator could be seen by the court as negatives, but with our connections in the legal field and our growing reputation as professionals in the detective business, we didn't think there would be a problem.

Larry endeared himself to the Lipset household and agency by the time he was five days old, and in three months he was something of a permanent — a word used gingerly — fixture among agents, family friends, and his older brother, Louis. Meanwhile, Hal got a break when the prestigious San Francisco law firm of MacInnis and Hallinan hired Lipset Service to conduct an unusual investigation in Palm Springs.

Hal: The case seemed pretty straightforward at the time: An alleged drug dealer named George Watson was arrested and charged with possession and sale of heroin. He wanted to hire Jim MacInnis to defend him, but he didn't have any money. A tax specialist in Jim's office advised Watson that now that he was under indictment, the federal government would probably hit him with an income-tax bill, too. So before MacInnis and his partners could agree to represent Watson, they had to make sure he could pay their fee.

When asked if he had any property, Watson said he had a garage in Palm Springs and about fifteen hundred dollars in a bank in Riverside. He offered to give MacInnis a lien against the property for services to be rendered. MacInnis said he would take the lien, knowing that if the government decided to slap their own lien on the property, he would get only services rendered up to that point. So MacInnis sent me down to Southern California to get Watson's money out of the bank and record the lien.

"Just one other thing," Watson said as I was preparing to leave. "I have some guns in that garage, in case you need to know." This was important. We didn't want bad publicity — say a story about some gangster's arsenal or cache of weapons — so I flew to Palm Springs with orders to pick up the guns while I was registering the lien. Further, Watson said, there were two locks on the garage where the guns were stored, but he had lost the key to one of the locks, so I was to break open that lock with a crowbar.

I went to Palm Springs with official letters giving me the right to break into Watson's garage and file the lien. His property happened to be located almost directly across the street from the local police station. I didn't want to complicate matters further, so I felt the best thing was to explain the matter to the chief of police.

When I found the chief, I showed him my letters. Since

this was a narcotics case and guns were involved, I asked the chief to send an officer in with me to witness the breaking of the lock. I even asked that the officer check the serial numbers on the guns to see if they were wanted for anything, and to search the garage for contraband.

The chief sent both a captain and a sergeant over with me, and *they* broke the lock. We found the guns where I had said they would be. They teletyped Sacramento [the state capital] and confirmed the guns were clean. No drugs were found.

A week or two later, government agents attempted to file a lien against Watson's property. When they found out that MacInnis's firm had filed its lien ahead of them, they got upset. Contending that filing the lien in anticipation of their action was illegal, they indicted all of us — the lawyers, their secretaries, and me — for conspiracy to cheat the government.

This was ridiculous, we all knew. MacInnis was perfectly within his rights to use this way of getting paid; his only "anticipation" of a government action was knowing that if the feds did file a lien, he wouldn't get any more money. The charge of conspiracy against so many of us was one of those obfuscation tactics you run into when government authorities have been outwitted and try to throw the book at you, even though there aren't any legitimate statutes in the book to throw. We got our pictures in the papers and our indictments registered, and everybody settled in for a long wait before the whole thing would be straightened out. Except me.

What complicated things for us was that Larry had become part of our family by this time but not officially adopted. The earlier "negatives" I had thought could be smoothed over now seemed real problems in light of the indictment and upcoming trial. No court in the world would approve an adoption if the prospective father might be hauled off to prison. And, of course, I was a private detective, wasn't I? Weren't private eyes always doing something sleazy, having run-ins with the law?

Larry's six-month birthday came and went, but we did

nothing about registering the adoption in court. In the MacInnis case, I made all kinds of motions to show why I shouldn't be under indictment, but none of them were honored. Then to top it all off, I was called downtown for "questioning."

"Come on, Lipset," the federal attorneys said. "Tell us what you know about Watson and his cronies. We've got a rap sheet on him a mile long, and you're in bad company. What was he doing with those guns? Who's supplying him? He's a rich man — where's his cash?"

When I didn't answer, they looked sympathetic and said, "It'd be a shame if the adoption court got wind of your lack of cooperation with law enforcement on this issue, wouldn't it?" I was sure they were bluffing — they wouldn't dare threaten the well-being of a child over an indictment that was doomed from the start. Then again, they were big-wheel federal attorneys acting like cops. They wanted this conviction; after all the publicity, they felt their reputations were at stake.

At night Lynn and I admitted that we were worried. It wouldn't be the first time prosecutors had tried to mess up the private life of a defendant just to win a case. We'd stand over Larry's crib and will him to stay with us.

When the trial finally started, the government put on its entire case without calling anyone to testify against me. When they finally got down to their last witness — the one they thought would put me away for good — who did they call but the very chief of police in Palm Springs with whom I had been so cordial.

The chief might have been a witness for the defense. He told the court what an honorable person I was and how I had handled the case with his cooperation. The prosecutor was taken by surprise. "But didn't *this man* (he would point accusingly at me) actually break and enter a property to retrieve a cache of guns?" The chief nodded and explained how a captain and a sergeant had broken the lock for me, searched for contraband without success, and identified the guns with my help.

This blunder on the part of the prosecution was the last

straw as far as the judge was concerned. He issued a judgment of acquittal for four of us — Hallinan, myself, and
two secretaries — and let the trial continue for the other
five. The prosecution's case continued to fall apart, and in
the end, all defendants were acquitted. Lynn and I immediately placed the adoption on the court calendar and,
with the publicity surrounding the case now in my favor,
officially made Larry a member of the family.

But the case was also a turning point for me. It was the
first time I really understood how someone accused of a
crime must feel. Before this, I hadn't had the experience
of sitting alone in the middle of a police interrogation wondering if my rights were being violated or if my lawyer had
forgotten my case or if I somehow "owed" it to my family
to go along with the system at the expense of what I
thought was right. In retrospect, it seemed clear the prosecution had brought on the indictment to manipulate
me — they thought they could use the system to scare out
the information they wanted. I resented that very deeply.
To this day I still resent it.

Hal's acquittal led him to other criminal cases as defense investigator for James Martin MacInnis, hailed after his successful
"obscenity defense" of novelist Henry Miller as "San Francisco's
Perry Mason." A tall, barrel-chested, wavy-haired Scottish orator,
MacInnis and his partner, Vincent Hallinan, had earlier hired Lipset
to work on the defense of longshoreman Harry Bridges, the famous
union organizer from Australia. Bridges was known to police and
federal agents alike as the rabble-rouser who led the "Big Strike" of
1934 that shut down San Francisco's waterfront for nearly three
months, leading to a general strike that stopped all city business for
three days.

Federal prosecutors tried to deport Bridges as a Communist in
four separate hearings. By 1949, after hiring Hallinan and MacInnis,
Bridges announced that the court was so biased against him that his
lawyers would go to jail before he did. He was right: Outraged by
the "witch hunt" they felt had been launched against their client,
Hallinan and MacInnis objected to "improper" rulings by a judge

they believed was clearly biased against Bridges. As a result, they both ended up in prison — Hallinan on several counts of contempt, MacInnis for boiling over at one point and "charging the bench."

Hal made a key telephone call during the trial and impressed MacInnis for his thoroughness and reliability.

> The prosecution had based much of its case on the testimony of a man named Lawrence Ross, who said he had seen Bridges at various meetings of card-carrying Communists. Ross, in identifying himself, said he had been born in a town back East, had gone to a certain college, and worked for a certain company — all of this to show credibility, but it sounded too pat, too smug for me.
>
> I got on the phone and called the college, the company, and the town. I said I was acting for an officer of the court, that a federal trial was under way involving an alleged Communist, that I was calling to verify the identity of a witness named Lawrence Ross, and that I was in a great hurry, which was all true. Everyone was very cooperative.
>
> It turned out that nobody had heard of a Lawrence Ross in the town, the college, or the company. MacInnis had a heyday pointing this out when Ross was on the stand and making repeated references to the fact that this man was a phony witness for the FBI. Ross even admitted on the stand that he had lied about himself all the way through the trial.
>
> But the judge interrupted the proceedings with the astonishing announcement that Ross's true identity was irrelevant. The important thing, he said, was that Ross saw Bridges at the meetings of card-carrying Communists. MacInnis, Hallinan, Bridges, and I sat there with our mouths open. We were dumbfounded by this judge. In any other kind of case, Ross's admission would have ended it right there — the judge would have thrown the case out of court. Instead, this judge took the entire system of American justice and threw it out the window.

The Supreme Court later agreed. In a 1953 judgment in favor of Bridges, the Court declared: "Seldom . . . has there been such a concentrated and relentless crusade to deport an individual because he dared exercise the freedom that belongs to him as a human being and is guaranteed to him by the Constitution." The ruling was a victory for Bridges but had little effect, Lipset believed, on the misuse of power by judges and prosecutors in lower courts.

MacInnis hired Lipset as his defense investigator frequently after the Bridges trial. In fact, the two were to make headlines for the next thirty years by bringing in acquittals in some of the most flamboyant "open-and-shut" criminal trials on record. Of them all, perhaps the one that seemed most doomed for conviction was the murder trial of Joe Clampitt.

> *Hal:* The murder had taken place during a political action [PAC] group meeting in the Western Addition neighborhood of San Francisco, which was essentially a ghetto at that time. A power struggle had been going on between two factions: On the one side was a radical activist named Lee Rogers, who was involved with a faction of the Black Panthers and a group called the Black Liberation Army.
>
> On the other side was Joe Clampitt, a political moderate and a member of Jim Jones's People's Temple. The two had tangled over what Clampitt called the "corrupt activities and questionable financial management" of the group's executive director, a person Rogers was always eager to defend.
>
> During the meeting, Rogers's sister, Michelle, began arguing with Clampitt's wife and, according to witnesses, hit her over the head with a 7-Up bottle. As Clampitt went to her defense, Rogers jumped in, and a struggle began. The two men fought viciously, and during a moment when Rogers was on the floor, Clampitt produced a gun and shot and killed Rogers, then shot Rogers's sister, who later recovered.
>
> I agreed to investigate the killing on behalf of two lawyers who were sent to me by Jim Jones. They told me that Clampitt had a criminal past on the East Coast, where he had been convicted of robbery. Instead of going to jail he had turned informant for the government, traveled to Cal-

ifornia to start a new life, joined the People's Temple, and given up drugs through Jones's personal help.

MacInnis was signed on to handle the trial, and I went out to interview witnesses who had been there during the fight. The case looked bad for us because so many people at the PAC had seen Clampitt shoot and kill Rogers. Worse, we found out that two Baptist ministers had agreed to testify for the prosecution that Clampitt pulled the gun from his pocket. This would mean he intended to shoot Rogers all along.

I found that one of the Baptist ministers' statement was unshakable — not only was he willing to say "Joe reached into his back pocket and got a gun," he was going to testify that when Clampitt shot Michelle Rogers, he said, "Yes, you, too, you bitch." The other minister wasn't so sure. He would testify that he saw Clampitt shoot Rogers, but he wavered on the gun. "I saw a gun," he said, "but I don't know where the gun came from."

Clampitt claimed that the gun fell out of Rogers's pocket onto the floor, and that he used it as a means of self-defense. If that were true, then it was Rogers, not Clampitt, who had carried the gun into the meeting that night, meaning that Rogers, not Clampitt, might have intended to use it.

Jury selection was going to be a crucial factor in Mac-Innis's defense. When we received the list of jurors' names and addresses in the Clampitt case, I went out to check voter registrations and criminal convictions — anything in public records that might indicate political leanings. I also did a "drive-by" to look at each prospective juror's place of residence. Naturally, the difference between "America — Love It or Leave It" and "Free Huey" bumper stickers could be significant.

The brilliance of MacInnis as a defense attorney was his way of making everyone appear guilty except his client. During the trial he convinced the jury that Rogers and the executive director had concocted a plot to kill Clampitt for trying to expose the director's financial corruption. He

made the minister who said Clampitt had taken the gun
out of his pocket sound like a spurned father figure. He
said Michelle Rogers had hit Clampitt's wife over the head
with a bottle to entice Clampitt into a fight with Rogers
"so that Clampitt, not Rogers," boomed MacInnis, "would
end up bleeding to death on the meeting-room floor."

Observers would say later that MacInnis pulled out all his considerable tricks on this case. He was notorious for singling out a
conventionally attractive woman on the jury and seeming to send
special winks or smiles to her alone. He had an endearing stutter
and a facial tic that appeared to reflect his deep concern over the
unjust plight of his client. He was merciless at attacking the prosecution and mesmerizing in his closing argument, injecting terrible
poetry ("Lawyers like scissors keen / Cut through the lies that come
between") into the record that made even the most hardened jurors
find him charming. But it was his power in the courtroom that was
a sight to see.

Jim left our star witness to the end. This was a man who
said he was not on anyone's side. When I had found him
near the end of our investigation, he had been interviewed
by the district attorney's office and did not need my American Flag speech to convince him to talk to me. "I told the
D.A., and I will tell you," he said. "If that had been me,
and I saw that gun on the floor, I'd have killed the SOB
too." By the time he said that in court, MacInnis had the
jury believing Rogers deserved getting shot before he murdered the defendant.

The jury took only seven hours of deliberation to come
back with a full acquittal. They didn't even bother finding
Clampitt guilty of being an ex-felon in possession of the
murder weapon. They just, as we say, "ate the gun."

MacInnis and I both charged a low fee for this case. At
the time, we thought we were doing a mitzvah for some
poor people who ran a church. If I'd known how much
money Jones had, I'd have charged three or four times the
amount.

In fact, later, when I looked back on the case, I began

to wonder why Jim Jones was so personally involved in Clampitt's defense. He had never sought an outside investigator and attorney in a criminal case before — he had an entire legal staff in the People's Temple to do that. Finally I figured that Jones himself must have wanted to get rid of Rogers, and that he might have asked Clampitt to commit murder on his behalf. We never asked Clampitt about this; he said all along he was innocent, but so does every other murder defendant in the world.

If Jones did commission Clampitt to kill Rogers, that means you got a murderer acquitted.

It's all how you weigh it. Putting a murderer back on the streets would not make me feel great, but I would rather be responsible for the acquittal of a person in a fair and open hearing than watch him go to prison for the wrong reasons. You can't convict on the say-so of the prosecution. The evidence must be overwhelming. It wasn't in this case.

Or was it MacInnis's charm? His personality and lousy poetry — rather than hard evidence — might have convinced the jury to acquit.

Well, he had many professional skills, but let's say it was his charm alone. If that's all it took to convince the jury in a case that was supposed to be "open and shut" from the beginning, good. That shows you the prosecution built a weak case, and acquittal was the only choice.

Does the actual guilt or innocence of a client make any difference to you as an investigator?

No real difference. To me, every case is a test of the system. If the prosecution can't prove its case beyond a reasonable doubt, what's the sense of having a trial? If you think anyone the police charge with a crime is guilty — and a lot of people do — get rid of the adversary system and throw them all in jail. But your civil rights are going to get locked up, too.

The more he worked with MacInnis, the more Hal began to develop a theory about the investigator's role in criminal cases. He called it his Detective as Manager theory and used it as a kind of working affirmation to give himself direction on each case.

> A trial lawyer in a courtroom is too busy planning his strategy and going over testimony to see what's going on in real life. So the detective becomes his link with reality. I go out and find witnesses, investigate the crime scene, locate evidence, get the police report, the coroner's report, medical records. And that's just for starters. A good detective manages the case by preparing witnesses for the forensic process, making sure they can get there on time, writing reports that fit the legalese of the court, making sure all documents and evidence are ready and in order for court submission.
>
> The joy of working with MacInnis was that he wanted me to manage the case so that he could stay inside those courtroom walls fighting the points of law with his adversaries. He knew I was better at preparing witnesses than he was because I had the patience and the interest in people and their problems, while he had the courtroom presence and the legal expertise. Few lawyers will give this kind of authority to investigators, and that's too bad. In a trial where you can afford it, a trained detective managing the case is the most efficient and effective legal weapon an attorney can have.
>
> There is also the benefit of getting there first. A witness who has been interviewed by the police and told not to talk to me because the police say they are the good guys and I am the bad guy is going to be a lot tougher to talk to, obviously, than if I had found him first.
>
> Take the famous example of the cop walking into a room to find a man standing with a gun in his hand over a dead body. The cop says, "You shot this person!" The man looks up and says, "*I* shot this person?" In the police report, the emphasis on the word "I" and the question mark are not recorded. In court, the cop testifies the de-

fendant admitted the crime by saying, "I shot this person." Clearly, if a private investigator had gotten there first, none of that confusion would have occurred.

A private eye can't often be the first one to talk to a witness, because the police are almost always the first on the crime scene, but when there's a chance to get out there and beat them to it, you've got to go for it. The second best thing is to approach witnesses so differently that they tell you things they didn't tell the cops. That's where the private detective's skills as a manager *and* a salesman come in — without the authority of police, you can't intimidate, so you have to convince.

This brings up the question of police morality. Would police really lie on the witness stand to get a conviction or protect their case? To see if they would, Hal becomes an adversary to the adversaries in the Case of the Boy with the Toy Gun.

Chapter 15

The Case of the
Boy with the Toy Gun

"Let me put in a word for the hard boiled officers. They're over-worked and have so many things to do, they simply don't have time to think of people as human beings."
— Erle Stanley Gardner, *The Case of the Empty Tin*

It was a case that would be fictionalized on *Hill Street Blues*, a case that had similarities all over America. It may also have been the only case of its kind that was given a complete investigation by a private detective whose revealing conclusions were ignored by officials yet vindicated by a later trial.

On a dead-end ghetto street, police in Oakland, California, fired thirteen bullets, killing a fifteen-year-old black youth who had seemingly "threatened" them with a toy gun. Hal Lipset, whose investigative methods had ranged from unconventional to unorthodox before, was hired to investigate the case and did so by conducting an unheard-of scripted reenactment of the crime, complete with astronomer, photographic engineer, psychologist, and stand-ins, to determine the truth of what happened.

Hal: Melvin Black lived in Oakland and had never been in serious trouble with the police. He had been caught playing hooky from school and had been rousted off a street corner once or twice, but he had no real police record. At the same time, he had no reason to trust the police any more than any other young person raised in a black ghetto did.

Melvin had somehow come into possession of a realistic-looking toy gun, the kind that fires pellets, although this one was broken, and apparently he was playing around with this gun outside of the housing project where he lived at dusk one evening.

On this night, the Oakland police received reports that a sniper was shooting at motorists on a nearby freeway. They had a description that said the sniper was a black man of average height wearing a dark coat and some kind of white hat.

Melvin was leaning against a parked car near his home in a government housing project when an unmarked police car drove onto the dead-end street. The two officers inside the car — let's call them officers A and B — saw him leaning against the car with his back to them. To these officers Melvin didn't fit the description of the sniper — his hat and coat were not quite right — so they drove slowly past him.

Another police officer, let's call him officer C, had heard the report on his car radio and was approaching Melvin Black from a hill above the project, where he had a wide view of the scene. There was still enough light to see, but night was falling rapidly.

At this point, another squad car entered the dead-end street, this one with officers D and E. They had their spotlight working, shined it on Melvin Black, and decided he did fit the description. They stopped their vehicle about twenty-five to thirty yards from Melvin just as the first car, with officers A and B, came back around from the end of the street and approached Melvin from behind.

According to early reports, officers D and E, who were dressed in plainclothes, got out of their car and yelled to Melvin that they were police officers. They both had their guns out and were standing behind their respective car doors for protection.

As Melvin turned toward them, both officers said they saw him pull a gun out of his waistband and that he extended his arm with the gun in hand, aiming it at them in the shooter's position — legs wide, arms raised and straight, one hand supporting the hand with the gun. Seeing this and believing their lives were in danger, they opened fire.

In the midst of the barrage of bullets, some of which hit him, Melvin turned around and ran back into the projects. At this point officers A and B had gotten out of their car and were also firing. The officers chased Melvin up the stairs to a porch area, where he slumped over and fell. In a few moments he was dead.

The cops looked everywhere for his gun — in his hand and pockets, in the bushes, along the path he had taken from the street — but they couldn't find it. Finally they backtracked his steps to the spot on the pavement where he had been standing and found the gun — a broken BB gun designed to look like an automatic weapon — on the trunk of the car where he had been leaning. By this time, other officers had arrived, taped off the scene, and impounded the gun.

The family and friends of Melvin Black were outraged. They believed Melvin's intention all along was to cooperate with police. They said the officers, who were all white, panicked when they came into the project, where everyone was black. They felt officers D and E had mentally arrested, tried, convicted, and sentenced Melvin Black as soon as they saw him.

Melvin's family and friends drew more supporters from the projects and picketed city hall, announcing to the media that Melvin Black may have been young and a truant, but he wasn't stupid. He hadn't been raised in the ghetto without knowing that if you point a toy gun at white police officers, you're committing suicide, and Melvin Black was not suicidal.

I got involved when John Burris, a prominent civil rights lawyer in Oakland, was retained by mayor Lionel Wilson

and the Oakland City Council to investigate the circumstances surrounding the shooting. The city council had decided the case was so hot they would have to hire an
outside team of investigators to conduct an investigation
parallel to that of the Oakland Police Department's detectives in its own internal affairs department.

Burris wanted me to oversee the investigation. He had
just come out of the D.A.'s office and was doing well in
private practice, but he was not an investigator and needed
someone experienced in pursuing this kind of case. I think
he also wanted to place a white person on the case, so that
his conclusions would not look racially motivated.

The case turned out to be an absolute blueprint on how
to investigate a police shooting. I don't think it had ever
happened before that an outside team of investigators was
given complete access to police records and personnel (and
I don't think it will ever happen again), so we were extremely lucky. The Oakland Police Department insisted
that every officer involved talk to us as soon as possible.
Some came with lawyers, some came alone, and all of them
gave us permission to tape the interviews.

We also talked to Melvin's family and friends, his teachers, his truant officer, and a cop who had rousted him off
a street corner one time. We found witnesses in the project
who said they had heard or seen some part of the event.
We found one woman who said she had been sitting down
the street in her car and had seen it all, but she turned out
to be unreliable. We got the telephone tape transcription
of the police dispatcher taking the complainants' calls
about somebody shooting a gun at cars on the freeway. We
got the police reports, coroner's report, and autopsy. We
got transcripts of the internal affairs officers' interviews
with the police hours after the shooting — and here's
where we began to run into trouble.

We kept running into discrepancies in many of the OPD
documents. The internal affairs transcriptions, for example, were so full of mistakes that my agent, Ellen Eagleson,
got the original tapes and started transcribing them her-

self. One statement, by officer E, had been transcribed by the OPD, "He [Black] was still running, going past the apartment house, when I lost sight of him."

But when Ellen got to that part on the tape, what officer E really said was, "He was still running, going past the second car, when I lost sight of him." Ellen froze with her hand over the rewind bar on the transcription machine. None of the cops had mentioned a second car.

Now when you make a discovery like this, it gives you pause. We knew the internal affairs people resented our investigation — why shouldn't they? To them we were interlopers. But did they resent us because they were trying to cover up something, like an admission about a second car?

The only way we could track it down was to transcribe all the tapes ourselves, and that meant hundreds of more hours. Already John and I were dropping six or eight interview tapes a day on Ellen's desk, and by now she had a team of transcribers working around the clock. As it turned out, there was no second car — officer E was referring to the unmarked police car. But the mistake on the OPD transcription was one of hundreds, all of which had to be checked out.

An important difference did exist in the way the internal affairs detectives approached the case and the way Burris and I did. The I.A. detectives wanted to know if the police had acted legally and according to regulations. We wanted to take what had happened in a few seconds and slow it way, way down so that we could see all the options the police could have taken, how their training might have influenced them, what they were thinking at the time, and how the actions of the other cops and Melvin had contributed to each officer's decision.

This was all approached from several angles. While we were in the field, Ellen was researching legal codes, police regulations, firearms discharge policies, training manuals, and other materials that pertained to OPD procedures and the use of deadly force in any police situation. It turned out this kind of shooting was occurring all over the country. By far, the majority of victims were people of color.

But we also wanted to understand the victim's point of view: Could Melvin Black have been the sniper they were looking for? Did it matter? What options did he have, and how did the officers' behavior contribute to his decision?

In this a real breakthrough occurred during our interviews with officers D and E. Both cops said they had their weapons drawn as they got out of the car, using the doors as protection. Officer D said he shouted, "Police! Freeze!" but officer E said he yelled, "Police! Put your hands on the car!"

These of course were contradictory commands. Here is Melvin leaning with his back against the car, looking at the cops over his shoulder as they get out of their car and shout their orders. If he follows the first command, to freeze, he does nothing. If he follows officer E's command, he has to turn around toward them, bringing his hands in front of his body to place them on the trunk of the car. Either way, he's going to disobey one of the commands.

Both officers said Melvin pulled a gun from his waistband and got into the shooter's position. Officer D said as soon as he saw the gun pointing at him, he started firing. Officer E said as soon as he saw the gun "flash" — meaning fire coming out of the barrel of the gun — he started firing. Now that was impossible. A BB gun, even if broken, does not flash. Officers A and B, coming around behind Melvin, said they also saw Melvin raise his arm as if to fire on the other cops, so they got out of their car and, as the others started firing, they also fired.

The key question was, did Melvin Black raise his arm as if to shoot at the police? All four police officers on the street said they saw him raise it. Officer C, coming down the embankment, said he didn't see the arm raise, possibly because it was getting too dark.

Logic would tell you Melvin would not have raised his arm: He knew he had a toy gun and would only be inviting fire he couldn't return. But then, logic flies out the window in a crisis situation. You don't know what it's really like or what you really see and feel unless you're there.

Officer E did give us an indication, however, and this we regarded as another breakthrough. He said he had been in a situation a short time earlier in which a suspect had pointed a gun right at him and pulled the trigger. The gun missed, saving him from fatal injury. At the moment he saw Melvin's gun pointing at him, he thought, "Oh, no, here we go again. . . . I was scared to death . . . because I'd experienced it once before." You can't ask for anything more honorable than a statement like that. He nearly admitted his bias from a previous shooting.

By this time we had woven all the details taken from our interviews, police reports, dispatcher's tape, and internal affairs interrogations into a single "statement of events." This broke down every second from the time the first call came into police headquarters to the time officer D called in with a "suspect in custody" report as Melvin was dying. The statement was completely factual: It was our bible of undisputed disclosures. It showed without doubt not only everything that did happen the night Melvin Black was shot, but everything the officers (here I borrow a word from my Watergate days) perceived had happened.

For example, at the moment officers D and E spotted Melvin, the statement of events (complete with footnote references) reads as follows:

. . . they "said to each other that's the guy" (45), because he "matched" (46) or "fit" (47) the description they had received [over the radio] from Officer C. E also said, "That's him because of the the, ah, the hat and clothing, it was based on the description of that tennis cap, it's something really distinctive, first of all people don't even wear caps when they play tennis, so I knew when I saw that, that pith helmet I, you know, I just knew that was him" (48).

D in a written statement given to OPD says it was, "obvious

to me that he was wearing the clothing [the hat and green coat] as provided by Officer C" (49).

Confusion over such things as the difference between a pith helmet and a tennis cap, or between a green and brown jacket, occurred throughout the case. The value of the statement of events was to show that officers A and B experienced the same confusion and decided not to proceed, while officers D and E ignored the confusion and went ahead. The basis for their decision should have been department policy and earlier training. The statement of events told us they had made an error.

At this point we could have stopped. We had slowed the incident down to a lengthy and deliberate sequence of events so the mayor and city council could judge for themselves what had happened the night Melvin Black was shot. We had isolated at least three mistakes on the part of the police: the contradictory demands made by officers D and E; the belief by officer E that he had seen a "flash" from Melvin's gun, which was impossible; and the fact that one or more officers had fired at Melvin Black as he was running away — Section 196(3) of California statute did not authorize police officers to use deadly force to apprehend suspects fleeing from nonviolent felonies.

This last was debatable, since the police believed Melvin Black had a gun and stated that he was firing at them over his shoulder as he ran away. We knew that couldn't have happened, since the gun had been left on the trunk of the car and, even if Melvin had taken it, he could not have "fired" it at anyone. Still, facts were not at issue as far as officers D and E were concerned — it was what they perceived to be the truth that counted.

I felt there were too many unanswered questions in this case. Could officers A and B really have seen Melvin raise his arm? Could officer C have seen Melvin's arm raise from his vantage point on the embankment? Was there something about the play of light — say, the way a street lamp might have shone on Melvin's gun — that contributed to the sequence of events? The only way to resolve these questions, I felt, was to stage a reenactment — a dramatic way to follow each of the steps of the shooting in slow motion. It seemed to me that we owed it to the community to at least try to iron out the areas of conflict in this way.

From our "statement of events," Ellen fashioned a script showing each of the moves that could have been made by everyone that night. She then found models of the exact height and weight of the participants to stand in for each person, and cars of the exact make and year to be placed on the street in accordance with OPD measurements and photographs.

I hired Alan Friedman, an astronomer at the University of California at Berkeley, who would advise us on the day and time the moon and cloud cover above Oakland would be the same as it was the night of the shooting; Paul Kayfetz, a photographic engineer, to supervise and photograph the placement of all participants at each stage of the reenactment; Slade Hulbert, a psychologist who specialized in such a thing as "the likelihood of human action," to help us understand what might have been going through everyone's mind at the time.

Details piled on details as we went about duplicating the conditions as meticulously as possible. Lighting was crucial, for example. Friedman advised us that the cloud cover must be 2,500 feet above ground, with scattered clouds covering two tenths of the sky.

With preparations complete, on the appointed night we all gathered at the housing project for the reenactment. There was a strange, ghostly feel about the scene. As the afternoon faded into dusk, people from the projects noticed what we were doing and silently appeared outside their homes to watch us. On the sidewalk where Melvin Black had been shot, "revolutionaries" had spray painted the words "AVENGE THE MURDER OF MELVIN BLACK."

Kayfetz placed our stand-ins in all the places the officers had been standing on the night of the shooting. We gave everyone a walkie-talkie so we all could communicate simultaneously. According to our astronomer, the cloud cover was perfect.

After trying to line up the police cars and the automobile Melvin had been leaning against, Kayfetz realized that the Oakland Police Department's measurements were wrong — off by about a foot in each case. I sent Eagleson back to the office to pick up the photos taken on the night of the shooting so that Kayfetz could "eyeball" the cars into the correct position. This took up precious time we couldn't afford to lose.

Meanwhile, we realized that three plainclothes policemen with hand-held tape recorders had gathered along the edge of the project to observe the scene. Every time a word was spoken by one of us, a plainclothesman would hold his tape recorder up in the air to pick up whatever was said. They would not talk to or look at us, but their presence was unnerving. They must have thought they were protecting the officers' rights or something, because they acted as though what we were doing was illegal.

Once their presence was noted, we tended to conduct our conversations in hushed voices, huddling together like a football team before breaking to move the cars or characters. This seemed to make the cops mad. Glowering at us, they stood around smoking, dropping their lighted butts and grounding them out with their heels while holding their recorders on high.

The moment officers A and B had first driven their car onto the dead-end street where Melvin was standing, we began our reenactment. What did they see as they drove past Melvin, turned around at the dead end, and started back up the street, stopping at the time officers D and E began their approach? We discovered that on the way down the street, they probably had been able to see Melvin close enough to decide he wasn't the suspect.

Now officers D and E arrived, moving their spotlight around until they spotted the Melvin Black stand-in. Once they got out of their car to yell the contradictory commands, we stopped the action to put the fifth cop in place.

The key question was officer C: He said he couldn't tell if Melvin had raised his arm. If we determined that C could have seen the arm raised that night, then C was telling the truth, which meant the other cops weren't. Burris and I took the astronomer, psychologist, and photographic engineer up the embankment to the freeway overhead and marked off the fence posts to number twelve, where officer C said he had been standing when the shooting occurred. We used a stopwatch to take us through the steps we had charted on Ellen's moment-by-moment script. Where it said, "MELVIN BLACK TURNS FROM HIS POSITION AGAINST THE CAR," Kayfetz made a check with his pencil and yelled down from our embankment to the Melvin Black model below.

"TURN!" Kayfetz shouted from above. Eagleson read from the script as the stand-in turned, pulled the BB gun from his waistband, and raised his arm. She waved in a wide arc to me, which meant that the turn had been completed. We hadn't seen it.

"TURN!" Kayfetz yelled again, not understanding Ellen's wave and figuring the Melvin Black stand-in hadn't heard him the first time. Once again, Ellen watched as the stand-in leaned back against the Plymouth, pushed himself off it, turned, and pulled the gun out, raising his arm in a shooting stance. "IS HIS ARM RAISED?" yelled Kayfetz. Ellen shouted back: "HE'S DONE IT TWICE, PAUL." Everyone's heart sank. Although we knew now that officer C was telling the truth, there was no way to know if the cops on the street had been lying.

At this time I asked over the walkie-talkie what the men acting as officers A and B could see. "Well, we can see part of the boy's torso," they said. "But we can't see if he's raising his arm. The top of our car and the top of the car he's leaning against obscures our view." This was interesting: Both A and B had testified that they had seen Melvin raise his arm.

We came down from the embankment to observe the officer D and E stand-ins go through their commands.

"FREEZE, POLICE!" yelled D. "POLICE! PUT YOUR HANDS ON THE CAR!" came from E. As Melvin's stand-in turned toward the cops, it became clear that he wouldn't have had time to pull the gun out of his waistband, raise his arm, and pretend to shoot. If he had, the gun would have ended up someplace else. The bullets had spun him away from the car so fast that he wouldn't have been able to get back to the trunk to put the gun down. The only way the gun could have been placed on the trunk was if Melvin put it there as he was trying to obey the police.

I will never, to my dying day, believe that Melvin Black lifted his arm to aim a toy gun at police the night he was killed. We had no proof — our reenactment was just that, a staged version of the facts — but we felt from our vast file of interviews and materials, by now thousands of pages in length, that we could make several conclusions to the mayor and city council. That officers D and E exercised "faulty judgment and poor police tactics" when they chose Black as their suspect; that they had not kept an open mind when they approached him; that they erred in giving him conflicting commands. Officers D and E, the report read, "must bear the responsibility for the shooting, because it was their own conduct which in large part contributed to the circumstances that led to their shooting of Melvin Black."

Finally, none of the cops had seen Melvin fire over his shoulder as he was running away. Shooting him in the back violated OPD's "fleeing felon" policy and endangered "the lives of persons not involved in the offense."

Burris did not want to call for criminal charges against any of the police officers. He wanted to show that these were human errors that could have, and should have, been corrected previously by rigorous police training. He wanted it made clear that when a cop is faced with a split-second decision regarding the use of deadly force, he has no time to think it through, so his training and his discipline must come to his aid. If there was a lesson to be learned from Melvin Black's death, it was that the Oakland Police Department, more perhaps than the officers involved, was responsible, namely, for not giving officers better resources to use in crisis situations.

On the day we bundled up our many boxes of files for the mayor and city council, we prepared a seven-page summary of "findings" and called a press conference to explain our conclusions as outside investigators. The media had a field day going over the killing as we presented it with our references to police error and our conclusions that responsibility rather than blame be placed not only on the individual officers but the Oakland Police Department.

Then everybody settled back to see what the mayor and city council would do about it. Their next public meeting was only weeks from the date we turned in our report, and it seemed to us that if they didn't bring criminal charges against two of the officers, they would certainly announce some kind of program to be instituted within the OPD so that nothing like this would ever happen again.

And, of course, the mayor and the city council did nothing. They scheduled no time for it, they made no announcement about it, they had no deliberations on it. As far as they were concerned, our six months of work had appeased the outraged families from the projects. Our boxes of interviews and carefully retranscribed internal affairs interrogations were stuffed into some archive somewhere, and that was the end of that.

A short time later, officer D got involved in a lengthy and very dangerous car chase across Oakland's freeways and downtown streets that led to the local NAACP office, where questionable use of deadly force again occurred. We were asked to investigate this incident as well, and after hauling Ellen's team back into place, we conducted a number of interviews and did some research and concluded officer D had used poor judgment again. Nothing happened after that either.

A year later, the family of Melvin Black, still outraged and still in mourning, consulted me about taking the matter to civil court. I told them everything we did was on public record and I would be glad to give them duplicates of all the stuff we had placed in the hands of the mayor and city council. They took this and sued the City of Oakland in a wrongful-death action that eventually got them about a million dollars. This helped, but there was no sweet victory for anyone.

There was, at least, a sense that the family had stood up for itself to bring some resolution to the death of Melvin Black. It is this idea — that an individual's integrity means something in the face of a system going wrong — which propels Hal through his next visit to Washington.

Chapter 16

His Anchor

"See the value of imagination!" said Holmes. "It is the one quality which [police inspector] Gregory lacks."
— Arthur Conan Doyle, *Silver Blaze*

Hal Lipset is not the only private investigator whose life reveals uncanny parallels to mystery fiction. In the annals of detective history, if there is such a thing, two others come close to living inside the fictional image.

One was François Vidocq, a nineteenth-century convicted felon who proved so adept at escaping from prison that the police eventually made him a paid informer. Later, when he opened his own agency, the "Information Office," in Paris in 1830, he employed a gang of thieves and cutthroats who took on the kinds of jobs the police couldn't handle. Vidocq was a master of disguise who outwitted both criminals and police, and the publicity surrounding his often sensational cases made him appear a romantic antihero embodying both good and evil.

The other was Allan Pinkerton, a Chicago strikebreaker who captured railroad thieves in the tumultuous 1850s, then opened his own office with his trademark of the constantly open, all-seeing, never-sleeping eye. Appearing to cooperate with the police, Pinkerton violated all sorts of laws in the pursuit of such famous criminals as the Molly Maguires and in the operation of a security force called the Pinkerton Protective Patrol.

Reputed to be personally abrasive, Pinkerton nevertheless promoted himself and his agency well, and if he stands for anything it is for transforming detective work into a well-organized, highly profitable business — and for his ability to appear as omnipresent as that all-seeing eye.

But Vidocq and Pinkerton are remembered primarily because they were real-life detectives whose reputations spawned fictional heroes.

Vidocq, it is said, inspired Edgar Allan Poe to write the first detective story, *The Murders in the Rue Morgue,* in which C. Auguste Dupin introduces a method of deduction called "ratiocination" that later found its most enduring advocate in Sherlock Holmes.

And it was Pinkerton's San Francisco office that in the 1920s employed a young loner named Dashiell Hammett, the first of the "hard-boiled" fictionalists, who almost single-handedly changed the American detective story forever.

What has not been pointed out about Vidocq and Pinkerton, however, is that they did act in the tradition of the fictional detective. First, they insisted on working outside the system by their own means of deduction, their own moral code. Second, they were driven to succeed in areas where others, especially the police, had failed.

Third, by their very presence on a case, they were able to create order out of chaos. This does not make heroes out of either of them, but it does suggest that at the moment a Vidocq or a Pinkerton took personal responsibility for a case, he became what Raymond Chandler described as that lone maverick who walked those mean streets, the existential model who was for that moment "the best man in the world."

A further comment that might be made about Vidocq and Pinkerton is that they were as angry — at the system, at society, at the police, and even their own colleagues — as the Sam Spades and Philip Marlowes were angry at the loss of their ideals. Disguised as cynicism, flippancy, belligerence, or wise-guy humor, the hard-boiled detective's driving force is a deep and abiding outrage at the corruption in society (and potentially in all of us), at the mess civilization with its misguided dependence on science has made of urban life, and at the betrayal of a (nonexistent) existential god. Every quip, every retort, every taunt at a cop or a client or a criminal is to say to the existing system, you betrayed us all.

Hal Lipset not only follows in the tradition of Vidocq and Pinkerton, he is the epitome of the outlaw hero in post–World War II America, and he still doesn't know what the term "existential" means. For Hal, the guns, gangs, thieves, and cutthroats of the Vidocq and Pinkerton eras have been transformed into the electronic monitors, professional agents, and computerized office procedures of the seventies, eighties, and nineties.

Unlike even the hard-boiled detectives, Hal looks and behaves respectably. He is guarded but likable; he respects individual cops but distrusts the system; he has the world-weary wisdom of one who has seen it all. But very much like Vidocq and Pinkerton, and certainly like Spade and Marlowe, he is deeply, irrefutably angry.

Hal laughs if you ask about his anger. "What's that? My anchor?" he asks, tapping his left ear (his one injury from World War II was a shattered eardrum) as if to make a joke. "I'm not angry, I'm driven. That's why I make so much money." The old smoke screen.

But it doesn't take a psychologist to deduce that a Depression kid who was never hugged by his mother, who lost his father to suicide, and who felt doubly betrayed by the paternalistic system of law enforcement that nurtured and abandoned him during World War II would come into his mature years with a great deal of anger stored up inside. In fact, it is his pure, pent-up rage that explains in some part why every time a prosecutor or police detective bends the law to get a conviction, Hal boils over.

To critics who ask: "What kind of man would *do* this work for a living — break into hotel rooms, kidnap children, chase ambulances, work with cult leaders like Jim Jones?" — the answer must be: a very angry man. To have the stomach for spying on errant spouses, bugging bedrooms, or working with lying clients and seedy informants, the good detective has to accustom himself to a steady diet of unsavory cases. Anger, as Hal knows perhaps more consciously than he will admit, is the iron lining that adapts to a lifetime of abuse from cases that result from a society gone insane.

Maybe that's the reason Harry Caul, the character who is partially modeled after Hal in Francis Ford Coppola's movie *The Con-*

versation, goes insane: He just isn't angry enough; he hasn't got enough rage inside to protect himself from "the kind of paranoia," as Hal says, "that creeps in like the fog."

Lynn had her own brand of anger, sometimes venting it at Hal in what Lipset Service agents at the time referred to as "binge arguments" — arguing as they came down the stairs in the morning, arguing over their desks, arguing over the coffee machine and over the file cabinets so loudly that one day somebody installed a rackety fan in the downstairs bathroom so Hal and Lynn could go have it out in private.

Hal would find an even deeper source of anger eighteen years after their marriage when Lynn, after years of good health in spite of her diabetes, suddenly became ill.

Hal: It happened on a Monday. Lynn abruptly went to bed with what appeared to be a case of the flu. Her doctor had died a few months before, but he had recommended another doctor who was well versed in cases of severe diabetes. Lynn hadn't seen him yet, but I had the new doctor's name. When she got too dizzy and weak to stand, I called him. He suggested we hospitalize her, but she could not make it to the car, so I called an ambulance. She was very sick.

The doctor was encouraging, though. After doing some tests, he said she had probably gone into insulin shock and would have to stay overnight so they could stabilize her. Her condition was serious, he said, but with the hospital monitoring her progress, she should come out of it by morning.

I hadn't eaten all day, so the doctor pushed me out the door. "Go have dinner," he said. "Call me around seven. Don't worry." I had dinner. I called him around seven — her condition hadn't changed — and worried. At nine the hospital phoned to say I should call the doctor immediately. I went to the hospital instead. A nurse told me the doctor had been "working on" Lynn for an hour. "Doing what?" I said as I raced down the hall to her room. "Resuscitation," she said. Lynn had stopped breathing.

A code blue alert was on. It seemed as though a hundred people were rushing in and out of Lynn's room with respiratory equipment. I waited in the hall gasping for air. Lynn had slipped away and there was nothing they could do. I couldn't believe I had left her alone with these people — with this doctor we had never met before. Here I was a detective and I could not find a doctor who could save her. I was a father and I could do nothing for my boys.

Hours passed, and people started leaving her room. They glanced at me as they tore off their surgical gloves in resignation. The doctor came out, shaking his head. He didn't have to say anything — the whole troupe before him had said it all. She was gone.

Lynn (from her diary): *I had been a diabetic for about a year when I began having frequent dreams that I was dead. This morbid thought haunted me during the days, even though I was busy caring for a year-old baby and helping Hal get Lipset Service off the ground. Perhaps it was the shock of knowing that a minor illness or accident for anyone else could be fatal to me. The dreams slowed over the years, but they never left me entirely.*

I came to the conclusion that death is a rather simple experience for the one who is dying. You just lapse into permanent unconsciousness. It is the survivors who have the traumatic experience, as my brother and I did after our mother died. Those who love you suffer for weeks and months and years. Eventually, the pain lessens and even disappears, but the void remains.

Roz (Hal's sister): Our phone rang at about three A.M. that night. I fumbled with the receiver in the dark and heard Harold sobbing on the other end. "We lost Lynn," he said. I got five words out: "Hang up. I'll be there."

Joe and I arrived in San Francisco the next afternoon. I remembered as we hurried up the steps to Hal's house the excitement I used to feel walking into that place, with so many clients and investigators and crazy people rushing

about, Hal bellowing at his desk, and Lynn calmly handling everything from grocery lists to new clients at her desk.
Now the house was like a tomb. Everyone was in shock.

Hal: We would never know why Lynn died. The hospital
put "heart failure" on the death certificate, but that meant
they didn't know either. Her heart had failed because she
stopped breathing. She stopped breathing because something else had gone wrong.

I found out later that the hospital, for all its state-of-
the-art technology, had discovered by accident that Lynn
had stopped breathing. A nurse walking by her room heard
Lynn gasping and rushed in too late to save her. This
sounded like negligence to me. They should have had
round-the-clock nurses if their monitoring system wasn't
reliable. They should have had a team of doctors if this
one couldn't hire a better staff.

I could hear myself saying, "Listen, you have a good
case for wrongful death," as though I were my own client.
I had said things like that hundreds of times to victims of
injury or loss. I knew just the lawyer who could do it, too.
We could probably get a million dollars. I almost laughed.
"You may think it ridiculous right now," my detective self
went on. "But a lawsuit could prevent this from ever happening again. Give the money to charity if you don't want
it. Set up a trust fund for your kids. But make this hospital
set itself straight before the next guy walks in here with a
sick wife."

But I was incapable of doing anything. The world had
stopped turning as far as I was concerned. It was hard
enough to go home and talk to the boys, let alone bring a
lawsuit that would mean nothing. I would do it only to
keep her alive, I realized. When I walked out of the hospital, leaving her there, I knew nothing would bring her
back. It was over. She was gone.

Roz: Hal decided to postpone the funeral so Lynn's father and stepmother could drive out from the farm (they
didn't fly). I answered all the condolences, cleaned out

Lynn's closets, talked to the kids — Louis was sixteen, Larry twelve — and cooked my heart out.

Lynn was a wonderful girl, but she always had this terrible sensation she wasn't going to live. She confided this to me because of the tendency to diabetes in her family and her mother's tragic death. One time she came to New Jersey to visit us with Louis and was acting very funny — not making sense, slurring her words. I was kind of annoyed with her until we had dinner, and then she came to. I realized she had needed food and was too polite to ask for something before the meal.

Lynn was a stabilizing influence because Harold's temperament and personality were so volatile. She took care of everyone from nasty clients to my own mother in a very calm, businesslike way, which was unusual for a woman under so much pressure. She wore well, grew well. You didn't just like her, you liked her very much. She didn't have that many women friends because, she said, she "didn't have time to be social." After all, she ran the business with Harold.

The funeral for Lynn was one of the largest in the history of San Francisco's Jewish community. The place was overflowing, and anyone who couldn't come — the governor and mayor included — sent personal messages that were read at the service. In several instances the courts in San Francisco adjourned in her honor. I think she had as much to do with Harold's position in the community, with the acceptance of who and what he was — being a private investigator was frowned upon at the time — as he did.

At ages sixteen and twelve, the boys did not recover from their despondency for a long time, but spending summers with Lynn's stepbrother, Eddie, and his wife, Gladys, helped them work off their grief and got them to begin thinking of their own futures. For Hal, the pain that had virtually destroyed him after his father's suicide returned in full force, but instead of receding into his former malaise, he threw himself into work with a vengeance.

In the next years, he became more productive, more efficient, more widely traveled, more popular, and more volatile than he had ever been — and, of course, richer. To say he was angrier than ever before would be an understatement. He was beyond feelings of abandonment and betrayal, beyond bereavement. His outrage was inexpressible.

Without Lynn, the atmosphere at Lipset Service became inflammatory. Agents knew better than to suspect the nature of investigative work as the reason for the outbursts that occurred almost daily — and sometimes still do. It was Hal whose temper could erupt if a bill went out improperly or an agent erred on a simple process service, Hal whose lashings-out stunned even veteran agents, Hal who once went through nine secretaries in two years because he had reduced them all to tears one too many times.

But like Vidocq and Pinkerton, Hal learned to use his anger as a wedge against conventional thinking. He might blow up privately, but at the same time he was an extremely congenial and creative investigator who surprised his clients with his unusual yet effective ideas. It was this combination of aggression and innovation that attracted him to Sam Dash when the Senate Watergate Committee began looking for a chief investigator.

Dash had observed Hal's flair for original tactics when the two worked together to investigate the Betterment Committee of Teamsters Local 107 in Philadelphia (see Chapter 3). Some years later, on the day he was sworn in as chief counsel for the Senate Watergate Committee (March 6, 1973), Dash telephoned from Washington, D.C., to offer Hal the job as chief investigator.

> *Hal:* I asked Dash if he was sure he wanted to hire somebody with my background in electronic recording devices, given the fact that part of the Watergate case included the bugging of Democratic headquarters. I mentioned my conviction in New York and reminded him that during one of my many arrests, I had been working for Dash himself — and I had been "wired" that time, too.
>
> Dash said his people had checked into all that. The committee chair, Senator Sam Ervin, had looked at my record and said, "Well, when you hire an outside private detective, if he's any good, he will have taken chances, and if

he took any chances, he's bound to have gotten into trouble once in a while. Let's get him."

Dash would later remark that the reason he did not hire FBI agents or police to conduct the Watergate investigation was that he felt many law-enforcement officers had become too dependent on the power of their badges. Government detectives, he said, ran the risk of becoming extensions of the very system the Watergate Committee was investigating. Even if they did not feel a loyalty to that system, they still depended on its clout to get them into areas where information was needed.

So Dash said he hired Lipset as chief investigator because he wanted a good detective in the old sense, someone who knew how to talk to people on their own terms, who relied not on official authority but on an ability to convince — and who was driven to succeed.

Hal: I flew to Washington to be sworn in and was swept up immediately by the pace of the investigation, a mountain of materials that needed sorting and an operation that urgently needed structure and direction.

We decided to coordinate three different phases of the committee's investigation: First, there was the break-in and the illegal placement of the telephone taps at Democratic headquarters in the Watergate building; second, there were the "dirty tricks" of Richard Nixon's 1972 campaign, such as the mailing of phony letters designed to create havoc among opposing groups; third, there were large amounts of cash that had been floating around, ostensibly used as payoffs, and a subsequent cover-up of the uses of that cash.

Ordinarily, I would have looked up and maybe stayed with Bernard Fensterwald, the lawyer who had been counsel to the Senate Subcommittee on Eavesdropping when I testified with my "bug in the martini olive" exhibit in 1965. We had kept in touch on and off over the years, and whenever I was in Washington, I had dinner with Bud or stayed at his house.

Dash felt that such affiliations should be placed in limbo

during the investigation. Nobody knew which lawyers had which connections involving Watergate, and Fensterwald especially, Dash thought, might have associations that could appear to compromise us as investigators. I disagreed: Everybody knew everybody in Washington, and the point was to keep the lines of communication open. If Fensterwald had had some kind of tainted association that might have a bearing on this case, we should know about it. The greater harm would be to maintain ignorance for the sake of appearances. Dash could not see this, and I deferred to him. Maybe I'd see Fensterwald next time around.

About this time, the Republicans on the committee selected their minority counsel, Fred Thompson, and he picked as his chief investigator a former FBI agent who had worked for the House Un-American Activities Committee. Politically, morally, socially, and politically (I felt), this FBI man was my opposite.

But Dash and Thompson agreed not to conduct the investigation along partisan lines, so that all of us would exchange information equally. I found the former FBI agent to be a hardworking investigator and was able to coordinate the case with him easily. Although sharing secrets and leads is not exactly my stock-in-trade, I figured this was my first glimpse at the ideal of compromise that seemed to be so popular in Washington.

At the beginning our staff consisted of Dash, myself, an assistant to Sam Ervin, and a secretary. The great frustration and challenge at that time was to structure the operation yet plunge into the case as though the office were up and running. I read thousands of pages of testimony from the Watergate trial even as I was interviewing investigators and researchers for jobs on our staff.

So much is at your disposal when you work for the government. Dash requested the Library of Congress to duplicate every newspaper article that had anything to do with Watergate since the break-in was discovered on June 17, 1972. The clippings began pouring in by the thousands as well. Each time I read an article, I would identify it, mark it, and pass it on to one of Dash's law students for cross-referencing.

The push in Washington, I found, is to do everything within the bureaucracy. This way you cover your position and risk nothing. By tradition, I should have stayed in Dash's office supervising the creation of a massive bureaucracy (the staff grew from five to hundreds) and delegating the fieldwork to various investigators. My goal was to manage the operation from the inside until I could free myself up, like the head of a detective agency, to do my own detective work.

But a few weeks later, on March 23, things changed dramatically. Dash told me that District Court Judge John J. Sirica was going to sentence some of the Watergate burglars and read a letter in open court from James McCord, the former CIA agent and CREEP (Committee to Re-Elect the President) security coordinator who had led the break-in.

Dash and I decided to go to district court and hear what it was about. Sirica read the now-famous letter from McCord, which was the first indication that there might be a cover-up, that threats had been made and money offered to some of the Watergate defendants to keep their mouths shut.

Perhaps just as important, McCord's letter echoed the words of Sam Dash about the integrity of investigators working for the federal government at that time. "I cannot feel confident in talking with an FBI agent," McCord wrote, "[or] in testifying before a grand jury whose U.S. Attorneys work for the Department of Justice, or in talking with other government representatives." The reason, according to Robert L. Jackson and Ronald J. Ostrow, who broke the story in the *Los Angeles Times,* was that anything McCord said in front of government investigators "would be made immediately available to White House officials."

Sirica himself said later that he read the letter in open court to force the Justice Department, which he believed had been less than diligent during the trial of the Watergate burglars, "to get to the bottom" of McCord's charges. It's no wonder that McCord, who also said his family expressed fear for his life if he were to "disclose knowledge of the facts . . . to any government representatives," gave his first interview to Hal Lipset and Sam Dash.

As Dash walked over to confer with Sirica's clerk, I turned into the aisle and found myself face-to-face with Bud Fensterwald, the attorney Dash had warned me not to see. "Hal!" he said. "What are you doing here?"

"I'm Dash's chief investigator," I said. "What are you doing here?"

"I'm McCord's new attorney," he said, beaming. "I wrote that statement you just heard."

I had to laugh. Had I called Bud a week earlier, I would have known that very fact. "Why, Bud, that's very interesting," I said.

"Isn't it, though?" he said. "Now I suppose the next thing you'll want is an interview with McCord."

"The thought is just crossing my mind."

"Well, if you take me to lunch, we can arrange it," Bud said happily. He liked to be at the center of things.

"Good idea," I said. "Now you wait right here." I found Dash and explained Fensterwald's proposal. Dash was now delighted to have me renew my friendship with Fensterwald, so I did take Bud to lunch and we did arrange for Dash and I to interview McCord secretly at Fensterwald's office the next day. Bud didn't need much convincing. He knew we were the only outlet that McCord could trust. But he also insisted on the tightest security possible: Any leaks to the press could endanger McCord's life.

The next morning we arrived at Fensterwald's office, where McCord permitted us to record the interview. I brought the tape recorder I had taken from my office in San Francisco, which was both lucky and amusing, because I had been informed it would take several weeks to get a tape recorder out of the Senate. This had been announced when I asked to be reimbursed for some cassettes and was told by a clerk, "Oh, no. You can't go out and *buy* anything you need. You have to get things like audio-cassettes through the Senate supply house."

"All right," I said. "Where is it? I need new cassettes in an hour, so I'll go there myself."

"Oh, no," he said again. "You don't go there — you *requisition.* Here are the forms. Figure one to three weeks for delivery."

"Thanks, but no thanks," I said. To hell with it.

I brought a box of my own cassettes to the meeting, which was a good thing. Sam and I spent all day with McCord in what proved to be an extremely difficult inter-view. There was a lot of hemming and hawing, with McCord saying, "I'm not prepared to answer this ques-tion," or, "I have to think about that question." McCord wanted to write out his answers so he could "shape" them properly, but we insisted on going right to the heart of the issue. He had dropped a lot of names of people he said knew in advance about Watergate, but did he have evi-dence?

The meeting ended late Saturday and resumed Sunday. On that day, McCord gave Dash a written statement that was so secret and so hot, Dash said he would show it only to Sam Ervin, who was out of town that weekend. Mean-while, both McCord and Fensterwald said they wouldn't mind if Dash released a statement to the press that McCord was talking to us. From their point of view, Sirica would see that McCord was cooperating with the committee and might reduce McCord's sentence.

From our point of view, as I told Dash, "The whole cover-up depends on a wall of silence and McCord is now cracking that wall. If we let it out that McCord is talking, there are going to be some pretty scared characters around town who may be able to make some bigger cracks in the wall, and it might all come down."

Dash agreed, called Ervin, and got approval to distrib-ute a "limited press release" stating that McCord had been secretly meeting with us and was giving us information and names. But Dash was not well versed in the operation of Senate selective committees and how they work. Once they got hold of the "limited press release," the media stormed into his office and blitzed him with cameras, lights, and questions, making it look as though Dash had called a full-fledged press conference to take credit for uncovering secrets he would not divulge.

This huge ruckus continued with TV people and reporters clamoring for interviews with the members of the Watergate Committee, and soon another hullabaloo took place behind closed doors, where Dash found himself on the hot seat. There you could hear committee members booming, "Counsel doesn't hold press conferences. *Senators* hold press conferences!"

To make matters worse, someone leaked McCord's secret memo to the *Los Angeles Times*, which reported that McCord had named Jeb Stuart Magruder and John Dean as Watergate planners during our secret meetings in Fensterwald's office. This was the crack that would make the entire wall disintegrate, since it was Dean's subsequent confession that pointed the finger at the President.

I hadn't seen the memo, so I had no idea who could have leaked it or how. But Fensterwald was furious. He called Dash and said, "Who's shooting his mouth off? I've been getting calls all morning about that leak to the *L.A. Times*. McCord is damn angry. He thinks he's been double-crossed." The upshot was that McCord refused to talk to Dash again and insisted upon testifying to the entire committee. Dash was against this, because the committee didn't know enough to question McCord thoroughly. He was right. When McCord did get his meeting, he was defensive and coy, while the committee was hostile and frustrated. He did offer yet another bombshell — that former U.S. Attorney General John Mitchell had approved the plan to burglarize Watergate — and for this and the other information, he hoped the committee would grant him immunity. (We learned later that McCord himself had planted the leak with the *L.A. Times*.)

At this point Dash got very upset, believing that Fensterwald had suckered him to a degree, and again ordered me not to see Bud. I thought this was an idiotic order and didn't totally abide by it. I was *getting* information from Fensterwald, not giving it to him, and although I told Dash that Fensterwald loved publicity and might himself have leaked that memo, he was still a valuable pipeline. Dash couldn't see it.

We then entered that terrible Washington syndrome of the media pounding on the door while we tried to stanch constant leaks to the press. Every senator who sat in on a meeting would drop a little bone to the media. The next day you'd read, "An authoritative source from Senator So-and-So's office says . . ." or, "A reliable contact close to the committee has revealed . . ." It seemed there were two campaigns going on: An investigation of Watergate and a frenzied need by politicians to use Watergate as a vehicle to get votes, make deals, accumulate power, or make friends with the media.

With McCord's information, we wanted to interview more CREEP leaders — not to confront them with direct accusations they would only deny but to find out where they had been on certain key dates, if they had sat in on meetings with, say, Mitchell when he was conferring with G. Gordon Liddy, or with Dean and White House aide Charles Colson, who had once employed E. Howard Hunt.

We couldn't interview Hunt, Liddy, or anyone who had been charged in Sirica's court because they were represented by counsel, as were most of CREEP's administrators. But I felt we should visit CREEP headquarters anyway and try to interview the clerical staff. In private investigations you come to depend on secretaries, file clerks, bookkeepers, receptionists, and the like as "keepers of the calendars," as it were, who can often tell you more about where their bosses have been on any given day than their bosses can remember.

I went out with the minority counsel's investigator, the former FBI agent, to interview as many clerical employees at CREEP as we could find. They were reluctant to talk, of course, but it was still early in the Watergate game, and no one had warned them away from us. Some warmed up eventually, but others had to be told they might be subpoenaed before we got them to cooperate. We tape-recorded, with consent, all interviews and came away with valuable names, dates, and links.

Things were happening very fast. We were gathering information and passing it along to Dash, who then reported to the committee. I was also sort of a liaison to Bob Woodward and Carl Bernstein of the *Washington Post*, who knew more about the subject than anybody. As time went on during their own investigation, if they ran up against a stone wall because they had no official power to get people to talk, Woodward would, ironically, become my own "Deep Throat."

We had lunch together weekly. Bob would tell me of people he or Carl had talked to who were weakening or were prepared to talk if "somebody official" marched into their office. I would give nothing to Bob in return, but he knew what would happen. I'd take the information to Dash, and we'd interview witnesses we might not otherwise have approached for several days.

It was amusing. As far as Woodward was concerned, the Senate Watergate Committee was a helpful means of stirring up the pot for his purposes as a reporter. As far as we were concerned, Woodward was a source with valuable recommendations we could not ignore. The further irony was that after we followed up on Woodward's recommendations and reported our findings to the committee, some senator or another would leak those findings back to Woodward. That's why Bob never asked for anything from me. He had senators unofficially plying him with informational favors. Such were the arcane politics of Washington.

I found it interesting the way Washington worked . . . for about five minutes. Since I was sworn in as an employee of the federal government, none of my living expenses in Washington were paid. I lived in a roach-infested basement apartment across the street from our office because I couldn't afford to stay in a hotel. Every night I'd stand around with a can of Black Flag in one hand and Roach Death in the other. At twelve, three, and six I'd wake up and aerosol the room.

That was endurable. Much harder, even painful, was the daily attempt to get something done in the midst of Washington's obsession with the Three P's — politics, protocol, and publicity. One day Dash and Thompson decided I should fly out to Los Angeles to serve Herbert Kalmbach (Nixon's attorney) and subpoena his banks for financial records. "Certainly," I said, and walked over to the telephone to call Kalmbach's office to see if he was in town. Dash and Thompson came running after me.

"What are you doing?" they said.

"I'm going to call Kalmbach and tell him I'm on my way to serve him a subpoena," I said. "I want to make an appointment with him."

"My God, Hal," they said. "Don't do that. You can't warn him ahead of time. You have to surprise him."

"Surprise him?" I was incredulous. "Suppose I fly all the way to Los Angeles, and it turns out he's in Washington? Then who'll be surprised? He's not going to destroy any records just because I'm making this phone call. If he wanted to destroy his records, he would have done that long ago."

They were exasperated. "Look, Hal, don't argue. We're telling you how we want it done," they said.

"Yessir." I saluted and got on the next plane to Los Angeles. Kalmbach was as cooperative as any man who had been waiting patiently for a special investigator to come out and subpoena him.

I felt I was effective as chief investigator, but it was as though somebody had tied my arm and leg behind my back. By April, about a month after I had arrived in Washington, Dash called me into his office. He had word that the press was going to do a big, splashy story on my conviction for eavesdropping in New York. I shrugged. That misdemeanor was no skeleton in the closet — we had discussed it long before I was hired. Dash nodded. Apparently the problem did not lie in the fact of my behavior but in people's *perception* of my behavior. A fourth P, of all things.

I told Dash I understood the situation perfectly, and I did. You don't work with lying clients for twenty-five years without realizing that people change their perceptions to suit their own needs. In the political cauldron of Washington, that meant I was out just as fast as I had come in.

I further informed Dash that it had never been my intention to stay in Washington for more than a few months. I had a business to run in San Francisco, and if it would make it easier on the committee, I would be glad to resign and go home. Inside I was nearly cheering. The idea of returning to investigations over which I had total control and no roaches to contend with sounded to me like a vacation with pay.

Dash went off to bear that message to Senator Ervin, and after more discussion they decided to accept my resignation "to keep the spirit of the committee clean." It's a joke in retrospect, because one of the senators on the committee was later convicted of taking bribes in his own state. That's not exactly keeping the committee clean.

Senator Ervin then issued a statement to the press that implied he didn't know about my arrest record when I was hired. Another changed perception.

In fact, Ervin made it pretty plain when he told the press, "I was not aware of his previous record in New York when [Lipset] was employed by the committee. Mr. Lipset has done very good work for us, all in a lawful manner. . . . Under the circumstances it was better for [Lipset] to sever his commitment to the investigation. I deeply regret this incident, but it's to be said that he didn't bug Watergate."

As far as I was concerned, the job worked out satisfactorily. I was in on the very beginning of the committee's investigation, and my recommendations were followed to the letter. I was able to say in advance that I thought the President of the United States was involved in Watergate — which was a good guess on my part — and I even reaped the public relations benefit of Nixon's anti-Semitism.

When Bantam published Richard Nixon's long-protected and much-censored White House tapes, comments on April 14, 1973, revealed that the day after Hal's resignation, Ehrlichman told the President he was going to "gig" Dash and Ervin "about the double standard" — meaning that here was an investigator in an eavesdropping case who was guilty of eavesdropping himself. It's clear from the transcript that Nixon, Haldeman, and Ehrlichman knew the pronunciation of Hal's name, but they use the term "Lipschitz" perhaps as a way of injecting a scatological dimension into the case (not for the first time).

In the end, it didn't matter what Ervin or Nixon or even Dash thought of Hal Lipset. Standing up for oneself in the face of criticism and rejection was nothing new to him, and, anyway, a new case was waiting that would again prove the value of personal integrity in a system gone mad.

PART VI

FREE WILL
VERSUS THE SYSTEM

Chapter 17

The Case of the Neglectful Police

"There they all were, caught and held in the meshes of the law. Bound together for a little while in the relentless aftermath of sudden and violent death. Each of them had his or her own tragedy and meaning, his or her own story."
— Agatha Christie, *Murder after Hours*

Free will is the foundation of all mystery fiction. Whatever chaos needs to be put in order, whatever system falls prey to corruption, whatever evil has generated yet another crime, the independent mind of the good detective, operating with complete autonomy in a world that wants to shackle it, is there to set things right again.

To understand free will, mystery writers often put a barrier in front of private detectives to keep them from solving crimes too easily. That barrier is called the law-enforcement system, and its representative is the police detective who relies on rule books, reports in triplicate, and a battery of law-enforcement personnel to help him apprehend culprits in his unending battle against crime.

The police detective believes in a civilized order of things, understands the need for bureaucracy to preserve that order, and sees himself as a small but important cog in the machinery of law enforcement that society has set up to protect itself.

But because he is dependent on the military hierarchy that supports him, the police detective is often portrayed as a bumbling bureaucrat who is constantly bewildered by conflicting evidence that never seems to fit the picture of the puzzle he has in mind. This makes him wonderfully inferior to the private eye, who seemingly by his wits alone succeeds in mastering each case without any of the resources the police detective has so slavishly garnered to support him.

The police detective represents one side of the detective process — the scientific method of collecting all the pieces of information and analyzing them according to certain disciplines of observation and objectivity. Perhaps the perfect example is Ellery Queen's father, Inspector Richard Queen, portrayed "like a bloodhound who follows the true scent in the clutter of a hopelessly tangled trail."

What the police detective can never grasp is the other side of the deductive process: the use of imagination — the mind's precursor to free will — in taking all those "bungled and torn" facts and making sense out of them. Thus "the intuitive sense, the gift of imagination," continues the author, "belonged to Ellery Queen" — the intellectual, the writer, the artiste.

Perry Mason and Hamilton Burger; Nero Wolfe and Inspector Kramer; Sherlock Holmes and Inspector Lestrade; Miss Marple and Chief Inspector Craddock — the barrier is everywhere in detective fiction, for one thing because it is fun to watch two practitioners of the deductive method go at it tooth and nail, and for another because the duel symbolizes that classic battle between independence and authority, maverick and institution, free will and the system.

This is why Inspector Queen plods along in his dully methodical way, barking orders and confusing everything, while Ellery zips in and out of each case with flashes of brilliance that outpace his father every time. So Sherlock Holmes observes that "were he but gifted with imagination, [the inspector] might rise to great heights in his profession."

Actually, though, he wouldn't. Imagination is the very antithesis of the ordered system within which the police detective must function as a willing piece of the larger apparatus — a kind of robot whose superiors have so structured his job that he dares not act independently. Even the sympathetic Inspector Queen, having bellowed orders to his men in a fit of rage, suddenly changes his tune when the police-station hierarchy snaps its fingers: "Once the telephone rang, the inspector's voice became a thing of beauty. It was the commissioner demanding information. Two minutes later the telephone rang again. The deputy chief inspector. Honey dripped from Inspector Queen's lips."

No wonder the police officer is so threatened by the private eye, who as a free agent can move with fluidity and grace around suspects and evidence without need or want of the bureaucracy of a police officer. "That is the advantage," as Holmes says, "of being unofficial."

No wonder, too, the police detective ends up blaming the private eye for interfering in official police business and ruining an otherwise orderly accumulation of evidence. This has occurred so many times in Rex Stout's novels that Nero Wolfe observes to Inspector Kramer, "I know that when I have been consulted by a person who is in any way connected with a death by violence you automatically assume that I have knowledge of evidence that would be useful in your investigation." Here the tables have turned: The police detective, with all the power of his rank and the resources of his office, must now turn to that loathsome interloper, the private eye, for information his massive machinery cannot obtain on its own.

Hal Lipset is one of a handful of successful private eyes to have sustained good working relationships with the police. But as we have seen, he has also been at odds with the police over what he considers a built-in tendency to abuse power. Perhaps the clearest and most conclusive example occurred when he investigated the Case of the Neglectful Police.

> I was called in on a murder investigation by a lawyer representing a large family in one of those bay towns north of Oakland that serves and supplies the shipping industry. The family was black and lived in a predominantly black neighborhood, and a few of the sons had links to the Black Panthers, who at the time were having many well-publicized confrontations with local and federal (FBI) law-enforcement agencies.
>
> The victim, Charles, was the head of the family and had been a member of the Marine Cooks and Stewards Union.

He had worked on various freighters, so he had traveled much of the year. His wife, Shirley, lived with their step-sons and a couple of adopted kids. Both had been married before.

The family believed the police had not done a good job investigating the killing or even showing an interest in pursuing the murderer. They didn't know if it was because of their Panther connections or simply that they were black in an all-black neighborhood and the police were white, but they felt nothing was happening on the case in an official manner.

Shirley told the police that Charles had been home on leave for a few days when late one night the doorbell rang and Charles got up to answer the front door. Shirley said she couldn't hear a conversation, only that suddenly two gunshots were fired. She ran out of the room and found Charles in the hallway, shot twice through the heart, the door still open. She called out to her children, got one of them to telephone the police, held Charles until the ambulance came, and only then accepted the fact that he was dead.

Shirley said she had not looked out the door and had not seen anyone running away or walking by outside. Later, when police detectives were interrogating members of the family, there was some conjecture (voiced by the police) that Charles in his travels might have been involved in something illegal, such as smuggling, but the family didn't think that was true. They had no idea who could have killed him.

They did feel after several weeks had passed that the police had dismissed the crime as "just another black problem" and had swept the matter under a rug. After finally giving up on the police, they contacted their attorney, and he called me in.

I started the investigation by going to the police to see what they'd actually accomplished. Ordinarily, a licensed private investigator representing the family of a murder victim is considered to have some right to ask questions, but in this case, the captain at the station was unfriendly. All he would say at first was that his investigators were "doing what needed to be done."

"Fine," I said. "The family will be relieved to hear that. Tell me what you've done, and I'll go fill them in." This annoyed him. "You know, Mr. Lipset, I don't have to tell you anything. You're interfering with police business just by coming around here. I'm advising you officially to keep your nose out of it."

Well, this was like waving a red flag in front of my face. Here the family had received no help from the law and had spent their own money to hire me to look into this murder, and I as their representative couldn't get answers to these very legitimate questions. When the captain even refused to let me see a copy of the police report, which is a routine document you give to any legal representative, especially someone hired by the family of a murder victim, I decided to switch directions. I knew the coroner's report would be a matter of public record and that it would contain most of the police report, so from that I began my own investigation.

Why doesn't law enforcement welcome Lipset's help? Because in another example of real life mirroring detective fiction, the police resent private eyes in the same way that bureaucrats resent entrepreneurs. Cops and bureaucrats may have power, but they don't have autonomy. "This is a murder and a police job," a cop says to Philip Marlowe, "and we wouldn't want your help, even if it was good."

Even if it was good. Forgoing the truth and letting a murderer go free is seen by the system as preferable to the embarrassment of accepting outside help, even if it is good.

The coroner's report stated that Charles had been shot twice at point-blank range and that the bullets had gone straight through his chest, indicating he wasn't turning away but was facing his assailant at the time of the shooting. It also stated that the police had canvassed the neighborhood for witnesses, but there was no record of the people they talked to, what neighbors had heard the shots, where the rest of the family was at the time of the killing, whether anyone had been seen running away from the house or anywhere in the neighborhood, whether Charles had indeed been involved in smuggling, who Charles's enemies had been, how his sons' and stepsons' Black Panther activities might have pertained, and so forth.

I began at the point where I felt the police should have started. I sent agents out to interview people around the neighborhood and really take their time. We wanted to be friendly and open about the case so we wouldn't intimidate anybody, and we wanted to have long talks with people about Charles and his family — about who used to come around, how the kids had gotten along with neighbors, any drugs or suspicious doings in the area, and what was going on the night of the murder.

Within a few days, we came up with two witnesses who had heard something that night but didn't want to get involved and hadn't told the police anything. Further talks with these people took place while we checked out Charles's friends and contacts at work, his union, local markets, and bars. We learned more about his relationship with his stepsons and whether or not he had any interest himself in the Black Panthers (he didn't).

Eventually it became clear that the neighbors who had heard the shots appeared to know something important about this family. One woman had seen one of the younger stepsons, Duncan, talking animatedly to Charles on two different days and knew of some connection concerning Duncan and a local drug dealer. We kept going back to her and to another neighbor who finally said that "everybody knew" Duncan had a habit and had asked his stepfather for money several times. Did he have a gun? She said it was possible: The Panthers had a lot of guns, and Duncan was proud of being a Panther.

I felt it was conceivable that this kid might have been an addict and was desperate for a fix the night of the murder. Maybe he called on Charles again, was furious when

Charles refused to give him the money, and in a blind rage shot Charles. It was hard to tell without further evidence, and doubly problematical since I didn't know how much the family, my client, knew or wanted to know about what appeared to be violations of the law (the drugs) and possible murder by one of their own members.

So I decided to call a meeting with the five men who had hired the lawyer who had hired me. They were sort of a family council, representing the various in-laws and relatives involved. Their spokesman was traveling at the time, so it took weeks to get everyone together in the same room. In the meantime I did nothing more on the case.

When the day for the meeting came and I greeted them at the door, they all looked at me quizzically. I'm sure they thought I had either run out of money and was going to call it quits, or I had the murderer all picked out and was about to put him or her under lock and key. I told them we had to have a talk and ushered them into the dining room, where they all sat around the dining-room table looking apprehensive as hell.

I explained that what I had done was a preliminary investigation without cooperation from the police. They nodded. I said I believed that I had found the person who had murdered Charles and that I felt I could prove it through the next two or three steps in the investigation. They nodded again. Or I could stop right now and walk away from the case. This puzzled them. "But why would you stop, Hal?" they asked. "Because I'm pretty sure the murderer is a member of this family," I said. It was as if I had hit them with a baseball bat. They sat back in their chairs and gasped, "What?" "What are you saying?" "This can't be true!"

I waited for them to calm down and said, "I feel I owe it to you to explain this much, because if I develop more evidence I'll be legally bound to give whatever I have to the district attorney. I can't conceal evidence of a possible felony, but at this point in the investigation, all I have now is conjecture. If you want to tell me to stop and not go any further, I'll end the case and walk away. Considering how the police have been acting, I'm sure they don't care. If you want me to continue, I'll need more money. I know you'll want to discuss this privately, so I'll leave you and go to my desk in the other room. Let me know when you want me to come back in."

I think that was the hardest news I have ever given to a client. The look on their faces as I left was enough to break your heart. They talked for about an hour before calling me back in. A check was ready for me. Their spokesman said they had gone over the pros and cons of the problem and understood the message I was getting across. It came down to the idea that as a family they felt they would never rest easy until they knew for certain who was responsible for the death of Charles. It was a very emotional moment for everyone.

It's interesting to see how easily the police, whose job is to solve murders, gave up the chance to find the truth by closing the case prematurely, while this group struggles to get past its sense of family loyalty and find the truth at whatever cost. Money acts as the lever on which the decision to act is moved back and forth; but make no mistake: At Lipset Service, it is the client, not the detective, who moves that lever at every stage of the investigation.

Within another three or four days we had our two reluctant witnesses tied down with tape-recorded interviews. We learned there had been bad blood between Duncan and Charles, for one thing because here was the father making his way in the white world while the youth was living strictly in the black world and becoming progressively more militant with the Black Panthers. We found other witnesses to testify that an argument between the two had started in a local barbershop and ended with Duncan going away in a fury. Apparently, he returned to demand money from his stepfather and was refused. Unable to control himself any longer, he shot Charles at the doorstep.

When the time came to turn over the information to the police so they could go over the same ground and make their own case, I wasn't about to go back to the police captain who had been so difficult the first time around. Instead I took the evidence directly to the district attorney, who accepted it (grudgingly) and went to work.

In a relatively short time the police arrested Duncan, who was seventeen years old, and charged him with the murder of his stepfather. I thought that my part of the case was over, but the family hired the same attorney who had initially recommended me. He called and asked if I would tell him all I knew about the case, since he didn't expect the district attorney and especially the police of that town to give him much information.

I was glad to give the lawyer all I knew. He represented Duncan, who was tried as a juvenile and convicted. He was sent to a youth center for four years and was released on his twenty-first birthday.

Everybody connected with the case wanted to know why those witnesses never told the police what they told us. I think it's simple: One of the primary aspects of being an investigator is that you genuinely have to like people, because if you don't, they know it. It comes through loud and clear. Being a good detective, I've always thought, is a matter of accepting people as they are.

The irony here, though, is not that the police were too racist or too lazy to investigate thoroughly — it's rather that they weren't lazy enough. "Family and friends still do about two thirds of the killing," says detective-fiction writer Lawrence Sanders's ex-chief Francis X. Delaney. "It's basic. If you catch a homicide, you look at the family first. . . . We'd be morons to disregard percentages."

Were the police "morons" to disregard this essential knowledge? Certainly they wouldn't have had to canvass the neighborhood, alienating everyone in their wake, if they had read the routine statistics. All they had to do was start with the family, and they would have found their murderer right there.

Why didn't the police do a better job? The usual answer in fact or fiction is that the system can't parcel itself out like some grocery list every time somebody in the community gets killed. With the whole city to protect, the police believe they know better than the individual. That is the stance of official authority: The system can't bend to suit each individual; individuals, on the other hand, must bend to fit in the system.

The position of the private eye has classically been to push back against that system. In this case, Lipset not only offers to step out of the bureaucratic loop, he gives the family members an opportunity to decide for themselves whether the truth really will make them free.

Unlike detectives in mystery fiction (and here is the last difference that separates Lipset from his hard-boiled counterparts), Hal is not a savior of situations or people. He is not a Spenser or Travis McGee or Sam Spade or Philip Marlowe or Mike Hammer who resolves cases, lives, and mysteries by himself.

He is rather the manager and salesman he has taught himself to be, an intermediary, a seller of information, an objective witness, a free agent who says to clients who come to him as victims, here is your chance: You don't have to endure this pain, this ridicule, this jail cell, this injury, this rape, this divorce, this ignorance, this stigma, this system. You can take control, if you want to, by your own free will.

Lipset's notion about being the kind of investigator who genuinely likes people brings us back to that scene in the dining room where the family realizes that one of its own has killed Charles. Lipset describes it as "a very emotional moment for everyone," but the fact is that such moments occur regularly during the investigations undertaken by Lipset Service.

Hal, it turns out, is a booster of human initiative. He doesn't want to be a hero to his clients. He wants his clients to stand up for themselves — that's the reason he believes he's hired in the first place. What an extraordinary occasion it must have been, among thousands of cases coming through Lipset Service over forty years, to hand that moment of destiny to each client. It not only means that free will can be extended beyond the restrictions of place and time, it also suggests that the detective himself can find his own release. Beyond the Professor Moriartys of this world, beyond the corruption of cities and systems, and beyond his own obsessions — money, anger, loss — he can be free.

Epilogue

Professor "Lips Set" Looks Forward

Hal and bookkeeper Dorothy Jansizian are preparing to "wire" a client in the dining room of Hal's Victorian home. Standing awkwardly without his shirt and with arms outstretched, the client waits to be armed with a miniature, highly sensitive Nagra tape recorder.

The Nagra is one of the many tailor-made devices that have (for better or worse) contributed to Hal's fame as an expert on electronic eavesdropping. To keep it hidden, he uses a wide, elastic belt with Velcro clasps that was originally made for sacroiliac or rib support. A pocket, or holster, has been stitched on one side to hold the tape recorder under the client's left arm. With an undetected movement of his right hand — reaching over as if to scratch his side or adjust a piece of clothing — the client can activate the Nagra without a sound.

Dorothy takes her place behind the client, ready to pull the ends of the belt snugly around his rib cage, while Hal makes sure the holster fits just below the client's left armpit. They feel a little like tailors working on an expensive suit or corset. As Hal begins describing ways of inducing a blackmailer to incriminate himself on tape, Dorothy is concerned that the client has suddenly broken out in a heavy sweat.

"The Nagra can run for as long as three hours," Hal says, "so you can take your time to get him talking." The client shakes his head. "That's too obvious. This guy's no amateur. He knows I'm too scared to argue."

"All right, let's figure out the scenario after you try this on." Hal takes the Nagra out of its box and begins to demonstrate its mechanisms to the client. The miniature spools turn silently inside an extremely thin (quarter-inch) case that's a bit larger than two side-by-side packs of cigarettes. Hal mentions that each Nagra costs him about four thousand dollars, and the client, nearly transfixed by the Swiss-watch precision of the instrument, shakes his head again. Dorothy watches his sweat staining the top of the elastic belt.

"There's an interesting story behind these Nagras," Hal says, adding a bit of diversion as he slides the Nagra into the client's holster. "We found them in Hollywood, did you know that? They're designed for movies where you don't want a heavy boom or microphone floating around the actors, say, if they're having a love scene at the end of a pier or on a beach. The Nagra has so much fidelity it can pick up a conversation in the middle of a noisy restaurant or a storm."

The client seems mildly intrigued. "Now bring your right hand over to the Nagra and find the metal lever I just showed you." The client points his index finger toward his armpit and almost involuntarily pushes it toward the holster. He finds the lever and stops. "OK, push down and back. Right through the cloth. You should feel it lock in place." Voilà: The client's eyebrows shoot up as though he's just performed a miracle. "Great," Hal says. "Do it again, but this time pretend you've got an itch." Momentarily, the client looks like an ape scratching himself. "With a little less enthusiasm," Hal says. "All right. Do it again. And again."

Meanwhile, Dorothy moves the Nagra's tiny microphone under the client's undershirt to hide the wire and secure its clip on the cloth directly under the right side of his chin. His sweat prohibits the use of tape to keep the wire in place, so she pushes the slack inside the edges of the elastic belt. Hal unlocks the lever on the Nagra. "It's off," he says. "Now let's talk about how you're going to handle this. What's a good way to get this guy to open up?"

The client shrugs. "I have no idea. He hasn't said two words to me since this thing started."

"Think about it," Hal urges. "You know him. You had to talk

to him at some point." The client shakes his head. Hal takes a step forward and stands directly in front of him. "I'll be the blackmailer. Say something that will make me stop doing this to you."

The client stammers, "I — I . . ."

"Come on, you bastard," Hal sneers, pushing himself closer to the client's face. "Pay up."

The client gets the idea. "Look, I can't go on like this. I'm running out of money. I believed you four months ago when you said a thousand was all you wanted. . . ."

"I don't care about your problems," says Hal. "Ask your mother. She's got money. Maybe your wife'll give you a loan. I don't care. Go steal it."

The client raises his hands, palms up. "I haven't got all of it this time. All I could bring you was half. For God's sake, let's end this now."

Hal nods — this is what he's waiting for. "Whattaya, cheatin' me? Don't you remember what I told you four months ago?"

Clearly shaken, the client breaks the spell. "This is crazy. I'll never pull it off. How do I know this damn thing" — he gestures at the Nagra — "is still working? Suppose I hit it on a chair or something. . . ."

Hal not-so-patiently repeats his instructions, stopping to demonstrate the Nagra again. "You're going to be fine," he says. "When in doubt, put your belief in this machine: Think of the money I paid for it." That remark wins him the smallest of smiles.

Dorothy's concern — that sweat from the client's armpit will drip onto the Nagra and gum things up for good — doesn't seem to bother Hal. What he sees is a client beginning to stand up for himself, maybe for the first time, and more important, a client who is willing to pay the fee.

It's after six P.M. by the time they send the client off to meet his blackmailer, so Hal and Dorothy decide to have a drink. "He's nearly hysterical," Hal says as they go into the kitchen, "but he's going to nail the guy."

"I knew it when I could see him interested in the Nagra," Dorothy replies. "He's not so worried that he can't think straight. He'll be OK."

"It's just a matter of experience. When he gets through this, he'll know he can do a lot of things. It makes a big difference. I remember how much it meant to me when I could see for myself how cases were handled by the big law firms." As they sit down with their drinks, Hal tells Dorothy about the difference between starting out today as a private eye and starting out as he did in the late 1940s.

> I was very lucky. Lawyers wanted me in their office when they met the client, when the client told his story, and when they told the client how the law might apply. They wanted to know everything about my investigation — witnesses who would be good for our side and witnesses who would be bad — and if the client could afford it, they wanted me to sit in the courtroom if the case went to trial.
>
> I didn't charge much in those days, so I could sit in on many trials. On the one hand, I was a glorified gofer for the lawyer; on the other hand, I could investigate the backgrounds of prospective jurors or make some key calls in the middle of the trial.
>
> The whole thing was an education for me. I heard the lawyer's opening statement, so I got the picture that the jury got. I listened to the witnesses I had interviewed earlier as they were examined by the lawyer and cross-examined by the opposition. I got to see what was important in testimony, how it was attacked, and how it was rehabilitated on re-direct examination.
>
> I got to hear opening and closing statements, the judge's instructions, and the jury's verdict. If we won, we took the jury out for drinks and talked to them at length about how they had made their decision. If we lost, I was sometimes hired to question individual jurors afterward.
>
> That's an education you can't get today. The private investigator doesn't have that kind of relationship with lawyers, often doesn't go to court (since not that many cases go to trial anymore), and doesn't get the big picture.

"Do you tell that to your students?" Dorothy asks, referring to the course in investigation procedures Hal teaches at the University of San Francisco Law School.

"Absolutely," Hal says. "Most lawyers don't know how to use a good detective. They take on the case management themselves and end up buried in a mountain of details. A good P.I. can take half the case off their shoulders and manage it far better than they can."

Dorothy smiles. After all his years of trying to professionalize his field, Professor Lipset is now enlisting the help of future lawyers to do the job.

After their drink, Dorothy drives off to Berkeley as Hal calls out to David Pham, a Vietnamese refugee who has worked as a housekeeper and cook for Hal while earning his degree in computer science. David has a pot roast warming in the oven.

It's a meal that always reminds Hal of Lynn, who used to make pot roast the old-fashioned way, by searing it first and roasting it with plenty of vegetables. Of course, the boys always ate the meat and hated the vegetables.

The kids have grown and left home long ago. Larry is an independent contractor in Mendocino County, up the coast about seventy miles from San Francisco. And Louis is — what else? — an assistant district attorney in a prosecutor's office Hal couldn't have abided for twenty minutes. "It just goes to show you there are good detectives in the system as well," Hal likes to say, "only they're called assistant D.A.s."

Though he has had several long relationships since Lynn's death, Hal never remarried, and the house still has the feel of her easy humor and vivacity. The dining room she refurbished retains her original design, and pictures of Lynn still line the mantel in Hal's bedroom. Sometimes, in a certain light, Hal's grandson, James Michael, looks exactly like Lynn when she was amused.

Hal remarked the other day to Louis that Lynn was actually responsible for the company name. She believed from the start that the agency shouldn't be called Ace Detective Company or Sleuth Investigations. "Let's use our name," she said. "It'll show we stand up for what we do because we put our name behind it."

Eating his pot roast, Hal remembers the dinner they all burst out laughing when he told them about the new client he had met that day.

"And how did you come to Lipset Service?" Hal asked. "Did someone recommend us?"

"No," she said. "I saw your name in the yellow pages, and I thought, what a gimmick! You folks can not only keep a secret, you keep yours *lips set* as well."

Lips set, Hal thinks, rinsing off his plate. Now why didn't we think of that? We could have put an ad in the yellow pages with a pair of lips pushed in by an index finger!

At seventy, never to retire, and now also an instructor of lawyers, Hal may yet think up an angle to put it to good use.

THEFT OF LIBRARY MATERIAL IS PETIT LARCENY
PUNISHABLE UNDER SECTION 61-3-13b OF THE WV
STATE CODE. UPON CONVICTION THEREOF, THE
PERSON SHALL BE CONFINED IN THE COUNTY JAIL
FOR UP TO ONE YEAR, FINED $500, OR BOTH.